MARY-ANNE
BOERMANS

DEJA
FOOD

SECOND HELPINGS
OF CLASSIC
BRITISH DISHES

◨ SQUARE PEG

1 3 5 7 9 10 8 6 4 2

Square Peg, an imprint of Vintage,
20 Vauxhall Bridge Road,
London SW1V 2SA

Square Peg is part of the Penguin Random House group of companies
whose addresses can be found at *global.penguinrandomhouse.com.*

 Penguin
Random House
UK

Text copyright © Mary-Anne Boermans 2017
Photography © Sean Limbert 2017
Author photograph © Alison 'Ali' Palmer 2017

First published by Square Peg in 2017

Penguin.co.uk/vintage

A CIP catalogue record for this book is available from the British Library

ISBN 9780224101325

Typeset and Designed by Anna Green at *www.siulendesign.com*
Photography by Sean Limbert
Food Styling by Yasmin Limbert

Printed and bound in India by Replika Press Pvt. Ltd.

CONTENTS

PREFACE

We all need to be able to provide food for ourselves and also, at some point, for others, too. It is a life skill that, personally, I value as much as being able to swim, but one which seems to have slipped from importance in the age of convenience foods. Whatever advantages such foods may possess in terms of speed and simplicity of preparation are, for me, far outweighed by their disadvantages: namely their cost, the quality of their ingredients and the additives used to prolong their shelf lives.

I firmly believe that traditional British food, refined over centuries from local and seasonal produce, can be tastier, healthier, more exciting and easier to prepare than anything mass produced. Moreover, by following this cumulative culinary wisdom we can both save money and drastically reduce the food wastage that has become such a problem in the twenty-first century. It's a concept that I like to think of as 'Deja Food', and it encompasses tradition, recipes, ingredients and a whole philosophy of cooking and eating.

Simply put, Deja Food is the return to our tables of food we have served before, whether it be the remains of the Sunday roast, our grandmother's favourite pie or some toothsome recipe from further back in time. It's how we used to eat, making use of the whole animal and not just the prime cuts, being creative with the less expensive pieces of meat, making the most of fresh, local, seasonal ingredients served simply in ways we used to enjoy but have forgotten over the passage of time. It's frugal, but full of flavour, deliciously different, yet proudly traditional.

In the latter half of the twentieth century the reputation of British food suffered greatly; years of rationing after the war saw both quality and quantity diminish. I have the dubious honour of having grown up just 15 miles from the restaurant in which Elizabeth David was famously served the dreary post-war fare that would ultimately inspire her to write her iconic book, *Mediterranean Food*.

It wasn't always thus. The recipes of the sixteenth and seventeenth centuries, for example, reveal a delightful complexity, juxtaposing sweet and savoury elements and surprisingly sophisticated sauces. Long before Moroccan tagines were fashionable in the UK, our ancestors were enjoying a whole range of spiced meat-and-fruit dishes such as plum pottage and mince pies with a sprinkling of actual meat, which were so beloved that they became feast-day treats. We still enjoy their greatly redacted descendants today, but how much more enjoyable would it be to savour the originals?

The iconic image of a sumptuous British Sunday lunch invariably includes a joint or poultry, resplendent amid a veritable cornucopia of vegetables and accompaniments. Enticing as this image is, it comes at a price which can, for prime roasting joints, be budget-bustingly expensive. However, a grand Sunday lunch is still affordable if we only take a little more care selecting the meat, choosing from the cheaper cuts, which can be both better value and just as enjoyable, and treating them with care and attention. As a general rule, the best cuts come from the upper hindquarters of an animal. The forequarters (lamb/pork shoulder, beef brisket, beef flank) are usually cheaper because they are either not as tender or fattier, or both. However, this makes them ideal for long, slow roasting and braising, the fat slowly melting and basting the meat so that they become incredibly flavourful and tender.

It isn't just the meat dishes of yesteryear that can offer tasty and economical recipes to delight our tables. A whole host of vegetables were enjoyed in different ways, and much use was made of items that we no longer regard as deserving a special place on the dinner table. Onions, celery, mushrooms and lettuces are nowadays seen mainly as accompaniments or garnishes, whereas in times gone by they were greatly relished and recognised as part of the regular vegetable course in their own right. Stewed Lettuce and Peas (page 279) is quite delightful and much more popular in our house than ordinary steamed cabbage, while a dish of Dressed Mushrooms (page 291) is a meal in itself when paired with some fresh, crusty bread.

And so to those leftovers, which can also be Deja Food. Centuries ago, many classic dishes utilised not only our British forte of 'big lumps of meat in the oven' (which, incidentally, earned us the grudging admiration of many other countries, including France), but any surplus was also used to create the now long-forgotten fricassees, hashes, ragoos and 'à la mode' delights that once populated our culinary repertoire. The cooks of previous centuries saw no lessening in the quality of food just because it had been previously cooked; old recipe books are full of dishes that begin with instructions to 'Take a fillet of beef half roasted...', 'Take some under-dressed [rare] mutton...', 'Take some cold, boiled potatoes...', and so on.

This thrifty and practical approach has resulted in some of the tastiest and most iconic British dishes, such as cottage pie (made with beef) and shepherd's pie (lamb), both of which emerged as recognisable recipes in the late eighteenth and early nineteenth centuries. Properly made, from the surplus Sunday roast trimmed of all fat, skin and sinew, generously moistened with gravy and meat juices and topped with feathery mashed potato, they are dishes sublime. The richness of flavour from meat that has previously been baked for hours in its own juices cannot be replicated in any other way.

In this book I apply the lessons from the past to the needs of the present. The reader will find that some great British dishes, such as the traditional Sunday roast, are not only the perfect way to make the most of fresh ingredients, but can also provide the basis for a range of fabulous family meals for later in the week. Also included are some long-forgotten recipes for the cheaper cuts of meat and less popular vegetables that are not only packed with flavour, but economical, too.

I hope that enjoying the delightful old recipes in this book will prove the inspiration to return to this way of cooking and eating, thereby helping to preserve the culinary wisdom of centuries past through simple enjoyment of all that this land has to offer.

'In all ranks, and at every table, one important art in housekeeping is to make what remains over from one day's entertainment contribute to the elegance or plenty of the next day's repasts. This is a principle understood by persons in the very highest ranks of society, and who maintain the most splendid and expensive establishments. Their great town-dinners usually follow in rapid succession, one banquet forming, if not the basis, a useful auxiliary to the next entertainment. But as this has been elsewhere recommended to the attention of the reader, it is almost unnecessary to repeat here, that vegetables, ragouts, and soups, may be rewarmed; and jellies and blancmanges remoulded, with no deterioration of their qualities. Savoury or sweet patties, potted meats, croquets, rissoles, vol-au-vents, fritters, tartlets, &c., may be served almost without cost, where cookery is going forward on a large scale.'

Christian Isobel Johnstone, Scottish journalist, editor and author, 1828

INTRODUCTION

The motivation for this book came from my dual interests of cooking and history. In the UK we have only been recording the food that we enjoy preparing and eating for just over 600 years, beginning with *The Forme of Cury*, a parchment scroll of dishes compiled by the Master Cooks of Richard II around the year 1400.

The history of the British Isles can be written in food. Over the last 2,000 years, immigrants and invaders have brought with them not only their recipes, but also the ingredients with which to make them, and all have been absorbed into the food canon of these isles with open arms. Without the constant stream of visitors to these shores, we'd be stuck munching on indigenous onions and a few berries. A surprising number of domesticated livestock, fruits and vegetables now so familiar to us as to be thought of as British were brought, in the first instance, by the occupying armies of Rome. Invading Saxons and Vikings brought their methods of fish preservation, the echoes of which are still with us a thousand years later in the smokehouses and fisheries of the east coast of Scotland. The Normans brought spices and wine while the bounty of conquered and plundered countries during the age of exploration reached these shores in the form of exotic spices, fruits and nuts.

In the twenty-first century, with the rise in popularity of the traditional foods of many ethnic communities, British food is hardly ever written about, which is a shame because there is also a richly spiced food heritage in this country that is being overlooked. We love to discover 'new' and exciting foods that are a little out of the ordinary and also, in these straitened times, easy on the pocket. How gratifying would it be to be able to do so with traditional British dishes? Many of the recipes in this book were enjoyed for decades, if not hundreds of years, before they fell by the wayside. Just as the culinary adventurer can be transported to foreign climes by exotic cookbooks, so can they explore mystical places by using recipes recorded in that far off and intriguing place: the past.

'The past is a foreign country: they do things differently there.'
L.P. Hartley, The Go-Between

HOW TO USE THIS BOOK

The recipes in this book are arranged by key ingredient, for example meat, cheese, vegetables, etc. The different meat chapters usually begin with a recipe for a roast dinner, followed by suggestions for how you might use any leftovers and then a selection of separate recipes. You will find a chapter on simple sauces to accompany your main meals, plus a chapter on what I have called tracklements. These are the elements, such as pastries, chutneys, accompaniments and others, that complete a meal, but don't necessarily fit naturally elsewhere.

SUNDAY BEST

Sunday lunch used to be a British institution, but its status slipped with the rise of convenience foods and a lack of skills as cookery lessons disappeared from the school curriculum. In an attempt to redress this decline, I have included a suggestion for a dish that is suitable to serve up to the family as a Sunday lunch in appropriate chapters, together with recommendations for accompanying dishes.

As a child, I was in awe of the cooking and serving of a full Sunday lunch, believing it to be a monumental feat of coordination requiring the dexterity of a card sharp. Now I know better. Rather than juggling ten different items at once, it can be so much more relaxed if the vegetables are cooked and the gravy finished while the meat rests.

Another of the pressures, as I saw it, was trying to find recipes for the various accompaniments served alongside the main course, which could result in as many as half a dozen recipe books, pieces of paper and web pages being consulted at any one time. To combat this, I have tried to make this book very much a one-stop resource for all trimmings for all occasions, be they sauces, gravies, stuffings or extras. You might be surprised at how a few simple recipes can be cunningly deployed to suit a range of meals: crunchy herb Stuffing (page 319) can be enjoyed with pork as well as chicken, for example; Spiced Apple Sauce (page 36) can be served with pork, bacon and goose and Veal Forcemeat balls (page 331) can accompany practically anything.

REUSING COLD MEAT

There are a couple of rules that should be observed when you're preparing meals with cold meat. Whether it is to be eaten hot or cold, you should take the time to ensure the meat is presented in the best possible condition. This means trimming it of all skin, excess fat, connective tissue and any odd gristly bits, which tend to be forgiven at a joint's initial outing to the table.

If you are eating the meat cold, whether in sandwiches or on a platter alongside baked potatoes and a massed rank of pickles and chutneys, then cutting it into wafer-thin slices will both display it to its best advantage and maximise its flavour.

If the meat is intended for a hot dish, understand that extreme heat will render previously cooked meat tough. You do not have to boil cooked meat for it to be safe to consume. Red meat must reach a temperature of 70°C, white meat and poultry 80°C. Slowly warming the meat in a sauce or gravy to these temperatures will make it perfectly safe to eat as well as a palatable temperature.

VEGETABLE SIDE DISHES

In the vegetable chapter I highlight some of the less well-known vegetables that used to be served regularly on our dining tables, and include recipes for cooking lettuces, celery, cucumbers and onions to serve alongside your main meal.

SERVING SIZES

Most of the recipes in this book will serve four adults generously. They can easily be halved to make two meals, or multiplied to make larger quantities.

DEJA FOOD

Wherever possible, chapters include recipes for how to use cooked food as a basis for completely new dishes.

INGREDIENTS

It was my aim, in the writing of this book, that the ingredients for the recipes contained within should be accessible on the ordinary British high street. This is certainly true if you have the luxury of being able to shop at your local family butcher, fishmonger, greengrocer and bakery. For many, however, the delights of an unhurried meander through traditional, specialist shops is no longer a possibility and the store cupboard is more often restocked following a single shopping expedition to a supermarket. My aim, nevertheless, holds true for the most part, and readers can be reassured that the majority of the ingredients in this book are easy to get hold of and the recipes do not require unusual, outlandish or expensive items.

Below is a comprehensive listing of the ingredients used in this book. In short, if you have everything on the list, you can make everything in this book. Alongside each ingredient is the number of recipes in which it is used, giving an indication of its importance (thus salt and pepper are key ingredients, pig's head not so much). The items in italics are suggested flavourings to tweak and enhance your dishes. It is down to your own personal taste whether you choose to use them. Hopefully, the list gives an idea of the reassuring familiarity of the foods we'll be working with on this culinary adventure.

STORE CUPBOARD
Salt (96)
Pepper (51)
Cornflour (33)
Vinegar (25)
Sugar (16)
Flour (13)
Anchovy fillets (12)
Puff pastry (7)
Mushroom ketchup (6)
Capers (5)
Oyster sauce (5)
Mustard (4)
Verjuice (4)
Basmati rice (3)
Barley (2)
Bicarbonate of soda (2)
Cornichons (2)
Flaked almonds (2)
Gherkins (2)
Macaroni (2)
Oatcakes (2)
Oatmeal (2)
Oil (2)
Pickled artichokes (2)
Pickled onions (2)
Pickled red cabbage (2)
Pickled walnuts (2)
Saltpetre/preserving salt (2)
Stock cube (2)
Worcestershire sauce (2)
Anchovy essence (1)
Angelhair pasta (1)
Chestnuts (1)
Chutney (1)
Cooked macaroni (1)
Cream of tartar (1)

Evaporated milk (1)
Filo pastry (1)
Honey (1)
Lotus biscuits (1)
Oat flour (1)
Olive oil (1)
Olives (1)
Pickled beetroot (1)
Pickled jalapeños (1)
Pickles (1)
Rosewater (1)
Sea salt (1)
Spice mix (1)
Spice paste (1)
Walnut ketchup (1)
Yeast (1)
Apple jelly
Blackberry jelly
Bovril™
Dark soy sauce
Henderson's Relish™
Light soy sauce
Marmite™
Redcurrant jelly

BREAD
Breadcrumbs (16)
Bread (9)
Toast (8)
Sippets (2)

DAIRY
Unsalted butter (64)
Egg (48)
Double cream (15)
Milk (13)
Fresh suet (9)

Strong cheese (8)
Parmesan (4)
Beef dripping (4)
Salted butter (4)
Cream cheese (2)
Crème fraîche (2)
Goats' cheese (1)
Plain yogurt (1)
Single cream (1)

FRUIT
Lemons (26)
Apples (10)
Currants (9)
Candied peel (6)
Orange (5)
Grapes (4)
Gooseberries (2)
Cranberries (1)
Elderflowers (1)
Limes (1)
Prunes (1)
Sultanas (1)

VEGETABLES
Onion (41)
Lettuce (23)
Celery (14)
Baby spinach (13)
Carrots (12)
Mushrooms (9)
Shallot (8)
Spring onion (8)
Cucumber (6)
Peas (6)
Potatoes (6)
Radish (6)

Turnips (6)
Garlic (4)
Swede (4)
Cooked potatoes (3)
Parsnips (3)
Samphire (3)
Asparagus (2)
Boiled rice (2)
Chard (2)
French beans (2)
Fresh ginger (2)
Lentils (2)
Savoy cabbage (2)
Beet greens (1)
Beetroot (1)
Broad beans (1)
Broccoli (1)
Celery leaves (1)
Chillies (1)
Coleslaw (1)
Cooked cabbage (1)
Curly kale (1)
Fresh beetroot (1)
Green split peas (1)
Pea shoots (1)
Red cabbage (1)
Rocket (1)
Salad burnet (1)
Sorrel (1)
Tomatoes (1)
Watercress (1)
Yellow split peas (1)

HERBS
Parsley (50)
Thyme (24)
Sage (18)

Bay leaves (13)
Marjoram (12)
Mixed herbs (10)
Rosemary (8)
Mint (4)
Chervil (3)
Chives (3)
Savory (3)
Celery seed (2)
Dill (2)
Oregano (1)
Pennyroyal (1)

SPICES
Nutmeg (33)
Ground black pepper (31)
Cloves (19)
Ground mace (13)
Black peppercorns (12)
Ground white pepper (12)
Blade mace (11)
Ground cloves (9)
Mustard powder (8)
Ground ginger (6)
Cayenne pepper 4
Cinnamon sticks (3)
Ground cinnamon (3)
Horseradish (3)
Allspice (1)
Green cardamom (1)
Paprika (1)
Saffron (1)

STOCK
Beef stock (14)
Lamb stock (12)
Chicken stock (8)

General stock (6)

ALCOHOL
White wine (13)
Red wine (10)
Ale (2)
Cream sherry (2)
Madeira (2)
Port (1)
Cider (optional in several recipes)

VEAL
Lean veal (1)
Sliced veal (1)
Veal (1)
Veal joint (1)
Veal mince (1)

BEEF
Cooked beef (2)
Sliced beef (2)
Beef brisket (1)
Beef flank (1)
Beef joint (1)
Beef marrow (1)
Beef mince (1)
Beef shin (1)

BIRDS
Chicken (6)
Turkey (5)
Cooked chicken (4)
Duck joints (2)
Cooked duck (1)
Cooked turkey (1)
Goose (1)

FISH

Brown shrimp (1)
Crayfish tails (1)
Marinated anchovies (1)
Pickled herring (1)
Prawns (1)
Rollmop herring (1)
Smoked mackerel (1)
Smoked salmon (1)
Smoked trout (1)

LAMB

Lean lamb (2)
Breast of lamb (1)
Cold lamb (1)
Lamb (1)
Lamb neck (1)
Lamb's liver (1)
Lean mutton (1)
Leg of lamb/mutton (1)
Minced lamb/mutton (1)
Mutton fat (1)

OFFAL

Pig's liver (3)
Caul (2)
Chicken livers (2)
Oxtail (2)
Black pudding (1)
Calves' liver (1)
Pig's head (1)
Pig's heart (1)
Pig's kidney (1)
Pig's lights (1)
Pig's trotters (1)

PORK

Pork belly (3)
Lean pork (2)
Pork joint (2)
Pork tenderloin (2)
Cooked pork (1)
Pork cheek (1)
Pork fat (1)
Pork leg shank (1)
Pork sausages (1)

CURED MEAT

Bacon (21)
Gammon (5)
Ham (5)

MEAT & BIRDS

Where it is relevant, I have suggested specific cuts of meat or type
of bird necessary for the recipe. Beyond that, I don't wish to be too
dictatorial. I am well aware of the irony of this statement, coming at
the start of several pages of instruction on ingredients.

OFFAL

Offal is becoming much more readily available, and even
supermarkets now have a pleasantly surprising range available. It
is also worth checking with your local abattoir, who may be able to
supply the more unusual items.

EGGS & CHEESE

Eggs should be large, and cheese should be strong. It is a false
economy to buy a lot of mild-flavoured cheese as you have to use a
great deal of it in order to imbue any flavour into your dish. A small
quantity of strong cheese is altogether more satisfactory.

FLOUR

The range of flours is becoming broader as manufacturers and
artisan mills find worth in diversifying away from ordinary wheat.
I've recommended several different flours in this book, but these
should not be treated as hard and fast rules, and experimentation
should be freely indulged. For pastry, there is still a need for gluten,
to a certain extent, but other flours can be mixed in to provide
variety in both taste and texture. As a general rule, to ensure the
chemical aerators are fresh and active, rather than keeping a stock of
self-raising flour I tend to use plain flour and add in baking powder
as and when required.

THICKENINGS

The consistency of sauces, gravies, soups, stews, etc., is very much
down to personal preference. I prefer a sauce or gravy that clings so,

for my tastes, a little thickening is always going to be needed. In the past, the standard method was either to stir in a paste made of equal parts of flour and butter or to use some of the fat from the dish itself to make a roux. Although this is an easy and straightforward method, it does have some drawbacks. Firstly, if too much heat is used, or cold liquid is added too quickly, the sauce or gravy can be prone to lumpiness. Secondly, it requires the flour to be cooked for long enough so that it doesn't impact the flavour, and thirdly, it makes the sauce opaque. There's nothing wrong with opaque, but sometimes what starts out as a rich dark gravy can be rendered a mediocre beige by the time a thickening roux has been added. There's also an increased prevalence of sensitivity to the gluten found in wheat flour, which then renders your sauce or gravy a no-go for anyone susceptible.

My preferred thickening is a cornflour slurry (cornflour mixed with a little water): it doesn't add fat to the sauce, there are no lumps or floury taste, there is no need to 'cook out' the cornflour and the sauce remains beautifully clear. It also allows whatever liquid you're thickening to be enjoyed by people with wheat or gluten intolerances.

FATS
All the recipes in this book use unsalted butter. This is purely my personal preference; I like to know how much salt is added to a recipe and, with some flavourings containing significant levels of salt, I find it is easier to control seasoning levels if the amount of processed salt is kept to a minimum.

Fat in pastry can be almost anything. The old-fashioned combination is for equal parts butter and lard. Lard really gives a great crispness (think pork pie crust) but, although not overly strong, it is still a little unrefined for sweet pastry. Tempering the mixture with butter gives the best possible combination for crispness and flavour.

For savoury pies, it adds an extra dimension if you can match the fat in the pastry with the meat of the filling – chicken fat for chicken pies, dripping for beef, and so on. Beef dripping and pork lard are both available in shops, but any additional fats need to be collected from the cooking of other dishes. Once separated from the meat juices, fats should be clarified (page 334) and stored in the fridge.

Suet is the hard, waxy fat that surrounds the heart and kidneys of beef and mutton. Its high melting and smoking points make it ideal for pastries and frying. Fresh suet can be obtained from your butcher and processed suet is available in supermarkets. Fresh suet requires refrigeration, but processed suet does not. Processed suet is dried and coated with flour to prevent clumping, which should be borne in mind when baking for those with gluten sensitivity. Much of this flour can be removed by rinsing the dried suet in a sieve under cold running water. Since it has been dehydrated, if you're using processed suet, reduce the quantity used to about 80–85 per cent of the weight of fresh suet. The equivalent fat in a pig carcass is known as leaf lard and can be used in a similar manner.

Marrow is the fatty substance found inside the larger bones of the beef carcass. Much prized as a delicacy by the Georgians and Victorians who ate it roasted and served on toast, it is ideal for making pastry for beef pies or indeed for adding to the filling with especially lean meat such as venison. Add richness to casseroles and stews by frying the meat in marrow fat either before or after cooking.

MILK
Unless otherwise stated, milk is whole milk.

SAVOURY FLAVOURINGS
Even the most expensive ingredients need dressing with a little seasoning or sauce here and there to bring out their best. Whether your larder or fridge is stocked with the season's finest or items at the bottom end of the scale in terms of budget, a little help never

goes amiss and judicious use of flavourings can go a long way to embellishing the food you produce.

There are numerous ingredients you can employ to adjust the taste of your sauces, but you will need to check their efficacy yourself. No matter how prescriptive the recipes, there will always be differences between the ingredients I used to create and test them and those that you have sourced. It is imperative that you taste your dishes before serving them. Only then will you be sure to get the absolute best out of your ingredients by seasoning accordingly.

Flavourings for improving sauces:
stock cube
Marmite™/yeast extract
Bovril™
Worcestershire sauce
Henderson's Relish™
anchovy essence
mushroom ketchup
dark soy sauce
light soy sauce
oyster sauce
redcurrant jelly
apple jelly
blackberry jelly
balsamic vinegar
red wine
white wine
cider
port

HERBS
Herbs were of great importance in the preparation of food in times past, but seem to have fallen by the wayside a little in the twenty-first century. Perhaps this is why British food is sometimes seen as plain, bland and even pedestrian. I generally prefer fresh herbs over

dried, simply for their bright flavours, but dried herbs are invaluable in the depths of winter, for last-minute meals and for injecting interest into run of the mill ingredients.

The range of fresh herbs available in supermarkets can be rather limited, with a wider selection available online. The easiest and most cost efficient approach is to grow your own, either in the garden or in a few pots on a windowsill. The range of herbs referenced in the book is probably larger than you will find in other books and includes some less familiar names. If you have limited space for growing your own herbs, I suggest you grow the less familiar ones and buy the more mainstream varieties.

You might be surprised at some of the suggested herb combinations, but if I have learnt anything from working with these old recipes it is that there are no rules. Beef with mint or lamb with sage aren't the combinations we would normally put together, but they work. Similarly, you might be perplexed by the seemingly vague 'bunch of mixed herbs'. Which herbs? How many? Fret not. Some supermarkets sell bunches of mixed fresh herbs ready packaged, or you can make your own by tying together whatever fresh herbs you have to hand. A 'bunch' is what can be easily held in a circle formed by index finger and thumb, about 25–30g.

A word or two about a couple of unusual herbs that I recommend:

Savory is a perennial plant that comes in both summer and winter varieties. It looks a little like rosemary in that it has thin blade leaves and grows in a bush. Summer savory has a lighter, almost sweet taste that's similar to marjoram. Winter savory is darker and stronger, an attractive mixture somewhere between thyme and mint.

Pennyroyal is a member of the mint family but with a much more pungent aroma and flavour. It is not to everyone's tastes. The herb can safely be used in cooking as the quantities are so small. The oil, however, is toxic and should not be used at all. Pregnant women should avoid pennyroyal.

SPICES

Many of the spices used in these old recipes are still available today, although they are usually found in pre-ground form in the supermarket spice aisle. This is convenient but, unless you're going to use them regularly, they run the risk of their flavours fading over time. Another approach would be to purchase whole spices and grind them, either in a pestle and mortar or spice grinder, as and when you need them. The flavours using this method are astonishingly bright and surprisingly fresh for what are essentially dried goods. Some recipes specify whole spices and some ground, as whole spices tend to impart a much more delicate seasoning than ground spices. If you're short of suitable storage space for both forms, whole spices might be the sensible choice.

ANCHOVIES

Anchovies have been used to season a whole range of dishes for hundreds of years. They could be said to be the umami of the seventeenth and eighteenth centuries; used in small quantities to flavour numerous rich sauces, ragouts, hashes and stews, they imparted a savoury note without a discernibly fishy aftertaste. Nowadays they are filleted and preserved in three main forms: in vinegar, oil or salt.

Anchovies pickled in vinegar retain their pale colour and have the most delicate flavour. They can usually be found at the deli counter and should be kept refrigerated. Anchovies preserved in oil or salt are much darker in colour and stronger than pickled anchovies. They should be thoroughly rinsed before use and are usually found in small jars or tins on the supermarket shelf. They do not require refrigeration unless opened.

Anchovy sauce is made with a mixture of salted anchovies and vinegar. It is possibly the most convenient form, but also the strongest flavoured, so use with restraint.

ONIONS, LEEKS, GARLIC & CHIVES

The onion family, or alliums, are available in a wide range of sizes and strengths, each of which will be more or less suited to your dish according to personal taste. Unless I feel a specific type of onion is the most suitable for a recipe, I have left the selection open as to what type to use.

I like to think of the onion family as a continuum of flavour strength, so if regular onions themselves are too strong for your tastes you can just select something towards the milder end of the scale. Personally, I love the rich sweetness of caramelised brown onions, but really dislike raw onion, so when a dish calls for just a gentle flavouring I will opt for chives or spring onions, whereas someone else might choose raw red onion.

There are hundreds of alliums, but a rough guide, from mild to strong, is: chives, wild garlic leaves (ramsons), spring onions, shallots, leeks, white onions, Spanish onions, red onions, brown onions, garlic.

You can tone down the strength of the onion in your cooked dishes by peeling off the papery skin and simmering them whole either in boiling water or milk until tender, about 20–30 minutes. You can also slice or dice the onion before simmering for an even milder taste. The onion-infused liquid can then be used for soup.

VINEGAR

Much as there is a sliding scale of intensity for onions, so it is with vinegars. At the mild end of the scale are the lightest vinegars, pale in colour, such as gooseberry, rice wine, white balsamic and white wine. Towards the middle are more robust types such as cider, pomegranate, distilled and sherry. The darkest vinegars include balsamic, malt, date and Chinese black. The type of vinegar you choose should be dictated both by your own personal tastes and by the recipe you intend to use it in, and whether the colour is going to affect the final dish.

VERJUICE

Verjuice is made from pressed sour or unripe grapes, crab apples or other sharp fruit. It is acidic, but not as harsh as vinegar, and is best utilised as a means of brightening rich sauces or fillings for pies. It can also be used in salad dressings. It is available commercially, usually made from grapes, but is also simple to make at home: press crab apples and pour the juice into a demijohn or large glass bottle, cover the neck of the bottle with a double layer of muslin to keep out fruit flies and leave to ferment; when fermentation ceases, what remains is verjuice. Decant carefully to avoid cloudiness from sediment, and use as required.

WINE & BEER

At first reading, cooking with wine in the seventeenth century seemed pretty straightforward: it was either white or claret. But after researching some of the wines mentioned in old recipe books, I found that neither 'white' nor 'claret' were as straightforward as they sounded. Both types came in such a range of hues and flavour profiles that the labels could almost be swapped and still remain valid, with dark coloured whites and light, pale reds. Some of the recipes in this book may call for a wine you wouldn't normally associate with a particular ingredient, but that is all part of the surprise and enjoyment. Bottom line: be guided by the recipe, but not constrained by it. Try with the suggested wine but, if it is not to your taste, try it with something else.

Beer was a popular daily drink in the seventeenth century. Small ale was the commonest drink for all and was considered to be more nutritious than plain water. With a low alcohol content and mild taste, golden ale is a good approximation. Again, it can be substituted for something more to your own personal tastes, but bear in mind the type of dish and proceed accordingly.

PICKLES & CHUTNEYS

Pickling was an important part of still-room seasonal activities as it preserved meat, fish, fruit and vegetables for the long, lean, winter months. Thankfully, in the twenty-first century we are able to rely on other sources for vegetables in wintertime, but the British love of pickles has endured, although not to the extent to which it was practised at the height of its popularity. They are a neglected accompaniment to a great number of dishes and can quickly and easily transform a snack into something of much greater complexity. Echoes of this enthusiasm for pickling are still with us in the range of pickles available in the supermarket. They are a great store cupboard standby for snacks and garnishing Deja Food dishes.

Chutneys became popular in the nineteenth century as expats returning from India tried to recreate the spiced condiments they had become accustomed to. Whereas Indian chutneys generally consisted of fresh ingredients, British chutneys are cooked fruits and vegetables preserved with vinegar, sugar and spices. They are fantastic accompaniments to cold meats and cheese, baked potatoes and sandwiches and, like pickles, deserve space in the store cupboard for their ability to transform the ordinary into something special.

SUGAR
Unless otherwise stated, sugar is granulated.

DEFINITIONS
OF OLD DISHES

There are a number of old recipes in this book that will be
unfamiliar. While there will always be some differences in
interpretation, the following is a brief guide to the different styles
of dishes as interpreted in this book.

RAGOO
An anglicised spelling of the French *ragoût*. A highly seasoned stew
of usually meat and vegetables, although it can also refer to just
vegetables in a sauce.

COLLOPS
Thin slices of meat for pan frying. Initially used in reference to
bacon slices, before broadening out to mean any thinly sliced meat.
If not bacon, the raw collops were usually scotched (see below) to
tenderise them.

FRICASSEE
Another French-derived word to describe meat in sauce. It's a pale
version of ragoo, using poultry, rabbit and lighter meats, and usually
cream to contribute to its paleness.

HOTCHPOTCH
A mixture, usually chopped small. Can be of meat, vegetables,
grains, pulses or any combination thereof.

SCOTCHED
A preparation method, usually for meat, whereby it is criss-crossed
either by slashes or by beating with the back of a knife, for the
purpose either of tenderising or for allowing marinade or stuffing
seasonings to penetrate the meat. It has nothing to do with
Scotland.

SAUCES

It might appear a little odd to begin a book with a chapter on sauces, but it is deliberate and intended to put you at your ease. You might be feeling understandably apprehensive at attempting recipes from long ago, some of which date back hundreds of years, so what better way to ease you into the world of deliciousness that is Deja Food than suggesting some sauces with which to garnish your meals. They can be served on the side and added in small quantities to your plate. I have deliberately selected recipes that are simple to make, in several cases involving little more than blending the ingredients together, in the hope that their speedy creation and delicious taste will serve as a reassurance of the joy to be found in old recipes. Think of the recipes in this chapter as culinary inflatable swim rings; initially giving reassurance, then being fun to return to play with when confident.

I love the sheer versatility of these first two sauces for those unplanned moments when the joint has failed to give up enough of its juices to create gravy, or even for use on quick-cook meats such as chops, minute steaks and sausages.

....

SAUCE FOR POACHED OR FRIED MEAT
Elizabeth Jacob, circa 1685

MAKES 500ML

500ml strong stock, whichever is
  most suitable for your dish
1 onion
2 sprigs fresh thyme
2 sprigs fresh winter savory
2 sprigs fresh marjoram
4 cloves
2 slices nutmeg

1 tsp black peppercorns
1 tbsp grated horseradish
1 strip lemon peel
1 anchovy fillet, rinsed
1 tbsp cornflour mixed with 1 tbsp
  cold water
salt and pepper

Put all the ingredients except the cornflour slurry into a small pan and simmer gently for 30 minutes to allow the seasonings to infuse. Strain through a fine mesh sieve. Taste and season appropriately. For a lightly thickened sauce, add the cornflour slurry, salt and pepper, and whisk as you heat gently, until the sauce thickens and becomes glossy. Taste again for seasoning and serve.

SAVOURY SAUCE FOR ANY MEAT

Jane Newton, 1675

This is a very chunky sauce, probably more of a moist vegetable ragoo, which I love not only for its versatility, but also for the way the turnips absorb the stock and become suffused with the aromatics. If you make this sauce the day or just the morning before required, the depth of flavour is much more pronounced, however the quantity of liquid is also much reduced. Consider using twice as much stock as the recipe demands. This can be a make ahead dish, by as much as 24 hours.

MAKES 500ML

50g streaky bacon, chopped
2 turnips, peeled and cut into
   5mm dice
1 medium onion, finely chopped
500ml meat stock, whichever is
   most suitable for your dish
1 bunch fresh mixed herbs

vinegar or verjuice (optional)
meat juices from the accompanying
   roast
1 tbsp cornflour mixed with a little
   cold water (optional)
salt and pepper

Cook the bacon in a frying pan over a medium heat until the fat starts to run. Add the diced turnip and toss. Cook until the turnip has softened, then add the onion and continue cooking until the onion has also softened and become translucent. Pour the stock into the pan along with the herbs. Mix all together and simmer gently for 15–20 minutes, stirring occasionally.

Remove the bunch of herbs and taste for seasoning. Add salt and pepper if required. Now you need to decide how to serve: to strain or not to strain. Personally I like the rich tumble of vegetables and little pops of bacon of an unstrained sauce, but you might prefer

Juices from Roast Beef (page 54)

something less busy. If so, strain through a fine mesh sieve, pressing down firmly to extract as much liquid as possible from the vegetables.

Return to the pan and taste for seasoning. If you're serving this with a fatty meat (e.g. pork, lamb, duck, goose), you might want to sharpen it a little with some vinegar or verjuice. Add any juices from the rested meat and check the seasoning once again. Thicken, if liked, with the cornflour mixture and serve in a warmed gravy boat.

GREEN SAUCE
Heppington Receipts, circa 1700
Serve with: veal, eggs, potatoes, salad

This subtle sauce is especially fine with hot or cold veal, but I love the colour and delicate flavour so much that I use it on almost anything. The original recipe suggested serving it hot, but keeping it closer to room temperature preserves the glorious colour and makes for a much more versatile sauce.

MAKES ABOUT 250ML

80–100g baby spinach leaves
2 hard boiled eggs
60ml verjuice

30ml cider vinegar
juice of ½ lemon
2 tbsp sugar

Put all the ingredients into a blender and blitz until the sauce is a smooth and vibrant green.

Pour into a pan and warm slightly before serving, although be careful of overheating as too high a temperature will cause the sauce to lose its colour.

EGG SAUCE

circa 1700

Serve with: chicken

This is a piquant sauce with the unusual addition of cinnamon.
It only makes a small amount, but a little goes a long way.

MAKES ABOUT 250ML

4 hard boiled egg yolks
100g unsalted butter
60ml white balsamic or a light
fruit vinegar
½ tsp ground cinnamon

½ tsp mustard powder
½ tsp ground white pepper
2 tsp icing sugar
salt

Pound the egg yolks with the vinegar in a mortar and pestle to
make a paste. Don't worry about it being completely smooth as it
will be blended later. Cut 50g of the butter into small cubes and add
to a pan with the egg mixture, spices and sugar. Warm over a very
low heat just until the butter has melted, then use a stick blender to
blend the mixture to a smooth sauce. Slice the remaining butter and
add it to the pan and use the blender to mix it into the sauce. Taste
and adjust the seasoning, adding more spice or salt as required.

DEJA FOOD
Use the sauce cold as a dressing. Pour it over a fresh mixed salad,
with or without chicken, or with the leftover chopped whites of the
eggs.

GOOSEBERRY &
PARSLEY SAUCE

1695

Serve with: chicken, goose, lamb

This unusual accompaniment to chicken is bright with wine and fresh herbs, with the added zing of sharp gooseberries. If you can't find small gooseberries or grapes, cut large ones into halves or quarters. This sauce also works very well with lamb.

MAKES 400ML

6 stalks curly parsley
250ml white wine
150ml strong chicken stock
2 anchovy fillets, rinsed
3 lemon slices
1 blade mace

2 slices nutmeg
1 tbsp cornflour mixed with 1 tbsp
cold water
100g small, sharp gooseberries or
green grapes
salt and pepper

Strip the leaves from the parsley stalks and set them aside. Cut the stalks into 5cm lengths. Put the wine, stock, anchovies, lemon, mace, nutmeg and parsley stalks into a pan and simmer gently for 30 minutes to infuse, then strain through a fine mesh sieve to remove the solids. Add the cornflour mixture, whisking as you do so, and heat gently until the sauce thickens and becomes glossy. Season with salt and pepper as required.

Finely chop the parsley leaves and add them to the pan along with the fruit. Warm through for 2–3 minutes before serving.

ONION GRAVY

Eliza Sleigh, circa 1650

Serve with: pork, sausages, lamb, mutton

Onion gravy is a wonderfully adaptable savoury sauce which pairs well with a number of grilled meats. The addition of vinegar lightly sharpens it to make it especially suitable for pork and lamb.

MAKES ABOUT 400ML

100g streaky bacon, chopped
4 onions, finely chopped
1 tsp coarse ground black pepper
250ml beef or lamb stock

1 tbsp homemade mustard
(page 46)
2 tbsp vinegar

Cook the bacon in a frying pan over a medium heat until the fat has rendered out, then add the onions and cook slowly until starting to caramelise.

Transfer the mixture to a fine mesh sieve and strain off the fat by pressing down gently with the back of a spoon. Rinse the pan and return the onion mixture. Add the pepper and the stock and simmer for 15–20 minutes. Add the mustard and vinegar and stir to combine. Taste and add more seasoning to your liking. Transfer to a warmed gravy boat and serve.

SPICED APPLE SAUCE

Seventeenth century

Serve with: pork, goose, bacon

Traditional apple sauce consists of chopped apples simmered slowly until they break down into a pulp and it forms a wonderfully tart accompaniment to fatty poultry, as well as meats such as pork.

This recipe, however, is an amalgam of two seventeenth-century apple sauce variations and boasts a little more interest in both the gentle spicing and the addition of the currants, which add sweetness but also retain the sharpness.

MAKES ABOUT 250ML

1 large Bramley cooking apple,
  peeled, cored and roughly chopped
2 cloves
2½cm piece cinnamon
1 tbsp soft brown sugar

2 strips lemon peel
4 tbsp currants, plumped in hot
  water
1 tbsp unsalted butter

Put the apple, spices, sugar, lemon peel and 60ml water into a saucepan. Cover and cook over a medium heat for 5–7 minutes, until the apple is softened and fluffy. Pick out the lemon peel and the whole spices. Drain the currants and add to the apple mixture with the butter. Stir until the butter has melted. Serve.

CARROT & SPINACH SAUCE
circa 1700
Serve with: lamb, mutton

As well as being a delightful change from the usual mint sauce accompaniment, this sauce is a great way to sneak through extra vegetables beneath the noses of unsuspecting children.

MAKES ABOUT 400ML

250g (1 large) boiled carrot   *250ml strong lamb stock*
80g baby spinach leaves   *pepper (optional)*
juice of 1 lemon   *vinegar (optional)*
½ tsp salt

Put the carrot, spinach, lemon juice, salt and stock into a liquidiser and blend till smooth. Taste and add pepper and/or vinegar, if liked.

MINT SAUCE
Traditional 1930s
Serve with: lamb, mutton

With the luxury of your own herb garden, or even a well-tended window box, mint sauce to accompany roast lamb is simple to prepare. The trick is to remember to make it far enough ahead for the mint to infuse into the sweet and sour vinegar. Ideally this should be two or even three hours before you intend to serve, but remembering this in the whirl of Sunday lunch, or indeed any other meal, is a whole other matter. Salvation comes in this recipe from a pamphlet of old Yorkshire recipes from the 1930s. After simmering the sugar and vinegar together to remove some of the harshness, simply pour over chopped mint leaves and leave to infuse. The type of vinegar and sugar have been left intentionally vague to allow you to experiment with different combinations. A joint of spring lamb might warrant a light white wine vinegar and caster sugar, while a robust shoulder of mutton could be best paired with a malt vinegar and muscovado. If your herb garden is especially abundant, there's also the possibility of experimenting with different flavoured mints. Best of all, this recipe will keep in a stoppered bottle for weeks.

MAKES 250ML

60g sugar   *30g fresh mint leaves, finely*
250ml vinegar   *chopped*

Simmer the sugar and vinegar uncovered in a small saucepan over a low heat for 15 minutes. Tip in the chopped mint leaves and leave to cool and infuse. Taste and dilute with water if required. Personally I love a feisty mint sauce, but even I need to tone it down a little from its 'neat' state. Pour into a clean bottle and serve or store in the fridge.

ENGLISH BUTTER SAUCE
Traditional eighteenth century
Serve with: boiled and steamed vegetables, poultry and meats

This is the basic butter sauce, the one complained of by the French, with a consistency of double cream. It is very plain. On the other hand, it is quickly made and can be flavoured either by using different liquids instead of milk or by adding more ingredients once cooked.

MAKES 150ML

5g cornflour   *60g salted butter, diced*
30ml milk   *salt and pepper*

Put the cornflour and milk into a small saucepan and whisk to combine. Add the diced butter and stir briskly over a medium heat until the butter has melted. Add 60ml water and continue whisking until the sauce comes to a boil and thickens. Taste and add salt and pepper to your liking.

MILK SUBSTITUTES
Replace the milk with any of the following liquids. Many of these alternatives are heavily salted so refrain from adding any salt until you have tasted the finished sauce.
Mushroom ketchup
White wine
Red wine
Worcestershire sauce
Henderson's Relish™
Lemon juice
Tomato juice

ADDITIONS
The following can also be added to a plain butter sauce.
Tomato purée
Mustard powder
Horseradish, powdered or freshly grated
Chopped fresh herbs such as parsley, thyme, chives, tarragon

BREAD SAUCE

Elizabeth Jacob, 1685

Serve with: chicken, goose, turkey, game birds

The traditional recipe for bread sauce (page 45) is a pale and delicate mixture of infused milk and breadcrumbs that is served as an accompaniment to a number of roasted meats. Its mild flavourings ensure it can be enjoyed both warm and cold, to be relished as much with the Sunday roast as the next day with the same, now cold, roast cut into slices and served alongside earthy baked potatoes and a selection of pickles, or even used as a spread in sandwiches.

This recipe, however, is a little different. I have great affection for Elizabeth Jacob and her manuscript cookbook.[1] If it wasn't for the fact that it is 350 years old, I'd liken this recipe to a modern reinvention of a classic. A number of details appeal to me: the use of water instead of milk, the sharpness of the lemon, and the inclusion of the meat juices from the roast, all of which make it possible to customise the overall taste to whatever joint of meat happens to be the star of the meal.

MAKES ABOUT 400ML

120g stale breadcrumbs
1 onion, peeled and quartered
15g unsalted butter (optional)
juice of ½ lemon or 2 tbsp white
*   wine or 2 tbsp vinegar*

strips of peel of ½ lemon
½ tsp ground black pepper
meat juices from the accompanying
*   roast, skimmed of fat*
salt and pepper

Put all the ingredients into a saucepan with 200ml water and simmer over a low heat for 20 minutes. You might need to add extra water if your bread is especially dry, but this can be evaporated later once the flavourings have infused. Remove the onion and the lemon peel and blend smooth. Return to the pan and heat through. Add the butter and stir until melted. Taste and add salt and pepper as required.

TRADITIONAL WHITE SAUCE

Serve with meats, vegetables—see variations

A simple white sauce could be made with as few ingredients as just milk and flour, but it would have no taste and little to recommend it. It strikes me that the traditional white sauce strives to appear just as nondescript but, on tasting, reveals a bouquet and richness of delicate yet complimentary seasonings. There is nothing in the various flavourings that will trespass on the appearance of the milky mixture. The spices are left whole, the onion uncut, so when they are removed, the milk appears just as plain and unadorned as it was at the beginning. It could almost be seen as a metaphor for British cooking as a whole: beneath a simple appearance lies subtle and delightful complexity.

MAKES 500ML

4 cloves	*parsley stalks*
1 onion, peeled	*1 blade mace*
500ml milk	*½ nutmeg, quartered*
1 celery stick, roughly chopped	*1 tbsp black peppercorns*
1 carrot, roughly chopped	*25g unsalted butter*
3 fresh bay leaves, crushed	*25g plain flour*

Stick the cloves around the base of the onion so that they will be under the surface of the milk to infuse. Put all the ingredients except the butter and flour into a pan and bring to a boil. Make sure the cloves on the onion are submerged. Remove from the heat, cover, and leave to infuse for 1 hour. Strain through a fine mesh sieve and set aside.

Rinse the pan and return it to the heat. Melt the butter and then stir in the flour.

Cook for 2 minutes, stirring. Gradually pour the flavoured milk back into the pan, whisking to avoid lumps. Continue whisking until the sauce thickens.

Having made your delicately flavoured white sauce, you can then choose to add a whole range of ingredients to adapt it to a number of uses.

RICH WHITE SAUCE

Serve with: cauliflower, leeks, braised celery, to bind pie fillings

1 × batch Traditional White Sauce   *salt and pepper*
1 large egg, whisked

Whisk the egg into the thickened sauce, taking care that the sauce is not too hot, otherwise it will cook the egg before it is blended. Taste and add salt and pepper.

PARSLEY SAUCE

Serve with: ham, broad beans, salmon, white fish, hardboiled eggs

1 × batch Traditional White Sauce   *salt and pepper*
4–6 tbsp chopped fresh parsley

Just before serving the sauce, stir in the parsley. (Cooking the sauce with the parsley added would cause it to lose both its vibrant colour and its freshness.) Taste and add salt and pepper as required.

EGG SAUCE

Serve with: salmon, white fish, cauliflower, potatoes, to bind pie fillings

1 × batch Traditional White Sauce   *salt and pepper*
2 hard boiled eggs, finely chopped

Add the eggs to the thickened sauce. Taste and season as necessary.

CHEESE SAUCE

Serve with: fish, chicken, pasta, cauliflower, broccoli, potatoes

1 × batch Traditional White Sauce   *½ tsp mustard powder or freshly*
60g grated Parmesan or vintage   *grated nutmeg*
* Cheddar*   *salt and pepper*

Add the cheese and mustard or nutmeg into the thickened sauce
and stir over a low heat until the cheese has melted and the sauce is
smooth. Taste and add salt and pepper as required.

ONION SAUCE

Serve with: chicken, turkey, salt beef, pasta

1 × batch of infused milk from the   *2 onions, peeled*
* Traditional White Sauce recipe*   *25g plain flour*
* BEFORE the flour and butter*   *25g unsalted butter*
* are added*

Simmer the onions in boiling water for 30 minutes. Remove and
allow to cool slightly, then finely chop. Add to the flavoured milk and
simmer for 10 minutes, strain then thicken with the flour and butter.

TRADITIONAL BREAD SAUCE

Serve with: chicken, turkey, goose, game birds, cold meats, in sandwiches

1 × batch of infused milk from the Traditional White Sauce recipe BEFORE the flour and butter are added

200–300g stale white breadcrumbs

Pour small amounts of the milk onto the breadcrumbs, stirring after each addition, until you achieve the consistency you like.

MUSTARD

Seventeenth century

Nowadays we are blessed with an over-abundance of different types of ready-made mustards. Nevertheless it is extremely easy to make your own, with the advantage of it being infinitely customisable to your own tastes. I remember as a child the weekly ritual of mixing up, in an egg cup, just enough eye-popping, fiery English mustard from the iconic little yellow tin kept in the cupboard to accompany the Sunday meal. The advent of online ordering has made it easier to source mustard seeds, both yellow and black, to grind and mix at home, but even with this customisation, the method is still as basic as grinding the seeds and mixing them with liquid (usually water).

The seventeenth century manuscripts in the Wellcome Library contain a range of homemade mustards from which I have selected, with admirable reserve I might add, just three examples to include here. As you will see, the ingredient you choose to mix your mustard with doesn't have to be limited to water; you can experiment with almost any liquid, sweet, sharp or neutral. There exist some old recipes for making mustard balls, which the gentleman or lady traveller would carry with them, shaving off a little at mealtimes before mixing with whatever they happened to be drinking. You can use ordinary mustard powder or grind your own mixture of yellow, brown or black mustard seeds.

As a general guide, use cold liquid for a hotter flavour, and hot, acidic liquids for a milder result. As always, adjust the flavourings to your own personal taste.

The following recipes make enough to serve with a main meal.

HORSERADISH MUSTARD
Jane Newton, 1675

4 tbsp mustard powder
1–2 tsp icing sugar
½–1 tsp grated horseradish

½ tsp ground white pepper
¼ tsp salt
white wine vinegar, to mix

MADEIRA MUSTARD
Amy Eyton, 1691

4 tbsp mustard powder
2 tbsp vinegar

1 tbsp Madeira
1 tbsp dark muscovado sugar

GINGER MUSTARD
1691

4 tbsp mustard powder
1–2 tbsp soft brown sugar

1 tbsp ground ginger
boiling water, to mix

Mix to the consistency of your choice and then set aside in a warm place until required.

MUSTARD SAUCE
1700

Serve with: pork, goose, duck or haslet

*50ml white wine, cider or rice
  vinegar
1½ tbsp mustard powder*

*2 tsp granulated sugar
25g unsalted butter
salt and pepper*

Warm the vinegar slightly and mix it with the mustard powder to form a paste. Add the sugar and butter and whisk to combine. Taste and season as liked.

Serving suggestion: with Mulberry Garden Beef [page 74]

SALAD CREAM
Newent WI, 1935

As a child I used to love drizzling salad cream down the length of a crisp cos lettuce leaf and then rolling it up like a cigar to munch on. I'm not sure whether it was my palate or the recipe that changed, but it has been decades since I last bought a bottle of salad cream because I found the vinegar overwhelmingly harsh. Happily, this recipe means that, once again, cos is back on the menu! It only makes a small quantity, perfect for mixing up fresh as you need it, and can also be tweaked to your own personal tastes.

The original recipe called for regular milk. When I first came across it, I was excited to try it and bounded into the kitchen, only to remember that I was out of milk. Necessity being the mother of invention (and being too impatient to cook to go out and buy milk), I experimented with alternatives that were to hand, hence the evaporated milk. I think it adds an extra creaminess, but you could certainly use ordinary milk or indeed cream or crème fraîche. If you're reluctant to open a tin just for this recipe I would suggest that the remainder could be whisked into boiled potatoes to make a creamy mash, or drizzled over fresh fruit.

MAKES SUFFICIENT TO DRESS A SALAD FOR 4

1 large egg	*30g unsalted butter*
2 tsp caster sugar	*2 tbsp white wine vinegar*
1 tsp Dijon mustard	*salt and pepper (optional)*
50ml evaporated milk	

In a small saucepan, whisk the ingredients together in the order given, i.e. add the vinegar last. Set over a low heat and continue whisking until thickened, taking care to ensure the mixture doesn't boil. If you prefer a pouring consistency, remove from the heat once the mixture has thickened slightly, as it will continue to thicken up as it cools. For a texture more akin to mayonnaise, stir over the heat a little longer. Set aside to cool. Once cooled, taste, and add salt and pepper if liked (I usually don't).

SALAD DRESSING
Stephen Switzer, 1727

Stephen Switzer was an eighteenth-century garden designer, a champion of the English landscape garden whose commissions included the parklands of great houses such as Castle Howard in Yorkshire and Blenheim Palace. This recipe comes from his book *The Practical Kitchen Gardiner*, a lengthy and detailed publication covering all aspects of horticulture, with entire chapters devoted to the best ways to cultivate and nurture every vegetable and fruit imaginable. Aside from its simplicity, this recipe is, to my mind, the perfect combination of ingredients to enhance everything it is drizzled upon. Potato salad is especially delightful, as the mildness of the potato is both complemented and contrasted by the sharp, creamy dressing. It is best poured over the potatoes when warm.

MAKES ABOUT 200ML

6 tbsp oil
4 tbsp vinegar
2 large hard-boiled yolks

2 tbsp Dijon mustard
salt and pepper

Put all the ingredients except for the seasoning into a small blender and blitz until smooth. Taste and add salt and pepper to your liking.

GRAVY
Traditional

Gravy is a time-honoured accompaniment to traditional Sunday lunches and should involve seasoning and (optionally) thickening the juices that emerge from the meat during the cooking. Even if there doesn't seem to be much in the pan when it is removed from the oven, once the meat has rested there will always be more. It will be full of flavour, so full, in fact, that you might need to dilute it with some liquid to make it more palatable.

The basic principle is the same for whatever meat or bird is being cooked: remove the fat from the meat juices, add flavourings and seasoning as required, thicken (or not) to your own personal taste.

Removing the fat
The best way to remove the fat from the meat juices is to let it cool enough for the fat to solidify. Rather than wait for this to happen at room temperature, pour everything from the pan into a shallow tin and chill in the freezer for 5–10 minutes then, when the fat has both risen to the top and solidified, either lift it off by hand or pour the liquid through a sieve.

Flavourings
Once your meat juices are fat free, you can adjust the taste by adding complementary flavourings, or by diluting with a suitable liquid, which can be as simple as water, especially that strained from any vegetables that have been cooked at the same time. Other options can be *wine, cider, apple juice, orange juice, sherry, Marsala, Madeira, port,* etc. Alcoholic additions will need to be simmered to burn off the alcohol and mellow the flavour.

A couple of tablespoons of *sharp fruit jelly* melted into the gravy (such as *apple, redcurrant, blackcurrant, blackberry* or *plum*) pairs nicely with both fatty (e.g. lamb, pork, goose, duck) and very lean (e.g. venison) meats. You can also sharpen an overly rich gravy with the light-handed addition of any of a number of different *vinegars* or *verjuice*.

More robust condiments such as *horseradish* and *mustard* can embolden a gravy, but might not be to everyone's liking. When in doubt, omit them from the gravy and serve alongside for people to help themselves.

Seasoning

Seasoning is extremely important; be bold but not heavy-handed with *salt and pepper* and they will add relish to the whole meal.

Thickening

Lastly, decide whether your gravy requires thickening. This is traditionally done by adding a little *flour* to the cooking pan and letting it absorb all the flavours from the fat rendered from the cooking of the meat. This fat and flour combination forms the thickener for the gravy. It also seems to provide the most problematic part of gravy making in that the subsequent mixing in of the cooking juices can create lumps, as well as cause the gravy to taste floury if it has not been cooked for long enough. Without experience, it is also difficult to judge how much flour to add, thereby running the risk of finding your gravy over-thickened once the liquid has been added. The only solution is to dilute to a more reasonable consistency, which, disappointingly, also dilutes the flavour. Far better, in my opinion, is to get the gravy tasting perfect and only then add the thickening. I prefer a mixture of *cornflour* and water, which has many advantages over the traditional flour and fat method (see page 19).

Gloss

Finally, for a high-gloss finish especially for lean meats, add a little clarified butter (page 335) to your gravy.

2

BEEF

Roast beef has become the quintessential British meal. Reading through old recipe books has me puzzling over why this should have come to pass, as historically there seems to be a great fondness for serving beef in a frankly startling number of completely different ways. Of the 250+ beef recipes in the seventeenth-century manuscript books at the Wellcome Library, only six are for roasting beef. More popular, or at least more frequently occurring, methods of cooking include baking, stewing, collaring, frying, potting, salting and drying, with recipes for hashes, puddings, ragoos, brawns, sausages, pies, pasties, and so on. There's a lot you can do with a cow, mostly because there's so much of it, and it doesn't always have to be limited to the one or two prime cuts of meat. For this chapter I've selected recipes based primarily on flavour, but also with an eye to budget and interest, and I hope you have as much enjoyment from them as I have done.

ROAST BEEF
Traditional

As a child, I used to think that getting a Sunday roast lunch on the table, with everything piping hot and cooked to perfection, was the most fiendishly difficult challenge in a cook's repertoire. All those vegetables, potatoes, gravy and sauces all coming together at the same time? It seemed to me something that would require field-marshal levels of planning and strategy. Consequently, I put off any attempt of my own for many years. Now, of course, I realise that it was much less complicated than it appeared, and one can be almost relaxed about the whole thing.

Search the internet for pictures of roast beef, and the most striking images will be of a magnificent 3-or 4-bone standing rib joint, a sirloin or a fillet of beef. All three joints are undeniably impressive, but also undeniably expensive. Nevertheless, a meal of roast beef can still be enjoyed without breaking the bank simply by choosing a better value cut of meat.

This recipe calls for either a silverside or a topside joint. These cheaper cuts of beef are best enjoyed sliced wafer-thin, so be sure to have your sharpest knife available for carving. When selecting your joint, check the face of each end and choose one that has little, or preferably no, connective tissue running through it. There's no guarantee you won't find some as you carve, but at least you can start with something looking the part. You should also select a joint with a regular shape that is chunky, rather than long and cylindrical; I've seen some very oddly shaped pieces of beef on the meat counter, which are invariably difficult to cook, the outsides all too easily becoming dry and the centre overdone.

The method of cooking is one I have settled on over the years because it is the simplest. There are numerous theories for how to cook beef, but many of them involve fiddling around with oven temperatures, times and calculations by weight, then adding some more time on at the end. A popular method is to put the joint into a hot oven and then turn it down after a while, but if you forget it, or initially have the oven a little too high, then the meat will be scorched, if not downright burnt, and there's practically no way back from there. It might seem odd to put the joint into a cold oven, but I find it is a much more reliable method for achieving tender, juicy, medium-rare.

The only calculation you need to make is how long to cook it for, and this is solely based on the weight of the joint: 15 minutes for every 500g. So a 1.5kg joint will take 45 minutes from the time you place it in the oven.

I use no seasoning on the meat: there'll be seasoning enough in the gravy. Salt will draw moisture from the meat and pepper runs the risk of burning, so it's best left until the end of cooking.

SERVES 4

1.5kg beef roasting joint, such as   *Equipment*
  topside or silverside   large roasting tin with a rack

About 1 hour before you would like to serve your meal, put your joint onto a wire rack over a roasting tin. This will allow the heat to circulate and make for even cooking. Put the meat into a cold oven, turn the heat up to 200°C/180°C fan/gas 6 and cook for 45 minutes. Remove, cover in foil and then a clean cloth and allow to rest for 15–30 minutes while the vegetables and accompaniments are cooked.

Once the rest of your meal is ready, transfer the joint to a warmed serving dish. Skim the fat off the meat juices that will have gathered in the roasting tin. Set the fat aside for use later and pour the meat juices into the gravy.

Serve with: Gravy (page 50), Light Baked Puddings (page 316), Horseradish Butter (page 316), Roast Potatoes (page 300), carrots, cabbage, buttered parsnips.

BEEF & CABBAGE PIE

Elizabeth Jacob, circa 1670

Beef and cabbage is a classic combination, more often served as a slow-simmered joint surrounded by cabbage cooked in the broth. This recipe requires much less preparation and allows the beef to retain more of its juiciness because, contrary to most pies, it is placed in the pastry raw. The pie filling is moist, but not overly so, so consider making a complementary sauce to serve alongside, such as one of the sauces for any meat (pages 30–31).

SERVES 4

½ savoy cabbage
½ red cabbage
600g beef slices
½ tsp salt
½ tsp white pepper
½ tsp nutmeg
1 × batch Beef Dripping Pastry
(page 327), chilled

30g butter, plus extra for greasing
50ml beef stock (or 1 tbsp Bovril™
in 2 tbsp boiling water)
1 egg, beaten

Equipment
20cm round loose-bottomed or
springform pie tin

Break off the outer leaves of the cabbages and cut out the stalks. These leaves have great colour, but the stalks are a little on the tough side. Shred all the leaves finely, discarding the central stalk. The cabbage will cook quicker and pack into the pie more neatly if it is in thin shreds. Steam separately over boiling water for 5 minutes each, until wilted but still bright in colour and firm to bite. Set aside to cool.

Beat the meat slices with a rolling pin or mallet until thin and tender, then cut into bite-sized pieces. Mix the salt and spices together and sprinkle all over the meat.

Grease a 20cm loose-bottomed or springform tin. You can use a wider tin, but there will be fewer layers and the pie will require longer cooking.

Roll out one third of the pastry for the lid. Cut it about 2cm larger than the tin to allow for shrinkage and overlap. Chill the lid in the fridge until required.

Roll the remaining pastry out to about 1cm thick. Lining a deep tin with pastry can be tricky, so here is the method I have come up with, which keeps fiddling to a minimum. Fold the top and bottom of the pastry towards the centre to form a rectangle, making sure the width of the folded pastry is the same as the diameter of your tin. Pick up the pastry by the ends and gently lower it into your tin. Make sure it is smooth and flat over the bottom of the tin, with no trapped air, and press the ends into the sides of the tin—the pastry will stick to the greased metal. Unfold the rest of the pastry, one side at a time, and ease it against the sides until the whole tin is lined and the pastry smooth. Let the excess pastry hang over the sides of the tin.

The height of this pie is very impressive once baked and served. Although the pastry is fairly robust, a little reinforcement is required. Take a scrap of pastry from the trimmings from the lid and roll it into a sausage shape about 1cm in diameter and 60cm long. It might be easier to make two 30cm lengths. Place around the bottom edge of the inside of the pie. Using the ball of your thumb, press it firmly into place. This will strengthen the bottom edge and help the pie to hold its shape, even when cut.

Melt the butter and brush it over the pastry base. Add a layer of one of the cooled cabbages. Sprinkle with pepper and add a few dabs of melted butter using a pastry brush. Top with a layer of seasoned meat. Repeat, this time using the other cabbage variety. Continue alternating the layers of cabbage with seasonings and meat until the pie is full, finishing with a layer of seasoned and buttered cabbage. Drizzle the beef stock over the filling.

Using a pastry brush, dampen the edges of the pastry with cold water. Lay the pastry lid over the pie and press the edges down firmly to seal. Trim the excess pastry using the back of a knife (so that you don't scratch your tin). Crimp the edges of the pie, either by hand or using a spoon handle or the tines of a fork.

Gather the scraps of pastry and arrange them on top of one another to preserve the layers. Roll out thinly and use to make decorations for the pie lid. A lattice is simple and effective. Brush the pie with beaten egg.

Preheat the oven to 200°C/180°C fan/gas 6 and bake the pie for 45–50 minutes, turning it around halfway through to ensure an even colour. Check at 30 minutes and cover with a sheet of foil or baking parchment if the pastry looks to be browning too much. Allow to rest in the tin for 10 minutes before transferring to a serving plate. There will be juices in the pie, so make sure your serving plate is large enough to catch them all.

SKINK
1680

A very old and traditional British dish, with versions occurring in English, Irish and Scottish recipe books. The most widely known version today is Cullen Skink, a thick soup of haddock, potatoes and onions, originating from the coastal town of Cullen in the north-east of Scotland. However, skink is not always a fish soup; I have found at least one (Irish) version that is made with vegetables only, and then there is the version I have for you here from a seventeenth-century manuscript that is made with shin of beef and appears to have been personalised from Robert May's recipe of 1660.

The variety of recipes can be attributed to the multiple meanings of the work 'skink', which can be the shin of an ox, a soup made of that particular cut of meat; to pour liquid, especially drink; a server of drink; and general liquid-based activities.

The amount of liquid in this dish can be varied according to taste, and it can be served either in bowls or on plates, with the extra liquid served on the side. It's probably most accurate to call it a pottage (or potage), a term that has also fallen into disuse over the years, but which is generally accepted to have meant a thick soup, although by modern standards it is closer to a thin casserole: large chunks of meat and vegetables in broth.

'Wee finde also that Scotch Skinck, *(which is a Pottage of strong Nourishment,) is made with the* Knees, *and* Sinewes *of* Beefe, *but long boiled.'*
Francis Bacon, Sylva Sylvarum, *or* A Naturall Historie: In Ten Centuries, *1635*

I am highly entertained by the idea of beef knees as an ingredient.

SERVES 4

1kg beef shin

1 bunch fresh mixed herbs

1 tbsp black peppercorns

2 blades of mace

4 cloves

6 carrots, peeled

1 swede, scrubbed and sliced thickly

stock cube (optional)

2 tbsp flour or cornflour mixed

   with a little water (optional)

1 savoy cabbage

salt and pepper

Put the beef, herbs and spices into a large pot with a well-fitting lid. Add the whole carrots and swede slices and sufficient cold water to cover the ingredients and bring to a boil. Cover, turn down the heat to a gentle simmer and cook until the meat is very tender (2½–3 hours). Remove the meat and set aside. Remove the vegetables and set aside.

Strain the braising liquid through a fine mesh sieve or wetted muslin to remove the herbs and spices. Remove the fat either by chilling and then lifting off the solidified fat or by using a fat-separator jug. Taste the liquid. If it is not strong enough, either simmer over a medium heat until it reduces and becomes stronger or add a stock cube. When you're happy, add salt and pepper. You could also add one or more of the enhancers listed on page 21. Thicken the liquid, if liked, using either a mixture of equal parts flour and butter or a cornflour slurry.

Peel the swede then cut all the vegetables into pieces. The meat will have naturally divided into chunks during the long cooking, so use these as a guide for the size of the vegetables. Return the meat and vegetables to the liquid and set over a low heat to keep warm while the cabbage cooks. Break off the outer leaves of the cabbage and cut out the tough stalks. Shred all the leaves finely, discarding the central stalk. Steam over boiling water for 5–8 minutes until tender.

Arrange the cabbage around a serving dish. Spoon the meat into the centre and arrange the vegetables over the top. Moisten with a little of the sauce, and serve, with extra sauce in a jug on the side.

DEJA FOOD

Skink pies (follow the recipe for Oxtail Pies on page 225).

VEAL RAGOO
1660s

Do not be hesitant in considering whether or not to buy and cook veal. Thankfully, it is over a quarter of a century since the cruel calf crates formerly used in its production were banished from these shores, and the animals that produce British rose veal now have a much healthier and happier existence.

A ragoo is a robust stew with a piquant sauce, heavily seasoned towards the end of cooking and served with an assortment of pickles. This ragoo is a milder version of the traditional beef dish, as befits the more delicate flavouring of veal. Instead of being sharpened with pickles, the dish is finished off with white wine and lemon juice.

SERVES 4

1 veal roasting joint, or 5–6 veal steaks (weighing at least 600g in total)
8 rashers back bacon
50g unsalted butter
1 litre beef stock
2 anchovy fillets, rinsed and chopped
1 batch veal forcemeat, made with the extra steaks or the joint trimmings (page 331)

2 lemons, sliced
1 bunch mixed herbs
150ml white wine
2 tbsp cornflour mixed with a little water (optional)
2 tbsp capers, drained
salt and pepper
2 slices white bread, toasted and cut into Sippets (page 333), to serve
fresh parsley sprigs, to garnish

If starting with a joint, set aside 125g for forcemeat and cut 4 thick slices. You can cut more but you will need more bacon for wrapping. Wrap the steaks in the bacon and fry in the butter until lightly browned. Add the stock, anchovies, half the lemon slices and the herbs. Cover and simmer over a low heat until the veal is cooked and tender, 1–1½ hours.

Roll teaspoons of the forcemeat into balls 'no bigger than a nutmeg', to quote the original recipe, and chill in the fridge until the meat is cooked.

Lift the meat from the broth and lay it on a serving dish. Cover and keep warm.

Strain the broth through a fine sieve and discard the lemon and herbs. Pour into a clean pan and bring to a simmer. Poach the forcemeat balls in batches in the stock. They are so small, they will be done in a minute or two. Don't cook them all at once, as they will cool the liquid too much. Once all the balls are cooked, cover and keep warm with the meat. Add the wine to the pan, turn up the heat and boil briskly to reduce by half. Taste and adjust the seasoning with salt, pepper and any of the seasoning sauces on page 21 you feel it needs. When you're happy, thicken with the cornflour slurry, if liked. Add the capers.

Spoon some of the sauce over the veal slices. Pour the remainder into a jug to serve separately.

Arrange the forcemeat balls and sippets around the edge of the dish, and garnish with lemon slices and parsley.

DEJA FOOD
Cut the veal into small pieces, similar in size to the forcemeat balls. Mix with the forcemeat balls and moisten with a little of the sauce. Pour into a deep dish. Add more sauce if available/liked. Blitz any sippets to breadcrumbs, or make fresh, and sprinkle over the top. Place in a cold oven and turn the heat to 200°C/180°C fan/gas 6. Allow to warm though for 25–30 minutes, until the meat is hot and the crumb topping has browned.

BEEF CAKES

Nineteenth century

This recipe is an adaptation of something I found in a nineteenth-century recipe book, and a great way for making cold roast beef into a tasty and appetising new dish. The recommendation was for it to be served hot for breakfast, but this might be a little too out of the ordinary for modern tastes. I can see it being a great brunch dish or an easy Monday-night supper, especially if prepared beforehand from the Sunday joint. The quick frying of the assembled cakes is only intended to colour the tops and bottoms of the potato; the heat won't reach the meat patty. The cakes can then be chilled until needed and then only require a thorough warming in the oven before serving.

SERVES 4

150g cold, preferably underdone beef
50g lean bacon
25g fresh suet
1 shallot or small onion, finely chopped
1 tbsp walnut ketchup (pickling liquid from a jar of pickled walnuts)

4 tbsp chopped fresh parsley
2–3 tbsp beef stock or 1 tbsp Bovril™ mixed with 2 tbsp hot water, cooled
400g mashed potato
salt and pepper
butter, for frying

Preheat the oven to 160°C/140°C fan/gas 3.

Mince or finely chop the beef and the bacon. Add the suet, chopped onion, parsley, ketchup and stock. Season with salt and pepper. Mix thoroughly and divide into 4 portions. Shape into patties.

Season the mashed potato and divide into 8 portions. Spoon a layer of mashed potato on top of each meat patty and pat into shape.

Turn the patty over and add a second layer of potato. The cakes should now resemble a burger in a bun, but with potato in place of the bun.

Melt a little butter in a pan and fry the cakes for 3–4 minutes on each side over a high heat, until nicely browned and starting to crisp. Transfer to a baking tray and warm through in the oven for 15–20 minutes.

BEEF COLLOPS WITH SIPPETS & FORCEMEAT BALLS

circa 1695

Collops means slices, and is used to refer exclusively to slices of bacon. The Monday before Lent was widely known as Collop Monday, when a meal of fried slices of bacon was eaten with eggs, the fat from the pan being reserved for the pancakes the following day. It later became a general term for slices of meat, and Scotch Collops survives to this day north of the border, although 'scotch' in this context has nothing to do with the dish being Scottish.

This recipe will suit any slices of beef, but especially those cuts labelled 'frying steak'. Be sure to tenderise them well by giving them a good pummelling with a rolling pin or meat mallet. The garnishes are crunchy sippets and savoury forcemeat balls. The forcemeat balls add another dimension to the meal and can also help stretch it a little further if necessary. You can prepare both the sippets and forcemeat balls while the meat is cooking.

SERVES 4

600g sliced beef
1 blade mace
1 large onion, chopped
small bunch fresh thyme
small bunch fresh parsley
3 slices of white bread
butter or beef dripping, for frying
fresh parsley, to garnish
lemon slices, to garnish

For the gravy
60ml white wine
1 beef stock cube or 1 tbsp beef bouillon
1 anchovy fillet, rinsed
1 lemon slice
1 tbsp mushroom ketchup
a grating of nutmeg
salt and pepper
1 tbsp cornflour stirred into a little cold water

For the forcemeat balls

150g beef mince	2 tbsp chopped fresh thyme
2 eggs	¼ tsp ground mace
50g fresh white breadcrumbs	½ tsp salt
50g fresh suet	½ tsp coarse ground black pepper
2 tbsp mushroom ketchup	light grating of nutmeg
4 tbsp chopped fresh parsley	zest of ½ lemon

Tenderise the meat by beating it with a wooden rolling pin or meat mallet. Put into a pan with the mace, onion and herbs and add enough cold water to cover. Stew slowly over a low heat until tender, 3–5 hours depending on the thickness and quality of your meat. Alternatively, cook in a slow cooker for 6–8 hours on low.

Remove the meat from the sauce and strain the liquid through a fine mesh sieve to remove the solids, which can be discarded. Skim the fat from the surface, either by chilling and then lifting off the solidified fat or by using a fat-separator jug. Add the ingredients for the gravy up to the nutmeg, and simmer for 10 minutes until the anchovy has dissolved. Taste and add salt and pepper as required. When you're happy with the gravy, add the cornflour mixture and warm gently. At first cloudy, when sufficiently heated the cornflour will both thicken the gravy and give it a rich and translucent gloss. Return the meat to the sauce and warm though.

Cut the crusts from the bread and then cut into cubes or use mini cutters to make shapes. Lightly fry in butter or beef dripping until crisp and golden. Drain in a wire sieve and keep warm.
Mix together the ingredients for the forcemeat balls. Check the seasoning by frying a little of the mixture and tasting it once cooked. If you're making these ahead, cover with cling film and chill in the fridge until required. Form the mixture into balls, patties, sausages or a selection of all three and dry fry over a medium heat until crisp on the outside and still moist in the middle. There's no need to use any additional fat as the suet will melt during cooking and provide sufficient fat for the pan. Drain in a wire sieve.

Spoon the collops into a serving dish and arrange the sippets and forcemeat balls around the meat. Pour over the remaining sauce and garnish with fresh parsley and lemon slices.

COLD BEEF & PICKLES
Traditional

When we were growing up, Monday was always washing day. We had an old twin tub with a spinner for squeezing out the water from smaller items of clothing and a free-standing mangle for large items and bed linen. It was a long, drawn-out process and took the whole day. And before you ask, no, I didn't grow up in the nineteenth century, merely rural Herefordshire in the 1970s. As a result of the extended wash day there wasn't much time for preparing an evening meal, so this became our standard Monday supper. It is a meal of contrasts, with hot potato, cold meat, salty butter, sharp pickles and fresh salad. A bonus is that, although the title mentions beef, it works beautifully with any joint of meat from the day before and, provided enough care and attention is given to the preparation of the cold meat and a reasonable store cupboard, is a veritable feast with the bare minimum of preparation.

SERVES 4

cold beef joint (or any meat)	a selection of chutneys
4 large baking potatoes, scrubbed and dried	coleslaw
	tomatoes
pickled onions	cucumber
pickled walnuts	radishes
pickled red cabbage	cold salted butter
cornichons or gherkins	Salad Dressing (page 49)

Using a skewer or a sharp, pointed knife, poke some steam holes into the potatoes. If the steam has nowhere to go, you run the risk of your potato exploding. Put potatoes directly onto the shelf of the cold oven, and set the temperature to 200°C/180°C fan/gas 6. Leave for 1 hour and test with a skewer. A fully cooked potato should have no resistance in the middle. If it does, leave for another 15–20 minutes.

Meanwhile, prepare the meat. Remove all the lean meat from the joint. If you can slice it thinly, then great! Otherwise, remove it in as large pieces as possible. Neatly remove all skin, fat, connective tissue, etc. before slicing thinly and arranging on a serving platter. Just because it is making a reappearance at the table doesn't mean it can't still look its very best.

Decant the pickles, chutneys and coleslaw into individual bowls; again, presentation is the key. You *can* just plonk the jars on the table, but you shouldn't. Wash the salad vegetables and arrange in a bowl for people to help themselves. Cut the butter into 'pats' for easy serving.

And that's about it. Serve all together when the potatoes are cooked; their skins will be hot, dry and crisp when taken from the oven, but will soften unappealing if made to hang about.

GEORGE'S PIE OR PIES
Mrs Mary Miller, 1660

This is an example of what appears to be a unique recipe. I've not been able to find any other instance of a pie with the same, or even similar, name. I found it in the manuscript book of Mrs Mary Miller.[1] At first I assumed that George was a family member, because it predates even 'The Pudding King' himself (George I) by about 60 years. Then I noticed that it wasn't called 'George's Pie' but 'A Georges Pie', and I started wondering whether Mrs Miller had been having a stab at spelling 'gorgeous'. As a word, it has been known in English since the fifteenth century, with a slightly less flamboyant meaning than modern times of 'elegant or fashionable'. However, even the most ardent pie-lover might hesitate to call something made with cold roast meat 'gorgeous', although this pie is, in fact, remarkably tasty. In addition, effusiveness of this type is noticeably absent from the recipes of the time and also much later. Plain speaking was the order of the day; they called a cake a cake, or if they were feeling especially exuberant, 'another sort of cake'. One delightful exception to this pithy approach was a recipe I found that rejoiced in the title 'The Puffs I Was Speaking Of Before In My Pottage'.

Whatever Mrs Miller was intending, this is certainly a very enjoyable dish, made all the more-so because you have a choice of ingredients with which to make it. The herbs add a freshness and brightness and the sharpness of the vinegar tempered by the sugar gives a delicate sweet/sour edge to the filling. You can make this as a single large pie, but I prefer to make small, individual pies, baking them in a cupcake tin. These pies are best served warm.

MAKES I LARGE OR I2 SMALL PIES

1 × batch Cornflour Shortcrust
  Pastry (page 326), chilled
160g cold lean roast beef or lamb,
  finely chopped
80g fresh suet, or 60g dried
80g fresh white breadcrumbs
4 tbsp finely chopped fresh
  marjoram
4 tbsp finely chopped fresh
  pennyroyal
2 tbsp finely chopped fresh thyme
100g currants

4 tbsp vinegar
2 tbsp sugar
1 egg
cold butter
1 large egg yolk mixed with 1 tbsp
  cold water, for the eggwash
salt and pepper

Equipment
20cm round pie tin or 12-hole
  cupcake tin
round cutters (for small pies)

Grease a 20cm pie tin or the holes of a 12-hole cupcake tin.

Divide the pastry into two and roll out one half to 3–4mm thick. Use it to cut 12 pie lids the same size as the holes in your cupcake tin, or the diameter of your large pie tin. I prefer to make the lid the exact size required and make the base much larger so that it can be folded over the edges of the lid to make a firm seal.

Gather the scraps together and roll them out with the rest of the pastry. Cut 12 pie bases and press them into the greased cupcake tin, or line the large pie tin, leaving the extra pastry overhanging the sides.

Preheat the oven to 200°C/180°C fan/gas 6.

Mix the finely chopped meat with the suet, breadcrumbs, herbs and currants. Beat the vinegar, sugar and egg together and pour over the meat mixture. Stir thoroughly. Season well with salt and pepper. If you're making a large pie, shape the filling into meatballs and arrange in the pie dish. An ice-cream scoop will help keep them evenly sized. For individual pies, divide the filling evenly between the pastry cases. Since the meat in the filling is already cooked, it won't shrink as much as a raw filling, so pile it high. Cut wafer-thin slices of cold butter and place over the filling, just to add a little richness to the pies.

Moisten the edges of the pastry lids and lay them over the pie or pies. Fold the excess pastry over the lid edges, pressing down firmly to ensure a good seal. Crimp the edges neatly and cut a small hole in the top of each pie to let out steam. Brush the lids with the eggwash.

Bake the small pies for 15–20 minutes, until the pastry is crisp and golden. A single, large pie will take 25–40 minutes, depending on the size. Allow the cooked pies to cool in the tin for 10 minutes, then remove and serve, or cool on a wire rack.

MULBERRY GARDEN BEEF
circa 1700

'In 1599, Oliver de Serres, a French agriculturist, published a work on the art of rearing silkworms, in which he urged his countrymen to the cultivation of the mulberry tree. This book caused a considerable sensation, and thousands of these trees were planted in the vicinity of Paris, while the King, Henri IV, embraced the scheme with such enthusiasm, that he ordered his orangeries to be destroyed, and mulberry trees to be planted in all the royal gardens. It is not improbable that it was this example which prompted our King James I to follow the same course in England.'

Jacob Larwood, The Story of the London Parks: St James's Park, *1872*

Inspired by King Henri, but prompted also by the need to create jobs, in 1609 James I not only sent thousands of trees out to the shires for cultivation, but also ordered 4 acres of St James's Park to be planted with mulberries. Alas, the scheme was not a success, the accepted wisdom being that the trees ordered were the black, instead of the white, mulberry, which the silk worms would not eat. With no viable use for the manufacture of silk, the area became a pleasure garden by the mid 1600s. Samuel Pepys visited the Mulberry Gardens in May 1668 and, in true Monty Python fashion, deemed it 'a very silly place', being filled with 'a rascally, whoring, roguing sort of people'.

This notwithstanding, a great many people enjoyed visiting the numerous pleasure gardens in London and refreshments were available for those that wished to drink and/or dine. This recipe appears to date from the latter part of the seventeenth century, if not a little later, and is a great example of something that could be made beforehand, and then served at short notice for a number of days.

Quite apart from the back story, an equally interesting aspect is that I have found this recipe in two entirely different handwritten manuscripts: one originally by Elizabeth Philipps, originating in Lincolnshire and now held at the Wellcome Library;[2] the other originally belonging to the Worcester-born Elizabeth Slany, whose manuscript book is now held by the Essex Record Office. This in itself is not unusual; in the course of my studies I have found a wide selection of recipes from printed books copied into household books. The detail that makes this particular recipe duplication interesting is that they are not the same recipe. They are similar, yes, but subtly different. One suggests brisket, the other beef flank. One recommends winter savory, the other suggests Rhenish wine is just as acceptable as claret for braising, and that the accompanying sauce be elder vinegar. To me this suggests that both were home-written attempts to reproduce something that had been personally tasted. Did both ladies dine at The Mulberry Gardens some time apart, perhaps? Did the recipe evolve over time? The possibilities are both entertaining and intriguing. Ultimately, the site of the Mulberry Gardens passed from being a pleasure garden and became the location of a series of ever more splendid houses, the latest of which is still standing today. It is known as Buckingham Palace.

The recipe itself is similar to that for salt beef. Beef is brined and then slow cooked and pressed until cold. It is served with mustard and pickles or, as Mistress Slany suggests, elder vinegar (page 77). It is fantastic in sandwiches or as part of a cold meat platter, served with hot baked potatoes.

If you can't get saltpetre, which will help keep the meat pink rather than grey, you can cheat by adding sliced raw beetroot to the braising liquid instead.

SERVES 4

Day 1
1.5kg beef flank or brisket   *25g saltpetre or preserving salt*
500g table salt, plus 2 tbsp

Day 3
2 bunches fresh sage
1 bunch fresh savory or a mix of
  thyme and mint
2 whole nutmegs, grated
2 tbsp coarse ground black pepper
20g ground cloves
20g ground mace

equal measures of red wine and
  water, to cover
sliced beetroot (optional)
200g fresh suet

Equipment
2 × large ziplock bags
butcher's string

Mix together 500g of the table salt and the saltpetre or preserving salt and dissolve in 2 litres of water. This will be easier if you heat the water a little, but you will then have to allow the brine to cool before pouring over the meat.

Unroll the beef, if applicable, and score the insides with a knife to allow the salt to penetrate the meat. Put the meat into a large ziplock bag and pour over the cold brine. Seal and place inside a second bag (in case of leaks). Put the meat into the fridge and allow to cure for 2 days, turning every 12 hours.

Strip the herb leaves from the stalks and chop finely. Grind the spices and mix with the herbs and remaining 2 tablespoons salt.

Remove the beef from the brine and rinse. Pat dry with paper towels. Spread the herb and spice mixture generously over the insides of the beef. Roll up the meat tightly and tie with butcher's string.

Put the rolled joint into a close-fitting pot. Add any remaining spice mix to the pot and then pour over sufficient wine and water to cover. Add the sliced beetroot, if using, and lay the suet over the top. Cover the pot with a double layer of foil and tie with string. The suet will gradually melt and form a liquid seal over the wine mixture, and help to prevent evaporation. Put the pot into the cold oven and set the temperature to 180°C/160°C fan/gas 4. Bake for 5 hours, then remove and set aside until cool enough to handle.

Remove the meat from the pot and tighten the string around the joint as it will have loosened during cooking. Wrap the joint in a double layer of foil and tie more string around the outside to secure. Lay the wrapped joint under a heavy weight overnight or until completely cold. Your Mulberry Garden Beef is now ready to be sliced and served.

Store in the fridge in a sealed container.

ELDER VINEGAR

To make elder vinegar, pick a large quantity of elderflower blossoms and allow to dry in the sun. Fill clean, sterilised jars with the dried blossom (no stalks) and pour over white wine vinegar to cover. Allow to infuse for 2 weeks, shaking every day. Strain out the flowers by passing through muslin and bottle for use in clean, sterilized bottles.

PONTACK'S COLLOPS
Johnson Family Manuscripts, 1695

Since the Middle Ages, wine from Bordeaux vineyards was grouped together and sold under the name of individual parishes. The price could vary by as much as 400 per cent between these localised areas and, since the quality of the wine sold within any one area would also vary, the producers of lesser quality wines would thus benefit from their association with a region that was well regarded. By the same token, producers of superior quality wines might suffer when grouped with a large number of wines of lesser quality. In the middle of the seventeenth century, one gentleman who believed the wine produced at his 'house on the little hill' should command a higher price than that set by the local parish of Pessac, was Monsieur Arnaud III de Pontac (1599–1681), and the wine was the soon-to-be renowned, Chateau Haute-Brion.

Monsieur Pontac's wine was already available in London. Entries for it can be found in the wine ledgers of Charles II in 1660[3] and M. Pontac may even have had a business arrangement with the Royal Oak Tavern, Lombard Street. Samuel Pepys's diary entry for 10 April 1663 includes the line:

'Off the Exchange with Sir J. Cutler and Mr. Grant to the Royall Oak Tavern, in Lumbard Street, where Alexander Broome the poet was, a merry and witty man, I believe, if he be not a little conceited, and here drank a sort of French wine, called Ho Bryan, that hath a good and most particular taste that I never met with.'

After the Great Fire of London in 1666, the ambitious Monsieur Pontac took advantage of the vast rebuilding programme and sent his son François-Auguste to London to promote his wines. Pontac junior opened a tavern on the site of the old White-Bear tavern in Abchurch Lane, which he named 'L'Enseigne de Pontac', or the 'Sign of Pontac's Head'. The tavern's sign consisted of a portrait of Monsieur Pontac senior, at the time President of the Bordeaux parliament.

The food in the tavern was a showcase for the wine, and made Pontac's famous and also the most elegant—and expensive—place to dine in London. For an idea of the haute cuisine served there we can thank the poet Elizabeth Thomas, who includes a list of food from Pontac's in her 1730 poem:

'Bird's Nest Soup, Snail Ragout, a day old piglet with a stuffing of hard roe perfumed with ambergris, peas stewed in gravy with cheese and garlic, a tart of frogs and forcemeat, crimped cod with a shrimp sauce and two-hour-old chicks 'in surprize'.' [4]

I suspect that this is somewhat satirical, since all the recipes that I have found associated with the tavern are much more accessible, including this one.

The culinary ghosts of this remarkable tavern have not completely disappeared from these shores. It is still possible to find recipes for Pontack Sauce, a highly spiced seasoning sauce in the style of Worcestershire sauce and Henderson's Relish™ can be made with elderberries, vinegar, shallots and spices. Slightly off-putting is the observation in more than one account that it is best enjoyed after being aged for seven years. I have some in the cupboard a mere two years from maturation, at which time I expect to be both delighted with the result and appalled that I haven't made it annually in the intervening years.

SERVES 4

4 veal escalopes
1 tsp Spice Mix (page 329) or a
  light sprinkling of cloves, mace,
  nutmeg, pepper and salt
1 × batch Veal Forcemeat (page 331)
50g clarified butter (page 335)
2 shallots, finely chopped
150g chestnut mushrooms, thinly
  sliced

2 anchovy fillets
1–2 tbsp oyster sauce
zest and juice of ½ lemon
1 tbsp cornflour mixed with a little
  cold water (optional)
orange and lemon slices, to garnish

For the cooking liquid
500ml chicken stock
500ml beef stock
250ml red wine
6 cloves
3 blades mace
½ nutmeg, sliced

10 sprigs fresh parsley
10 sprigs fresh thyme
1 sprig fresh rosemary
1 tsp coarse ground black pepper

Equipment
cocktail sticks or butcher's string

Put all of the ingredients for the cooking liquid into a pan and simmer gently for at least 30 minutes to allow the flavours to develop.

One at a time, lay the escalopes onto a sheet of cling film and cover with a second sheet. Tenderise the meat by pounding with a meat mallet or wooden rolling pin until thin. Sprinkle the spices over both sides of the veal slices.

Divide the forcemeat into 4 equal portions and form into sausages. Roll the veal slices around the forcemeat and fasten, either with cocktail sticks or butcher's string. Form any excess forcemeat, or any that falls out of the rolls as you tie them, into walnut-sized balls.

Strain the cooking liquid through a fine mesh sieve and pour back into the pan. Bring to a gentle simmer and then add the rolled veal. Poach the rolls in the liquid until cooked and tender, about 25–30 minutes, adding the forcemeat balls for the last 10 minutes. Lift the rolls and forcemeat balls from the liquid and keep warm.

In a separate pan, heat the butter. Toss the veal rolls in the hot butter until lightly browned, then remove from the pan and keep warm.

Add the shallots to the pan and cook over a medium heat for a few minutes until translucent. Add the mushrooms and chopped anchovies to the pan. Continue cooking until the liquid from the mushrooms has evaporated. Add 500ml of the cooking liquid, the oyster sauce and lemon zest and bring to a simmer. Taste and season with salt and pepper and the lemon juice, if required. Add any of the other seasoning sauces listed on page 21 at your own discretion. Thicken, if liked, by adding the cornflour slurry and bringing to a gentle boil.

Remove the string or cocktail sticks from the veal rolls and slice each roll into 2 or 3 pieces.

Stand the rolls on a warmed serving dish with the forcemeat balls arranged around. Spoon over the sauce and serve garnished with orange and lemon slices.

BIRDS

3

This chapter is a collection of a range of recipes for both wild and domestic birds. It is interesting that birds encompass our most elaborate feasts (the Christmas goose or turkey) as well as one of our simplest and most comforting meals (roast chicken).

Chicken is hugely popular and very straightforward to cook, with none of the fussing and fretting about times and degrees of done-ness that accompanies other meats such as beef or game. In times past, the eggs that chickens produced were valued more than the chickens themselves, so outside of the great royal kitchens, having a bird to cook quite often meant that it was either going to be a cockerel or a hen past its laying usefulness. In short, the chicken was unlikely to be in its prime and, over time, recipes evolved to make the most of these less-than-ideal ingredients. The most popular methods involved lots of moisture, by poaching the bird, baking it with rich sauces or encasing it in pastry. If the bird in question was too unpalatable even for these methods to rescue, there was always the popular seventeenth-century drink that involved adding the cooked and spiced carcass of a cockerel to a barrel of ale and allowing it to steep. This made what was known as cock ale, mentioned by Pepys in his diaries and described by both Nathan Bailey in his *Dictionarium Britannicum* (1736) and Francis Grose in his *A Classical Dictionary of the Vulgar Tongue* (1785) as 'provocative', meaning, in the usage of the time, encouraging of strong desires. Hopefully the following recipes will prove sufficiently inspiring without having to resort to a slug of cock ale.

ROAST CHICKEN & GRAVY

Nowadays, while we are blessed with a plentiful supply of chicken, the quality is still, if we're honest, usually not the finest. Modern breeding methods tend to produce a bulky but fatty chicken—the couch potato of the poultry world. Consequently, as in previous times, the method of preparation needs to be adapted in order to get the most out of the chickens that are available.

This method, of my own devising, is not only incredibly simple, with practically no preparation time, but will also result in meltingly tender chicken. It takes the perceived negative of fatty chicken and turns it to an advantage by slow baking in the oven for several hours. Thus the fat renders down, basting the lean meat as it does so and enriching the juices in the pan. The one downside, if any, is that the chicken ends up fall-apart tender and is nigh on impossible to transfer to the serving dish in one piece. However, it makes it incredibly easy to separate the chicken from the bones etc. and thus create a sumptuous and easy-to-serve platter instead.

For a beautiful colour and crispy skin, you can follow Jane Newton's tip (*circa* 1675) and baste your chickens with whisked egg white.

To take advantage of the long oven time, buy the largest chickens you can. The lengthy bake means that you don't have to worry about timings or weights, they will definitely be cooked by the end. Cook them side by side and you'll have plenty of cooked chicken ready to use in other dishes.

SLOW COOKER METHOD:
If you have a busy day ahead, if it's not convenient to spend 4 hours in the kitchen, or if you only want to cook a single bird, cut 1 onion, 2 carrots and 3 sticks of celery in half and lay in the bottom of a slow cooker. Rest the chicken on top, cover and cook on low for

8 hours. No additional liquid is required, as there is more than enough in the vegetables and the chicken itself, which make enough juices for the basis of a tasty gravy.

SERVES 4

2 large chickens   *2 large egg whites*

Put the chickens side by side on a wire rack in a roasting tin. Pour about 500ml water into the bottom of the tin to keep the chickens moist. Whisk the egg whites and brush over the chicken skins, making sure they are thoroughly coated. Put the pan in a cold oven and set the heat to 140°C/120°C fan/gas 1. Cook for 3 hours, brushing over more egg every hour.

Remove the cooked chickens from the oven and lift them into a warmed dish.

Cover with foil and a clean cloth to keep warm. They will retain their heat for almost an hour, so you can prepare the rest of the meal without a panic. The skin will soften under the foil, so if you like to serve it crisp, remove it now and keep warm.

Strain the meat juices from the pan into a plastic jug. Remove the fat either by chilling and then lifting off the solidified fat or by using a fat-separator jug. Alternatively, the juices might be the first to set into a rich jelly, in which case, the liquid fat can be poured off. Either works.

Use some hot water from cooking your vegetables to splash into the chicken pan to help loosen any caramelised bits stuck there. Pour this and the chicken juices into a small saucepan. Warm though and taste. If good, and there is sufficient liquid for your gravy needs, serve as is. Otherwise you can use one of the following methods to fine-tune the gravy to your own personal taste:

—*Not enough gravy:* add chicken stock, if you have some, or more hot water, or a splash of either sherry or Madeira wine. Adding more liquid will dilute the strength of the gravy.

—*Flavour not strong enough:* add more chicken stock and simmer to reduce until strong enough, or add a commercial stock cube. Stock cubes are rather heavy on the salt, so add no seasoning until just before serving, if at all.

Taste and season as required and pour into a warmed gravy boat.

Unwrap the chickens and separate the meat from the carcass. Arrange neatly on a serving dish together with the crispy skin and serve the gravy on the side.

Serve with: steamed cauliflower, steamed cabbage, Savoury Pudding (page 323), Bread Sauce (page 41), Celery in a Cream Sauce (page 274) and Clapshot (page 310).

POACHED CHICKEN WITH BACON & CELERY

Hannah Glasse, 1747

Poaching chicken, or indeed any meat, is a great way to get it meltingly soft and moist with the minimum amount of attention. As a bonus, you get lots of beautifully clear stock with which to make your sauce, as well as to use in other recipes. This recipe comes from the doyenne of eighteenth-century cooks, Mrs Hannah Glasse. Hannah suggests cooking and serving two chickens side by side, but in this day and age we're more likely to be limited by the size of our kitchenware. Nevertheless, I have actually managed to successfully employ my preserving pan and a tin foil 'lid' to successfully poach both a medium-sized turkey and, on a separate occasion, a whole goose.

SERVES 4

3 thick slices bacon or gammon
    (about 200g total)
1 whole chicken
2 small onions, peeled
3 cloves
2 carrots, scraped and cut into
    thick slices
1 tsp celery seeds
4 fresh bay leaves
1 tbsp whole black peppercorns
6 stalks fresh parsley

10 sprigs fresh thyme
8 celery sticks

For the sauce
125ml double cream
chicken stock granules (optional)
salt and pepper

Equipment
large, deep saucepan with a lid

Put the bacon into the bottom of the pan and put the chicken on top, breast down. This ensures the fleshiest parts of the bird stay submerged as it cooks. Add cold water to cover, bring gently to the boil and simmer for 5 minutes, removing any scum that rises. When all the scum has been removed, add the rest of the ingredients except for the celery and reduce the heat to a very gentle simmer, where the surface of the water is just rippling. If you don't have a lid for your pan, cover it with foil and crimp the edges tightly round the pan. Leave simmering for 1½ hours, or until the chicken is cooked through. Let the chicken cool in the broth for 30 minutes, then remove, together with the bacon, and set aside on a plate. Cover with foil and keep warm.

Strain the chicken stock through a sieve. Strain again through damp muslin if you want it especially clear. Cut the celery into 5cm lengths, and then into 2cm wide batons. Put the celery into a pan with a close-fitting lid and add just enough stock to cover. Bring to the boil, then cover and reduce the heat to a gentle simmer for 20 minutes, or until the celery is tender. If you prefer a softer bite to your braised celery then simmer it a little longer but be warned, it will lose some of its colour. Remove the celery with a slotted spoon and set aside. Boil the stock until it has reduced to about 125ml. Add the double cream for the sauce and salt and pepper to taste. If it needs extra flavour, add a teaspoon of chicken stock granules.

Cut the fat off the bacon and dice the lean meat. Melt a little butter in a pan and quickly cook the bacon cubes until crisped. Drain on kitchen paper.

Divide the chicken into pieces—cut each breast into 2, 2 drumsticks, 2 thighs, 2 wings—and arrange on a serving plate.

Add the braised celery and bacon to the cream sauce and warm through. Spoon the sauce over the chicken and serve.

DEJA FOOD
You don't need to wait 3+ hours to enjoy this dish. If you have some cooked chicken, you're more than halfway there. Skip down to cooking the celery and making the sauce.

Keep the stock for use in other dishes. If you have nothing planned then freeze it in suitable containers or sealable plastic bags.

BUTTERED CHICKENS
Mid seventeenth century

This recipe caught my eye initially because of its similarity in name to the modern Indian dish, however, it is just about as far removed from that rich, spicy creation as it is possible to be: delicately poached chicken with a buttery, creamy sauce, served with parsley and crunchy toast sippets. I found several versions of this recipe and, after studying them, the general impression was that the quantities of butter used were purely down to individual taste. I've been quite restrained in the recipe below, but feel free to add extra for additional richness.

SERVES 4

1 large chicken, poached (see preceding recipe) or 600g cooked chicken
toast sippets, parsley sprigs and lemon slices, to garnish

For the braising liquid
150ml milk
100ml white wine
2 blades mace
peel of 1 lemon, in large strips
salt

For the sauce
150ml double cream
75ml white wine
120g unsalted butter, diced
1 rounded tbsp cornflour mixed with a little water
salt and ground white pepper
5–6 tbsp chopped fresh parsley
zest of ½ a lemon

Remove the chicken from the poaching liquid and separate the meat from the carcass. Cut into bite-sized portions. Warm the braising ingredients in a separate pan. Add the chicken pieces, lower the heat to the lowest possible setting, cover and simmer to warm through, 5–10 minutes, then remove the chicken from the pot. Discard the mace and lemon peel. Cover the chicken and keep warm.

To make the sauce, add the braising liquid to the cream and heat gently. Add the white wine and butter and stir until the butter melts. Taste and add salt and white pepper as required. Add the cornflour slurry and stir briskly until the sauce is thickened. Just before serving, stir in the parsley and lemon, add the chicken to the pan and toss to coat it in the sauce.

Pour the chicken and all the sauce into a serving dish and garnish with sippets, sprigs of parsley and slices of lemon.

CHICKEN WITH ORANGES
Mrs Carr, 1682

I liked the sound of this recipe because orange is more often associated with the much richer duck, its sharpness a perfect match for the richness of the meat. This is an altogether more relaxed dish, ideal for a midweek supper because it uses already cooked chicken. You do, however, need to begin the day before you plan on serving it.

SERVES 4

500g cooked chicken, either jointed or in bite-sized portions
2 oranges
250ml red wine
250ml strong chicken stock

1 rounded tbsp cornflour mixed with a little water
sugar
salt and pepper
parsley sprigs and orange slices, to garnish

Day 1: Zest the oranges. Simmer the zest in the wine for 7 minutes, then add sugar to taste.

With a sharp knife, slice off the top and bottom of the zested oranges. Stand the oranges on end and remove the pith by cutting

down, from top to bottom, between the pith and the flesh. Separate the segments by slicing down the side of each membrane. If you do this over a dish you'll catch any juice that drips down. Sprinkle a little sugar over the oranges, then cover both the orange segments and orange wine and set aside overnight.

The following day, put the chicken into a pan and pour over the orange wine and the chicken stock. Cover and bring to a simmer, shaking every now and then to keep the chicken from sticking. Since the chicken is already cooked, you don't want to use a utensil to stir, if at all possible, as it might break up the meat. When hot, lift out the chicken and transfer to a warmed serving dish. Cover with foil and keep warm while you finish the sauce.

Taste and season with salt and pepper as liked. Add the cornflour slurry to the pan and stir briskly until the sauce is thickened, translucent and glossy. Add the orange segments and any juice that's collected and warm through. Taste again and adjust the seasoning if necessary. Pour over the chicken and garnish with parsley and orange slices.

DURRYDE PASTIES
Eighteenth century

This is one of a number of forgotten recipes that I have stumbled across in dictionaries of lesser-known and obsolete words and other less culinarily-oriented texts. Despite several mentions of the pastries I have yet to discover a single recipe. All descriptions seem to be in agreement that they consisted of chicken, onions and spices cooked in pastry, and were supposedly great favourites as portable food, as pasties were in the West Country. This recipe can be tweaked to your own personal tastes merely by varying the spice paste you use.

SERVES 4

50g clarified butter (page 335)
2 tbsp favourite spice paste
4 onions, peeled and thinly sliced
  (on a mandolin if you have one)
½ tsp salt
½ tsp ground black pepper

1 × batch Cornflour Shortcrust
  Pastry, chilled (page 326)
300g cooked chicken, cut into 1cm
  cubes
1 large egg, beaten

Melt the butter in a pan over a medium heat and fry the spice paste gently until aromatic, about 5 minutes. Add the onion and toss to coat. Sprinkle with salt and pepper and cook slowly until softened. This will take 25–30 minutes. Remove from the heat and set aside to cool.

Preheat the oven to 200°C/180°C fan/gas 6 and line a baking sheet with parchment paper.

Divide the pastry into 4 portions and roll out to a thickness of 5mm.

Stir the diced chicken into the spiced onions and mix thoroughly, then divide between the 4 pasties and spread evenly over the middle of the pastry. Dampen the edges of the pastry with water and fold each one over the filling. Press the edges together firmly to seal and crimp using a pinch-and-fold method or by pressing with the tines of a fork. Brush the pasties with the beaten egg and cut a small slit in the top of each one to let out the steam. Arrange on the prepared baking sheet and bake for 25–30 minutes, turning halfway through baking to ensure even colouring, until fully baked and the pastry is crisp and golden, then transfer to a wire rack to cool.

LUMBER PIE
circa 1690

Lumber Pie is one of a surprisingly large number of named pies that have fallen out of fashion in the past 300 years. It can be difficult to define what exactly a Lumber Pie is, because the recipes that abound in old cookery books and manuscripts all vary from one another to a greater or lesser extent. This variation can be frustrating if you are the sort of person that relishes order and absolutes. On the other hand, it can also allow you the freedom to be creative with whatever you have to hand. Having read over 70 recipes for just this one pie, I am confident that I can summarise the key points.

Lumber Pie is made from chopped meat, either raw or cooked, mixed with suet, herbs and spices and bound together with eggs. This mixture is formed into balls or small sausage shapes which can contain pieces of marrow or fruit in the middle. The meatballs are used to fill a pie dish or pastry crust and sprinkled throughout are small pieces of chopped candied peel and sometimes dried fruit. Sharp fresh fruit such as small grapes, gooseberries or barberries are used to cut through the richness. The whole is covered with a pastry lid and baked. Before serving, a caudle or thickened egg sauce is poured into the pie.

This mixing of fruit and savoury is common in old recipes, and is not so far removed from the fruity tagines and curries we enjoy today. The grapes used would have been the bunches pruned from the vines in order to allow the remaining fruit to ripen fully, and would have been eye-poppingly sharp when raw, but perfect to cut through the richness of the pie filling when cooked. Fresh cranberries are an ideal substitution, as well as adding a cheerful pop of colour.

SERVES 4

500g turkey mince
125g fresh suet
½ tsp salt
½ tsp black pepper
4 tbsp chopped fresh parsley
1 tbsp chopped fresh thyme
½ tsp nutmeg
¼ tsp ground cloves
¼ tsp ground mace
75g fresh white breadcrumbs
85g currants
30g candied citron, finely chopped

30g candied lemon peel, finely
   chopped
3 large eggs, plus 3 large egg yolks
1 sheet ready-roll puff pastry
200g small, sharp grapes or
   gooseberries or fresh cranberries
100ml white wine or verjuice
50ml cream sherry
50g butter

Equipment
large, deep pie dish

Mix together the turkey, suet, seasonings, herbs, spices, breadcrumbs, currants, candied fruit and two of the eggs to form a smooth paste and then shape into balls. A small ice-cream scoop will help to ensure consistency of size. Cover lightly with cling film and chill in the fridge.

Roll out the pastry. Select a deep pie dish large enough to hold the meatballs and grapes. Turn it upside down and place it on the pastry. Cut out the pastry lid a little larger than the size of your dish. Gather the scraps and use them to make a rim of pastry to fit around the edge of your pie dish. To get a really show-stopping effect, make 2 layers, which will allow the pastry to puff up really high. Use the remaining pastry trimmings to cut out decorations for the lid.

Preheat the oven to 200°C/180°C fan/gas 6.

Butter the pie dish and arrange the meatballs inside, scattering the grapes in between. Dampen the edges of the dish with water and lay the pastry rim over it, gently pressing the pastry against the rim of the dish. If you made 2 rims, dampen the bottom layer and place the second rim over the top.

Dampen the top of the pastry rim and lay the pastry lid over the pie. Press lightly but firmly all the way around, ensuring a good seal, but do not squash the edges of the pastry together as this will hinder the rise in the oven. You can turn the edge into beautifully curved scallops in the following way. Holding a sharp knife in your right hand and with the pie in front of you, reach across and place your left index finger onto the pastry so that the tip is on the edge of the pastry. Put the knife against the side of your finger. Press down gently with your fingertip whilst at the time drawing the knife blade back towards you. Move your index finger to the right of the cut made by the knife and repeat. Continue until the whole pie edge is scalloped, turning the dish around as you work.

Beat an egg and brush it over the top of your pie lid, then stick on the decorations. The egg wash will make the lid golden brown and glossy while the decorations will bake matt and pale and really stand out against the darker lid. Cut a vent in the middle of the pie with a sharp knife or an apple corer. Bake the pie for 45–50 minutes until the filling is cooked through and the pastry puffed and golden. While the pie is baking, whisk together the wine or verjuice, egg yolks, cream sherry and butter in a pan over a low heat until thickened. When the pie is cooked, remove from the oven. Pour the caudle into the pie through the vent hole in the pastry and serve.

MODISH TURKEY

Elizabeth Philipps, circa 1699

Initially it was the title that attracted me to this recipe; that use of -ish is refreshingly vague. 'A la mode' means 'in the fashion (-able way)' and over the centuries has been used to describe the preparation of a number of meat dishes, and bizarrely, in America the tradition of serving ice cream alongside a dessert. 'Modish' turkey is fashionable-ish turkey.

The original instructions describe a method of cooking more frequently known as 'stoved' or 'jugged', where meat, flavourings and seasonings are cooked in a close-fitting vessel in a water bath. This method requires the pan to be constantly watched to ensure that it doesn't boil dry, and can extend over the course of several hours. Thankfully, in the twenty-first century we have a not so much time-saving, but certainly effort-saving, device: the slow cooker. I don't propose to cook an entire turkey in the slow cooker, but you can certainly cook a turkey leg. Turkey legs are such good value and, if you use the slow cooker, take so little effort. Low and slow overnight makes for fall-apart tender turkey meat and a luscious stock.

You can serve this with a creamy egg-thickened sauce for special occasions, but for everyday I prefer just to thicken the meat juices in a pan and serve with some wilted spinach and poached mushrooms.

SERVES 4

1 turkey leg, thigh and drumstick
separated
250g bacon, either chopped or in
rashers
3 celery sticks
2 carrots, peeled
1 large onion, quartered
2 strips lemon peel
2 blades mace
80ml white wine (optional)
1 tsp anchovy essence (optional)

1 tbsp cornflour mixed with a little
water (optional)
500g mushrooms, preferably
chestnut, halved or quartered
150g baby spinach leaves
25g unsalted butter
salt and pepper

Equipment
slow cooker

Check that you can fit the 2 joints of meat into your slow cooker. You might have to chop or break the drumstick bone if it's a little on the large side.

Loosen the skin of the turkey with your fingers and put a layer of bacon between the skin and meat of both the thigh and the drumstick. This will add seasoning to the turkey meat and the preserving salts will help to keep it an attractive pink colour. You can remove the skin if you like, but it is helpful for keeping the bacon in place. Season with pepper and a light sprinkling of salt.

Lay the celery, carrots and onion over the bottom of the slow cooker and put the turkey on top. Add the lemon peel and mace and 150ml water. Cover and cook on low for 8–10 hours or overnight. The tendons in the drumstick will pull out easily when the meat is done.

Remove the meat from the slow cooker and set aside. Keep warm if you're eating immediately. Remove the vegetables and flavourings.

Strain the cooking liquid and skim off any fat. Pour into a pan and add the wine and anchovy essence, if liked. Stir in the cornflour slurry and bring to the boil, stirring continuously, until the sauce thickens and becomes translucent. Turn the heat to low and cover while the vegetables are prepared.

Boil some water in a pan and add a teaspoon of salt. Add the mushrooms and simmer for 10–15 minutes until tender. Steam the spinach over the pan for 1–2 minutes, until just wilted. Strain the mushrooms from the water and add to a dry pan.

Toss the mushrooms over a low heat to evaporate any excess water, then add the butter and shake the pan gently until the butter is melted and the mushrooms lightly coated. Season with pepper and a little salt.

Arrange the wilted spinach and the mushrooms around the edges of your serving platter. Pile the turkey in the centre of the dish and pour over a little of the thickened gravy to coat. Serve with the rest of the gravy in a separate dish.

THATCHED HOUSE PIE

Elizabeth Raffald, 1769

This pie has such a simple but effective decorative device that I couldn't bear to leave it out. It seems to have sprung straight from the mind of Mistress Raffald, for I have been unable to find anything similar in any contemporary cookery books. I think there is a strong case to be made for a variation on Mrs Raffald's recipe being the elusive and mysterious Cottage Pie referred to in Parson Woodforde's diary (See Sanders, page 141), for thatch was certainly a cottage roofing material. At some point during the nineteenth century the recipe appears to have undergone a subtle change and the pasta ended up on the inside of what was now being referred to as a Roman Pie. I have decided to combine the best aspects of these separate pies into a single recipe. It is very much a blank canvas, with the only conventions being pastry, pasta, meat and a cream sauce. The most popular variations tend to feature pale meats such as rabbit or chicken.

SERVES 4

100g cooked macaroni
4 tbsp chopped fresh parsley
300g cooked chicken, cut into bite-sized pieces
200g cooked ham or bacon, diced
20g unsalted butter, softened for greasing, plus 100g melted butter
100g angel hair pasta
1 × 250g packet filo pastry

Equipment
20cm round loose-bottomed or spring-form tin

For the sauce
1 onion
4 cloves
1 bay leaf
500ml milk
¼ nutmeg, grated
sprig of fresh thyme
zest of ½ lemon
¼ tsp salt
½ tsp black pepper
60g butter
60g plain flour

To make the sauce, first peel the onion and stick 3 cloves into it, slightly closer to one end than the other to ensure that the cloves sit under the surface of the milk. Use the last clove to pin the bay leaf to the onion. Put the milk and onion into a small pan and add the rest of the flavourings. Bring to a boil, turn off the heat, cover and set aside for 30 minutes to infuse. Strain the milk through a sieve, taste and add more salt, pepper and nutmeg as required.

Put the butter and flour into the same pan and pour over the flavoured milk. Put the pan over a gentle heat and stir with a whisk until the butter has melted and the sauce has thickened. Simmer for at least 5 minutes to cook out the flour. Taste again and adjust the seasonings if necessary. Remove from the heat, lay cling film over the surface of the sauce and leave to cool.

When cold, fold the macaroni, parsley, chicken and bacon into the sauce.

Grease the tin with the 20g butter, making sure the bottom is especially thickly covered. Lay the angel hair pasta over the base of the tin so that it looks like the spokes of a wheel (it is probably easiest to remove the base to do this). Make sure the whole base is well covered. Return the base to the tin.

Brush a sheet of filo with some of the melted butter and lay it carefully over the pasta, being careful not to dislodge the pattern. Allow a generous 5cm of filo to overhang the sides of the tin. Repeat until the whole of the bottom and sides of the tin are covered with buttered filo.

Spoon the filling into the pie and smooth the top. Butter any remaining sheets of filo and lay them over the filling. Fold in the overhanging edges of pastry and press flat. Transfer the pie to a baking sheet, cover with a sheet of tin foil and set a weighted baking tray on top. Leave for 30 minutes. Preheat the oven to 220°C/200°C fan/gas 7.

Remove the weight from the pie and bake for 25–30 minutes, until the pastry is crisp and golden. When cooked, remove the pie from the oven and allow it to cool in the tin for 10 minutes. Put your serving plate over the top of the pie and turn it out so that the thatched top is uppermost. Serve at once.

TURKEY IN BEEF BROTH
1699

This might be considered an unusual combination but, I have to say, it works beautifully. The turkey is tender and moist and imparts its own distinctive flavour to the broth for making fantastic gravy. It's a very low-impact way of cooking, needing practically no hands-on attention from the moment it is set on the heat to the moment it is taken off. The lack of stuffing means that the broth can get inside the turkey and help cook it from inside as well as out, so it is done in a fraction of the time usually required for roasting. The meat can be arranged artfully on a large platter for ease of serving, and any remaining after the meal can be used for sandwiches or other meals. True, there's no grand entrance of a whole bird, but the huge stress of having to babysit a turkey roast for hours, with the potential for tough dark meat and dry white, means I would choose this recipe every time.

The only potential awkwardness with this recipe is finding a vessel large enough to cook a whole turkey. There are two solutions. Firstly, you can use a very large saucepan such as a preserving pan or large stock pot and instead of a lid, tent some foil over the top to keep in the moisture. Secondly, you could opt to cook a turkey crown, if you're a fan of white meat, and/or a turkey leg which, being smaller, might be easier to accommodate. The advantage of cooking a whole bird, of course, is that you usually get a bag of giblets with which to help flavour your gravy but, to be honest, the broth takes on such a lovely flavour from the turkey itself, the bag of giblets is almost redundant.

SERVES 4

1 turkey or a mixture of turkey
legs and crown or a whole turkey
breast (3–4kg in total)
turkey neck and heart from the
giblets (optional)
3 sticks celery, chopped
2 carrots, chopped

1 onion, chopped
3 bay leaves
1 tbsp black peppercorns
2 litres beef stock
1 tbsp cornflour mixed with a little
water (optional)

Put the turkey into a large pan with the giblets, if using, and add
the vegetables, bay leaves, peppercorns and beef stock. If the meat is
not submerged, add more stock or water. Cover with a lid or, if your
pan has no lid, a foil tent. Bring to the boil, turn down the heat and
simmer until the turkey is cooked through. Since the stock can go
into the bird and cook it from the inside out, the length of time
required is much shorter than traditional roasting, no more than 2
hours for a 5kg bird. When the meat is cooked, lift it from the stock
and set aside until cool enough to handle.

Strain the stock twice: once through a fine sieve and then again
through muslin to remove all the unwanted solids.

When the meat is cool enough to handle, separate and discard all
skin, bone and connective tissue. Be sure to remove the coarse tendons
in the drumsticks. Arrange the meat neatly on a serving platter.
I suggest putting the white meat at each end, either slices or whole,
and the darker meat in the middle. Cover with foil and keep warm.

Taste the stock and decide if it needs reducing in order to
concentrate the flavour. If so, then measure out 1 litre and simmer,
uncovered, over a low heat until you are happy with the way it
tastes. You can thicken the stock if you want to by adding the
cornflour slurry and then bringing it to the boil, stirring as it
thickens. Pour a little gravy over the platter of meat before serving.

Serve the turkey with: Season or Savoury Pudding (pages 321 and
323), Stuffing (page 319), Bread Sauce (page 41), roast parsnips,

Braised Red Cabbage with Sausages (page 170).

As an alternative to the gravy, you may wish to try the much punchier sauce below.

SAUCE FOR TURKEY IN BEEF BROTH
E.S. 1739

1 turkey liver
2 blades mace
500ml turkey or beef stock
60ml white wine

60ml oyster sauce
1 tbsp cornflour mixed with a little
  cold water, (optional)
salt and pepper

Put the liver, mace and half the stock into a pan and simmer for 15 minutes. Remove the mace.

Purée half the liver (use the rest for something else) and the stock, either in a liquidiser or with a stick blender. Season with salt and pepper and pour back into the pan. Add the white wine and oyster sauce. Simmer for another 5 minutes. Taste and add more stock if liked. Check the seasoning. If a thicker sauce is preferred, add the cornflour mixture and gently bring to a simmer to thicken.

CHOOK WEED
Mrs Pick, circa 1700

This recipe is definitely a family favourite, since I have not been able to find another with even a remotely similar title. Instinctively you know that this is a dish created at home, possibly by Mrs Pick herself, or perhaps passed to her by someone else. It's a curious name, because Chook Weed, while close-sounding to chickweed, doesn't have any obvious link to what the dish is. Chickweed is a low-lying plant with herbal and culinary uses, and is also very much enjoyed by poultry. However, to even suggest that this dish earned its name because people enjoy eating bits of chicken as much as chickens enjoy eating bits of chickweed would be a little ghoulish.

This recipe is very similar to what would later become popular as rissoles or croquettes and is perfect for stretching a relatively small quantity of protein into a meal. The meat is bound together with a thickened white sauce made with just half the usual quantity of liquid, before being allowed to cool. Once cold, the mixture is then formed into sausage shapes and coated with breadcrumbs and either fried or baked. Although I have made it with as little as 140g of chicken (you can always make it stretch by adding some finely chopped cooked vegetables), the quantity given is frugal without being miserly.

Although this recipe is in the poultry chapter it could just as easily fit elsewhere as, once again, the basics of the recipe fit almost any main ingredient. Mrs Pick recommends pale meats such as cooked chicken, turkey or veal.

SERVES 4

250g cooked chicken or turkey,
  finely chopped
1 shallot or spring onion, finely
  chopped
2–3 tbsp chopped fresh parsley
2 large eggs
1 × batch White Sauce (page 42),
  made with 30g butter, 30g flour,
  250ml milk and a stock cube

100g fresh white breadcrumbs
1 tsp sweet paprika
1 tsp dried thyme
1 tsp dried marjoram
½ tsp salt
½ tsp ground white pepper
olive oil, for frying
fresh parsley, to garnish

Put the chopped chicken, onion, parsley and one of the eggs into a bowl and stir through the cold white sauce. Cover with cling film and chill in the fridge until completely cold. If you have suitably shaped silicone moulds, you could freeze the mixture in them. It makes the breading a little easier.

Mix together the breadcrumbs, paprika, thyme, marjoram, salt and pepper. Whisk the remaining egg in a separate bowl. If you haven't already shaped them, form the chicken mixture into small sausage shapes and dip them in the beaten egg before rolling in the breadcrumb mixture. Chill, or freeze, until required.

Heat some oil in a pan until shimmering and fry the rissoles until crisp and golden on all sides. Serve garnished with parsley.

BOILED GOOSE

Elizabeth Jacob, 1685

Many of you will gasp in horror at the thought of boiling such a magnificent bird for the table, but let me assure you it is not quite the heresy it seems. Firstly, the goose isn't boiled in the modern sense, it is delicately poached. Gentle cooking in barely simmering liquid, in this case a sturdy beef broth, allows the tender breast meat and tougher leg meat to cook through without drying out. Then, as cooking in liquid tends to make unseared meat rather anaemic, the bird is subjected to high heat after poaching in order to caramelise and darken the outsides. Since goose is a fatty bird it is ideal for this flash-roasting method. Not all the fat renders out during the poaching, and that which remains protects the flesh from the high heat of the oven for the short baking period. The result is a beautiful mahogany bird with tender, juicy meat.

SERVES 4

1 × 4–5kg goose
50g salt
6 bay leaves
4 sprigs fresh rosemary
10 sprigs fresh thyme
4 Bramley apples
2 large onions
1 bunch fresh sage
150g fresh white breadcrumbs
3–4 litres beef stock

150ml white wine
flavouring sauces (page 21)
  (optional)
cornflour (optional)

Equipment
large plastic bag or lidded pot
large pot, big enough to fit the
  whole goose
large roasting tin with a rack

Remove the giblets from the goose and set aside. Rinse the goose, inside and out, and sprinkle with the salt, inside and out. Place in a large plastic bag or lidded box and chill in the fridge for 24 hours.

Remove and rinse. Pat dry.

Divide the bay, rosemary and thyme into 2 equal bundles and tie firmly with twine or a clean elastic band.

Peel, core and finely chop the apples, onions and sage. Mix these together with the breadcrumbs and use to stuff the goose. Close the loose flap of skin over the opening using a cocktail stick to secure and put it into a large pot, breast-side downwards. Add enough beef stock to cover. Add the 2 bunches of herbs either side of the goose, cover, using foil if necessary, and slowly bring to a gentle simmer. Cook for 2 hours or until tender.

Preheat the oven to 220°C/200°C fan/gas 7.

Remove 1 litre of the cooking liquid and place into a pan for gravy. Add the wine. Remove about a quarter of the apple stuffing from the goose and add it to the liquid in the pan. The stuffing will have absorbed the juices from the meat during cooking and will enhance the flavour of the gravy. Bring to a gentle simmer and leave to cook while the bird crisps in the oven.

Remove the rest of the stuffing to a serving dish and keep warm.

Put the goose onto a rack over a roasting pan and bake at high heat for 25–30 minutes. You will need to drain off the fat as it renders, every ten minutes or so, otherwise your oven will become rather smoky.

Taste the gravy and season with pepper if necessary. Since the stock cubes will have been seasoned and heavily salted, additional salt will probably not be needed. Use any of the flavouring sauces on page 21, if liked. You can then choose whether to strain the stuffing pieces, and whether to thicken the gravy with cornflour.

Serve with: Braised Red Cabbage with Sausages (page 170) and Haricot of Root Vegetables (page 313).

DEJA FOOD
The rich, dark meat is ideally suited to a salmi (see page 124).

BRAISED DUCK WITH TURNIPS

Mrs Sarah Phillips, 1758

Duck is becoming more widely available, with supermarket shelves now offering a choice of whole birds as well as lesser joints such as crowns, legs and beautifully prepared duck breast. A whole duck is difficult to cook perfectly; the legs retain moisture and flavour best when cooked long and slow, while the breast should ideally be cooked pink, its rich layer of covering fat and skin rendered to perfection. In olden times, roasting before an open fire allowed a certain degree of control as the turning of the spit directed the heat towards the areas needing the most cooking and judicious use of a basting liquid ensured the tenderest parts didn't dry out. The very detail that we treasure in the modern oven, the constant and relentless dry heat, is no friend of whole ducks. Either the bird has to be cosseted, pampered and cajoled throughout its cooking time or a not-all-that-happy medium is reached where no part of the bird is cooked perfectly. The former is an awful lot of work, and the latter seems a bit of a waste of something special. The solution is to braise; gently poach in a seasoned broth to ensure succulence and flavour throughout the whole bird. You are, of course, limited by the size of your pan, but this method works well with both whole birds and joints, so adapt it to what you have to hand. The advantage of using smaller joints and cuts of meat is that they can be removed from the cooking liquid when required, although I rarely observe this myself, preferring a much more democratic (and easier on the cook) 'everyone gets the same' approach by using only duck legs.

SERVES 4

*8 pieces of duck, or as many as your
 cooking pot can hold
1 bunch mixed fresh herbs
½ nutmeg, left in one piece
4 cloves
strong beef or lamb stock, enough
 to cover
8 turnips*

*2 tbsp cornflour mixed with a little
 cold water
200g garden peas, boiled until
 tender
chopped fresh parsley, to garnish*

Equipment
large cooking pot

Put the duck, herbs, spices and stock into a large pan, cover and
cook over a low heat until tender, 2–3 hours.

Peel the turnips and cut into 1cm dice. Put them into a pan and
cover with cold water. Bring to the boil, then cover and simmer
until tender, 15–20 minutes. Strain and set aside. Keep warm.
When the duck is cooked, remove from the broth and set aside
to drain. Strain the cooking liquid from the herbs and spices and
remove the fat, either by chilling and then lifting off the solidified
fat or by using a fat-separator jug. Pour 500ml into a pan, add the
cornflour slurry and bring to a boil, stirring constantly.

Remove the skin from the duck and discard. Arrange the pieces in
a serving dish. Pour over the thickened broth and surround with
a border of white turnips and bright green peas. Sprinkle with the
chopped parsley.

DEJA FOOD
Strip the meat from the bones and set aside. Put the bones and any
skin back into any remaining cooking liquid. Simmer for another
hour or more to extract as much flavour as possible. Strain and
remove the fat, which can then be clarified and retained for use for
frying and in pastry. Use the meat and stock to make Duck Salmi
(page 124).

DUCK WITH LENTILS & CHESTNUTS

Jane Newton, 1675

Jane Newton's manuscript book is one of my favourites to browse through.[1] It is beautifully presented, each page laid out with bright red margins, the recipe titles similarly embellished and it has an alphabetical index at the front. When first inscribed, its appearance must have been striking, however the passage of time has mellowed the once black ink to soft mid brown. There's no rigid pattern to the order in which the recipes appear, which lends the book a personalised air, as if they have been jotted down as they are remembered or discovered. Occasionally, there are flurries of special interest, where a dozen tarts or puddings are recorded in as many pages. This particular recipe has an earthy quality, very autumnal with the chestnuts, mushrooms and lentils.

SERVES 4

4 duck legs
8 rashers unsmoked streaky bacon
1 litre strong beef stock
1 bunch fresh mixed herbs
250g portobello mushrooms
50g unsalted butter
250g puy, green or brown lentils, rinsed

240g cooked chestnuts, peeled
4 medium cooked turnips, diced
1–2 tbsp mushroom ketchup
1–2 tbsp cornflour mixed with a little cold water
chopped parsley, to garnish
salt and pepper

Preheat the oven to 180°C/160°C fan/gas 4.

Put the duck legs in a roasting pan and drape the bacon over them. Roast for 45 minutes, then remove and transfer to a casserole or saucepan. Add the beef stock and herbs and simmer gently for 1 hour, or until the duck legs are tender.

When the duck has been simmering for 30 minutes, cut the mushrooms into thick slices. Melt the butter in a pan and fry the mushrooms until softened, then add to the duck legs with the chestnuts.

Put the lentils into a pan with 500ml water and bring to a rolling boil, then immediately turn down the heat to a very gentle simmer and cook, uncovered, for 20–30 minutes, until tender. Drain and return to the pan. Sprinkle over ¼ teaspoon salt and stir thoroughly. Add the cooked turnips and mix through. Cover and keep warm.

When the duck is cooked, remove the herbs and discard, then strain the cooking liquid. Keep the duck and vegetables warm while you finish off the sauce.

Remove the fat, either by chilling and then lifting off the solidified fat or by using a fat-separator jug. Return to the pan and add the mushroom ketchup. Taste and adjust the seasoning if required. When you're happy with the flavour, add the cornflour slurry and bring to a boil, stirring, until the mixture thickens and becomes translucent. Return the duck and vegetables to the sauce and warm though.

Put the lentils and turnips into a warmed serving dish, or individual dishes, and arrange the duck legs on top. Pour over the sauce and vegetables, sprinkle with a little chopped parsley and serve.

DUCK SALMI
Nineteenth century

Some dishes are created from scratch, lovingly prepared using the finest fresh produce. Some dishes take as their ingredients food that has already been cooked, and make use of them in delightful and creative ways. And then there are foods that are lovingly prepared from fresh produce and then allowed to cool, untasted and untouched, because, in the cook's opinion, the second dish is much better than the first. Duck Salmi is just such a dish.

When I described it to my husband as being made with previously cooked duck, he reasonably asked, 'Who leaves cooked duck uneaten?' Quite. So you may find yourself wanting Duck Salmi without having any cooked duck to hand. If so, simply follow the recipe for Braised Duck with Turnips (page 119) and continue here as soon as the duck is cooked.

A salmigondis, to give it its full name, was originally a twice-cooked, highly spiced and seasoned ragout of game, most usually game birds. Shortened to 'salmi' in the UK, it was especially popular during the nineteenth century, when the frugal Victorians found it an ideal way of using up cooked duck. It was frequently served as a final dinner course, known as a 'savoury', the small amounts of cooked duck providing ideal portions for this piquant end to a meal. Traditionally salmis were served on toast, but I've opted for puff pastry cases, like giant vol-au-vents, to make this deja food snack into a main meal that's a little bit special.

This recipe can also be used for goose, pheasant and any other well-flavoured game bird.

SERVES 4

500g cooked duck, skin and bones
  removed
2 sheets ready-rolled puff pastry
2 large egg yolks, lightly beaten

For the sauce
30g butter
1 small onion, finely chopped
100g streaky bacon, chopped
1 bay leaf

3 cloves
1 blade mace
200ml red wine
300ml duck stock
  flavouring sauces (page 21),
  to taste
1 rounded tbsp cornflour mixed
  with a little cold water
salt and pepper

Preheat the oven to 220°C/200°C fan/gas 7 and line a baking sheet with baking parchment.

Unroll the pastry sheets and cut them into even rectangles. Set aside in pairs. If the pastry has cracked or split in places, use those pieces for the bottoms of the pastry cases. For each pair of pastry rectangles, cut out a smaller rectangle from the middle of the better piece of pastry, leaving a border of roughly 2cm. Discard the centre. Brush the uncut piece all over with egg yolk and lay the cut piece on top, making sure the sides are aligned neatly. Brush the border with egg yolk, taking care not to let it drip down the sides as this will prevent the pastry from rising in the oven.

Arrange the glazed pastry cases on the prepared baking sheet and prick the centres with the tines of a fork. Bake for 7–10 minutes, until risen and dark golden brown. Remove from the oven and set aside on a wire rack to cool. The centres will have risen, even with the poked holes. With a sharp knife, run the point of the blade around the insides of the cases and lift out the risen centres. You can use these as lids for the contents, or discard.

Reduce the oven temperature to 150°C/130°C fan/gas 2. ·

To make the sauce, melt the butter in a pan and add the onion, bacon, bay leaf, cloves and mace. Fry for 10 minutes over a medium heat until the onions have begun to caramelise, then add the red wine and simmer for 5 minutes. Add the stock and let all simmer together for a further 10 minutes, allowing all the flavours to mingle. Strain through a fine mesh sieve and return the liquid to the pan. Taste and add salt and pepper as required, along with flavouring sauce, if liked. Add the cornflour slurry and slowly bring to the boil, stirring, until the sauce clears, thickens and becomes glossy. Reduce the heat to low and add the duck meat. Allow the meat to warm though in the sauce, but make sure it doesn't boil as this would make it tough.

Warm the pastry cases in the oven for 10 minutes, then fill with the meat and sauce. Serve any extra sauce in a sauce boat on the side.

4

MUTTON & LAMB

Mutton used to be tremendously popular, but fell out of favour in the latter part of the twentieth century. Thankfully, it is becoming more readily available, as people relish the maturity of flavour that comes from an older animal. The meat from sheep is generally classified according to age:

Lamb—under 12 months old
Hogget—12–24 months old
Mutton—over 2 years old

Although the recipes in this chapter will specify a particular meat, they are also interchangeable. The only difference should be in the seasoning. Since lamb is the more delicate meat, have a light hand as regards seasonings if you are using it with a mutton recipe. Conversely, mutton can take powerful flavours, so be prepared to add more seasonings when making a lamb recipe with mutton.

BRAISED NECK OF MUTTON

Joseph Cooper, 1654

This recipe is, as the frontispiece of the book from which it came proudly proclaims, *'Collected from the practise of that incomparable Master of these Arts, Mr.* Jos. Cooper, *chiefe Cook to the Late KING'*,[1] the then recently deceased Charles I. Joseph Cooper is rather an enigmatic person, since food historians have yet to find any trace of him whatsoever in the household accounts. Of course, with all of the upheaval of the time it's quite possible for him to have slipped though the cracks, but it is a curious detail, nonetheless.

Neck of mutton or lamb is an economical cut of meat that is packed with flavour, and the boneless fillets are readily available. It is pleasantly striped with layers of fat that allow it to become fall-apart tender when gently cooked and as such makes it perfect for long braising, especially in the slow cooker; use timings of 2 hours plus 2 hours on low.

This recipe can be made with either lamb or mutton. This is an ideal dish for the slow cooker.

SERVES 4

800g neck fillet of mutton or lamb
3 onions, sliced
12 sage leaves, finely chopped
2 turnips, cubed
150g bacon, chopped
1 bunch mixed fresh herbs, finely
  chopped

50g fresh ginger, peeled and cut
  into matchsticks
3 tbsp capers
1 tbsp caper pickling liquid
60ml white wine vinegar
1 tbsp cornflour mixed with a little
  cold water (optional)

Slice the fillets into coins and tenderise them by covering with cling film and pounding them with a wooden rolling pin or meat tenderiser. Put the meat into a casserole dish and add sufficient water to cover. Bring to a simmer and skim off any bubbles of scum that rise. Add the sliced onions, sage and turnips, cover and cook on a low heat for 2 hours, then add the rest of the ingredients, except for the cornflour slurry, and cook for a further 2 hours.

Lift the meat and vegetables from the cooking liquid and transfer to a warmed serving dish. Keep warm.

Skim off any fat from the cooking liquid and reduce to about 500ml by boiling over a high heat. Taste and adjust the seasoning with pepper and salt. The bacon will have added salt, so be careful not to over-season. Thicken the reduced gravy with a cornflour slurry, if liked, and pour over the lamb and vegetables.

COLLARED BREAST OF LAMB WITH PICKLED WALNUTS
circa 1700

Breast of lamb is a very economical cut of meat which, due to its relatively high fat content, is also one of the most flavoursome. It is ideal for long, slow cooking and is almost impossible to overcook. After braising until tender, it can be crisped and browned in the oven to give great textural crunch. I found a lot of recipes for breast of lamb in old manuscripts, but this one caught my eye with its use of pickled walnuts. Once a staple of the store cupboard, they are little made today, but happily still available on the supermarket shelf. Dark, earthy and sharpened with brine, they are a perfect foil for cutting through the richness of the lamb and make for a striking appearance once the rolled joints have been sliced.

SERVES 4

2 breasts of lamb
2 large egg yolks
2 pickled walnuts
1 tsp freshly grated nutmeg
1 tsp ground black pepper
1 tsp salt
2 onions, peeled
6 cloves
2 litres lamb stock
300g fresh samphire

For the sauce
6 sprigs fresh thyme
12 stalks fresh parsley
3–4 sprigs fresh marjoram or 1 tsp dried oregano
½ tsp ground black pepper
1 tsp grated nutmeg
1 pickled walnut, mashed
1–2 tbsp mushroom ketchup
2 tbsp cornflour mixed with a little cold water (optional)

Equipment
butcher's string

Remove the bones from the lamb breasts. Set aside.

Grind together the egg yolks, walnuts, nutmeg and seasoning to make a paste, either in a mortar with a pestle or in a small food processor. Spread the paste all over the inside of the lamb breasts. If the lamb pieces are large, you may need to double the recipe for the paste.

Cut 8 pieces of butcher's string. Roll up each breast and tie with 4 pieces of string; after braising the breasts will be cut into 4, so tying the string tightly and evenly spaced will help the rolls keep their shape when sliced later.

Put the meat into a slow cooker or large saucepan. Stick 3 cloves into each of the onions and add to the pan with the lamb stock and bones. Cook on low or over a low heat for 4 hours.

Preheat the oven to 200°C/180°C fan/gas 6.

Remove the lamb from the braising liquid and transfer to a roasting pan. Roast for 20–30 minutes until the skin is crisp and brown.

Meanwhile, remove the fat from the braising liquid, either by chilling and then lifting off the solidified fat or by using a fat-separator jug. Measure out 600ml and pour it into a saucepan. Add the thyme, parsley, marjoram and pepper and simmer while the meat is browning. Strain through a sieve, then add the nutmeg and walnut and blend to a smooth purée with a stick blender. Add 1 tablespoon of the mushroom ketchup, taste and add more of the seasonings, if liked. If you prefer a thicker sauce, add the cornflour slurry and bring to a boil. Keep stirring while the sauce thickens and becomes translucent. Keep warm.

Bring a pan of water to the boil and blanch the samphire. To keep some texture, it should take only 1–2 minutes to cook. Drain and keep warm.

When the meat has crisped, remove from the oven and allow to stand for 10 minutes before cutting each breast into 4 slices. Discard string. Put the cooked samphire on a warmed serving platter and arrange the slices of meat on top. Serve with the gravy in a separate bowl.

CHINA CHILO
Maria Eliza Rundell, 1808

'This dates from the East India Company's time, and was a clear, white and green dish much fancied by the ladies of that period, and also thought to be good for the blood after the sea voyage back from the East. It was one of the dishes you made a little boastfully—to show you had overseas connections and to point out the new lacquered tea caddy, the Cashmere shawl, and the gossamer fine Indian muslin that he had sent to you last season … It makes a pleasant summer evening meal, with a flavour of white muslin and spinets.'
Dorothy Hartley, Food in England

Cooking lamb with lettuce makes for a very delicate dish, however, after prolonged cooking lettuces do tend to lose their vibrant colour. Enchanted by Dorothy Hartley's description, I've modified the classic recipe to include a second batch of greenery later in the cooking process, in order to emphasise the delicate colour of the meat, and to accentuate the lightness of the dish. It is the cook's choice whether to serve the stewed vegetables to the table. I include them because I hate waste; the colour will be a little faded, but full of flavour. It's your call.

SERVES 4

1kg lamb on the bone or 800g
  lamb neck fillet
4 Little Gem lettuces
2 O'So or Romaine lettuces
12 spring onions
300g basmati rice
4 tbsp salt, plus extra for seasoning
1 tbsp cornflour mixed with a little
  cold water (optional)

30g unsalted butter
500g frozen garden peas
pepper & salt

Equipment
slow cooker

Put the meat in the bottom of a slow cooker. Shred half the Little Gem and half the O'So or Romaine lettuces and add to the pot with half the spring onions. Pour over 500ml water, cover and cook on low for 8 hours.

Rinse the rice thoroughly in several changes of water. It might take as many as 6 or 7 rinses. When the water runs clear, put to soak in a bowl of cold water. Add the 4 tablespoons of salt and stir until dissolved. Soak for at least 30 minutes.

Remove the vegetables from the pot and set aside. Carefully remove the meat; it will be fall-apart tender. Separate the lean meat from the fat, bone and skin.

Strain the stock through a fine mesh sieve and remove the fat either by chilling and then lifting off the solidified fat or by using a fat-separator jug. Simmer the stock until reduced by half, then taste and season with salt and pepper. Use additional seasonings if liked. When you are happy with the flavour, stir in the cornflour slurry, if preferred, and heat, stirring, until the sauce is thickened and glossy. Add the meat and stir gently. Cover with a lid and leave on a low heat to warm through.

Shred the rest of the lettuce and finely chop the spring onions. If you would like to add the vegetables that have stewed with the meat, then chop those as fine as the fresh ones.

Melt the butter in a pan over a low heat and add all the vegetables. Cover and allow to wilt gently for 5 minutes.

Bring a pan of water to the boil. Drain the soaked rice and tip it into the boiling water. It will cook in 2–4 minutes so don't leave it unattended or it will quickly overcook. Drain through a sieve and then set the sieve back over the pan and cover with a lid. Allow to steam for 10 minutes while the rest of the dish is being finished.

Bring a second pan of water to the boil, add the peas and cook for

4 minutes. (I like my peas to have both a little texture and drum-tight skins and have suggested a cooking time to suit. You might want to cook yours a little longer, so be sure to taste the peas for texture before you drain them.) Drain thoroughly and then fold into the wilted vegetables. Lift the meat from the gravy and fold through the vegetables.

Make a ring of rice around the edge of a warmed serving dish and fill the middle with the meat and vegetables. Strain the gravy through a sieve and serve in a jug on the side.

MUTTON PIES
Thomas Dawson, 1587

At the end of the seventeenth century, a London publisher by the name of Jacob Tonson encouraged his friend Christopher, a baker, to move his premises from Grey's Inn Lane and open a Pudding Pye Shop in Shire Lane, just off the Strand. As a gesture of support for his friend's new venture, Mr Tonson agreed to hold weekly gatherings for his young, impoverished clients above the new shop and to feed them with baked goods purchased from the shop below, so that they might 'Storm the Crusty Walls of his *Mutton-Pies*, and make a Consumption of his *Custards*'.[2]

This generosity wasn't entirely altruistic on the part of Mr Tonson, for the price he exacted from his guests for this feast was the right of first refusal to publish their works, once completed.

These informal gatherings went on to become the gentleman's club known as the Kit-Cat Club. The origin of the name is disputed, but probably involves some combination of the following snippets of information:
—The name of the shop was 'The Cat and Fiddle' or 'Cat and Kit'.
—Kit is the (now obsolete) name for a small fiddle, of the kind preferred by dancing masters.
—Kit is an abbreviation of Christopher (the pastry cook).
—The last name of the pastry cook is listed variously as Cat, Catling, Kat or Katt.

According to Edward 'Ned' Ward:
'And the Cook's Name being Christopher, for brevity call'd Kit, and his Sign being the Cat and Fiddle, they very merrily deriv'd a quaint Denomination from Puss and her Master, and from thence call'd themselves The Kit-Cat-Club.'[3]

Then there is...
'One Night in Seven, at this convenient Seat,

Indulgent BOCAJ *did the Muses treat,*
Their Drink was gen'rous Wine, and Kit-Cat's *Pyes their Meat.*
Here he assembled his Poetic Tribe,
Past Labours to Reward, and new ones to prescribe;
Hence did the Assembly's Title first arise,
And Kit Cat *Wits sprung first from* Kit-Cat's *Pyes.'*
Sir Richard Blackmore, 1708

Alternatively this, from John Dryden:
'*The fact is, that on account of its excellence, it was called a Kit-Kat,*
as we now say—a Sandwich. So, in the Prologue to the REFORMED
WIFE, a comedy, 1700:
'*Often, for change, the meanest things are good:*
Thus, though the town all delicates afford,
A Kit-Kat is a supper for a lord.'' [4]

It is also interesting to note that Katt Pie is the traditional food
served for centuries at the fair in Templeton, Pembrokeshire. A
couple of my cookery books claim that the unusual name originates
with Mr Katt, a baker in Templeton who originally made the pies,
however I feel a stronger argument can be made in favour of the
London origins.

The modern recipe for Katt Pies consists of equal quantities of
minced lamb, currants and brown sugar baked in a hot water crust.
This combination is far too sweet for my tastes, but still wishing to
acknowledge the great esteem in which mutton pies were held over
many centuries, in its stead I here present the Elizabethan recipe of
Thomas Dawson. This recipe contains no sugar, but is flavoured with
both spices and a mixture of currants and prunes. The dried fruit
offers sweetness but with an accompanying sharpness that enhances
rather than overpowers the meat. The topping of hard boiled egg,
or eggs, makes for an attractive appearance once the pie is cut.

This recipe makes 4 individual pies, as was the traditional serving
size. However, the quantities are sufficient for a single large pie,
which would need a little longer, say 45–50 minutes, in the oven.

SERVES 4

400g mutton or lamb, roughly	*1 × batch Hot Water Crust*
minced	*(page 328)*
200g lean lamb, chopped	*4 hard boiled eggs*
60g currants	*1 egg, beaten*
60g prunes	
1 tsp Sweet Spice Mix (page 330)	<u>*Equipment*</u>
1 tsp salt	*4 × 10–12cm pie tins*
100ml strong mutton or lamb stock	

Preheat the oven to 200°C/180°C fan/gas 6 and grease the pie tins.

Put all the ingredients except the pastry and eggs into a bowl and mix thoroughly.

Set aside a third of the dough. Roll out the rest of the pastry and use it to line the pie tins. Spoon in the meat filling and smooth over. Separate the hard boiled eggs into yolks and whites and chop each separately. Sprinkle the yolk over the meat filling, and top with the chopped whites.

Roll out the remaining pastry and cut 4 pie lids. Dampen the edges of the pastry bases with a little water and lay the lids over the pies. Press to seal, crimp the edges and use any scraps to make decorations, which can be stuck to the lids with a little water. Cut a steam vent in the centre of each pie and brush the tops with the beaten egg.

Put the pies onto a baking sheet in case any of the cooking juices bubble over and bake for 25–35 minutes, until the pastry is crisped and golden. Once cooked, remove from the oven and allow to stand in the tin for 10 minutes before removing to a wire rack to cool, or to serve.

SANDERS

Maria Eliza Rundell, 1806

This recipe appears to go some way towards establishing the origin of the dishes we know today as Cottage Pie and Shepherd's Pie. The Reverend James Woodforde, famous for *The Diary of a Country Parson, 1758–1802*, is credited by the OED with the first mention of Cottage Pie, on 29 August, 1791: 'Dinner to day, Cottage-Pye and rost Beef'. Indeed he goes on to mention its appearance on the dinner table several times throughout his diary, with such combinations as 'Boiled Pork and Cottage Pye', 'Boiled Pike & Cottage Pye', 'Cottage Pye and a Neck of Mutton Rosted', and 'Cottage Pye, Tripe, a fine Pheasant Rosted and an Apple Pudding'. Alas, he never expands on what, precisely, Cottage Pie is, so it will forever remain a mystery. Personally, I think it unlikely that it is the dish we know today, since it is mentioned alongside such substantial accompaniments. Then again, it might have been some form of thatched house pie (see page 108).

Appearing in the first edition of Mrs Rundell's bestselling book *A New System of Domestic Cookery* (1806), this recipe is one of a number of thrifty suggestions for making meals out of the remains of a joint:

> *'To dress ditto, called Sanders. Mince small beef or mutton, onion, pepper, and salt; add a little gravy: put into scallop shells or saucers: make them three parts full; then fill them up with potatoes, mashed with a little cream: put a bit of butter on the top, and brown them in an oven, or before the fire.'*

I'm right with Mistress Rundell in this regard; the absolute best way to make this dish is with meat that has already been cooked, for a number of very good reasons. Firstly, it's economical, because you've got all the main ingredients, ready to go. Also, there's simply no duplicating the richness of roasted meat, short of actually roasting meat. In addition, the long cooking has allowed the meat to both develop flavour and be basted with its own fat, which is again difficult to duplicate via a shortcut. Making this dish with raw meat just doesn't have the flavour, plus the fat content is going to be significantly higher, whereas it is easy to trim away any solidified fat from a cooked joint and retain only the flavoursome lean meat. Finally, your gravy has already been flavoured, seasoned and skimmed of all fat and tastes so much better than anything that started life as a stock cube can hope to replicate. I'm pretty much a purist when it comes to Shepherd's Pie in that I believe this dish should contain only meat and well-seasoned potatoes, so I must confess to a moue of disapproval at Mrs Rundell's use of onion, since a well-flavoured gravy should be all that is required.

While Mrs Rundell's serving suggestion is a little unusual, hunting out some scallop shells to make an everyday dish appear that little bit special is a nice, decorative touch. However, the everyday and, to my mind, most practical serving suggestion (no washing-up!) is to present the meat inside hollowed-out baked potatoes; the natural containers also handily providing the mashed potato required for the topping.

In addition, don't limit this dish to just beef or lamb/mutton; any cold meat or fish, carefully prepared, can be used to make, for example, Beef Sanders, Salmon Sanders, Sausage Sanders. For beef, lamb, mutton, pork, chicken and turkey, the gravy from the roast will be ideal to provide richness and moisture to the dish. For gammon, ham or bacon, or any white fish or salmon, I suggest substituting parsley sauce (see page 43).

SERVES 4

400g cooked meat or fish
4 large baking potatoes
300ml gravy or appropriate sauce
  (white, cheese, parsley, etc.)

60ml double cream
unsalted butter
salt and pepper

Bake the potatoes using the method on page 299.

Prepare the meat or fish by removing all skin, bone, fat and connective tissue and cutting into small pieces. Resist the temptation to blitz it in a food processor, for that way lies over-processed meat purée that cannot be rescued. Moisten with the gravy or sauce and fold in thoroughly. Again, vigorous stirring will break the pieces down further, so gently does it. Taste and adjust the seasoning, but remember that when hot the seasoning will be more pronounced. Alternatively, if you're preparing this for immediate consumption, warm the meat and sauce in a saucepan and then taste for seasoning.

Cut a slice from the top of each baked potato and scoop out the cooked insides, leaving walls at least 1cm thick. Add the warmed filling, cover and keep warm while the potato topping is prepared. Pass the cooked potato through a ricer or mash thoroughly to remove all lumps. Mix in a little butter and the cream and season to taste. Add the potato topping to your filling, making sure it is completely covered. A plain or star nozzle and a piping bag can make this easier, but if you use this method, add a little milk to soften the consistency so that it is easier to pipe. Brush with a little melted butter and put back into the oven at 180°C/160°C fan/gas 4 and bake for 10 minutes, until piping hot and the potato topping is starting to brown. Serve at once.

SPRING LAMB PIE
E. Kidder, circa 1740

Edward Kidder was a renowned master pastry cook who taught
at several schools in London in the early years of the eighteenth
century. His obituary notice in 1739 read, 'In Holborn, aged 73, Mr
Edward Kidder, the famous Pastry-Master, who has taught nearly
6000 Ladies The Art Of Pastry'. He published only one piece of
work, *Receipts of pastry and cookery*, which, although undated, is
thought to have been printed around 1720. It is unusual in that,
although greatly plagiarised throughout the eighteenth century, the
recipes themselves appear original and serve as fine examples of the
range of dishes of the time. Not only this, but Kidder's recipe for
puff pastry is the first in print that is comparable to the modern
method used today. A copperplate version of his recipe book is
available online from the University of Pennsylvania.

This pie is an alternative way to enjoy spring lamb without the
stress of wrestling with a full joint. It is a combination of tender
lamb and fresh spring vegetables wrapped in richly flavoured pastry.
Unlike many meat pies, it is very light and, although the ingredients
are placed in the pie raw, cooks in a refreshingly short amount of
time. This is a particular favourite of a friend of mine due to the
fact that the gravy, or 'lear', can be served separately. As someone
who does not enjoy gravy, she was delighted when I served this pie
with the lear on the side, where she could cheerfully ignore it. It has
the added bonus of lowering the possibility of soggy pastry.

SERVES 4

400g lean lamb leg
½ tsp salt
½ tsp coarse ground black pepper
½ tsp freshly grated nutmeg
¼ tsp ground mace
pinch of ground cloves
1 × batch Cornflour Shortcrust
    Pastry, made with lamb fat
    in place of butter, if possible
    (page 326)
3 Little Gem lettuces, shredded
30g unsalted butter, melted
250g young asparagus, rinsed and
    cut into 3cm lengths
1 × sheet all-butter puff pastry,
    chilled
1 large egg, beaten

For the lear

250ml strong lamb stock (or make
    with 250ml hot water and a
    lamb stock cube)
2 spring onions, chopped
12 sprigs fresh thyme
1 anchovy fillet or 1 tsp anchovy
    essence
4 tsp mushroom ketchup
2 tsp Worcestershire sauce
1 level tbsp cornflour mixed with
    a little cold water (optional)
course ground black pepper

Equipment

20cm round loose-bottomed tin

Cut the meat into thin slices and beat with a rolling pin or meat mallet until thin and tender. Cut into bite-sized pieces. Mix together the salt, pepper and spices and sprinkle over both sides of the meat.

Grease a 20cm diameter, loose-bottomed tin. You can use a wider tin, but there will be fewer layers and the pie will require longer cooking. Roll out the shortcrust pastry to about 8mm thick and use it to line the tin using the method on page 59, letting the excess pastry hang over the edges and reinforcing the base with pastry trimmings.

Melt the butter and brush it over the base of the pie.

Put a layer of shredded lettuce at the bottom of the pie. Sprinkle with pepper and add a few dabs of melted butter using a pastry brush. Add a layer of asparagus pieces, followed by a layer of seasoned meat. Press down firmly. Continue layering the lettuce, asparagus and meat until the pie is full. Finish with a layer of seasoned and buttered lettuce. Be sure to press the filling down well because the greenery will wilt during baking and you don't want to end up with a half-empty pie when you cut it open. Packing the filling firmly now will ensure there's enough 'body' in the pie once cooked. The filling should be at least level with the top of the tin and preferably slightly rounded above it.

Preheat the oven to 180°C/160°C fan/gas 4.

Moisten the edges of the shortcrust pastry with a pastry brush and lay over the chilled sheet of puff pastry. Press the edges together to seal. Cut the excess pastry from around the edge of the tin, crimp the edges and brush generously with the beaten egg. Cut a steam vent in the centre of the lid. Use the shortcrust offcuts to make decorations and press them firmly onto the lid. Do not glaze the decorations. The lower fat content of the shortcrust pastry, together with the lack of glaze, means that the decorations will bake paler than the puff pastry and stand out against the dark and glossy lid. Bake for 50–60 minutes, turning the pie after 30 minutes to ensure even colouring, until the pastry is cooked and the top crisp and golden.

Meanwhile, put all the ingredients for the lear into a small pan and bring to the boil. Reduce the heat, cover and simmer gently for 30 minutes. Strain through a sieve, return to the pan and add the cornflour mixture to thicken if liked.

When the pie is cooked, remove from the oven and allow to stand in the tin for 10 minutes before removing and transferring to your serving dish. You can pour some of the lear into the pie through the vent before serving, or just serve it all in a gravy boat alongside for everyone to help themselves.

STUFFED LEG OF LAMB
Anon., 1700

A leg of lamb is a beautiful joint for a weekend family meal or any special occasion. My only gripe is that it can be relatively fatty, which hinders my personal enjoyment somewhat. This recipe provides a great solution. It requires a little more preparation, but the rewards definitely make it worth it. I found many similar recipes in my hunt through the seventeenth-century archives, so it would appear to be a popular choice for the table for a number of decades. You will need a sharp knife, a butcher's needle and some butcher's twine.

For this recipe, the skin is cut down the back of the leg, and the thigh bone is removed. The majority of the meat is cut away, leaving only a 1cm-thick layer against the skin, which is then sewn back together to create a large pocket. All fat and connective tissue is removed from the lean meat, which is then mixed with herbs and spices and stuffed back into the skin. The skin is then sewn shut around the stuffing, thereby giving the outward appearance of an ordinary leg of lamb. Once roasted, the joint can be sliced and served cleanly and easily. The meat is beautifully moist and any excess fat can be poured off before using the collected meat juices to make gravy.

This recipe works equally well with lamb, hogget and mutton. If using more mature joints, consider increasing the seasonings to match the stronger flavour of the meat.

SERVES 4

1 large leg of lamb or mutton
—about 2kg
150g fresh suet
4 anchovy fillets, rinsed and finely
  chopped
zest of 1 lemon
60ml thick oyster sauce
½ nutmeg, grated
½ tsp ground mace
1 tsp coarse-ground black pepper
20g parsley

12 sprigs fresh thyme, leaves
  removed and finely chopped
10g fresh marjoram, leaves
  removed and finely chopped
6 sage leaves, finely chopped
½ tsp salt

Equipment
sharp knife
butcher's needle and twine

Turn your lamb leg so that the flat side is facing you. Cut the skin cleanly in a straight line from the joint of the shank along the thigh bone. Cut down through the meat to the bone, then work the knife along and around the bone until you can cut it free. Leave the shorter shank bone attached. Cut away the meat from inside the skin, leaving only a 1cm layer, and set aside. Sew up the original cut in the skin with a butcher's needle and twine to form a hollow cone. There will be a large flap of skin from the end of the thigh; this will be used to close the skin around the prepared meat once the leg has been stuffed.

Trim the reserved meat of all fat and connective tissue and chop it into small pieces. The original recipe calls for it to be pounded into a smooth sausagemeat consistency, but I think it is nicer when the pieces of meat can be distinguished. Put the trimmings and thigh bone into a pan and cover with cold water. Cover and simmer while the meat cooks.

Put the prepared lean meat into a bowl and add the suet, anchovies, lemon zest, oyster sauce, spices, herbs and seasoning. Mix everything together well. Test the seasoning by frying a little patty of the meat mixture in a pan and tasting. Add more flavouring as required. When you are happy, spoon the meat mixture back into the skin, pressing it in firmly but making sure the flap of skin from the thigh can still close around it. Sew the flap shut, enclosing the filling. If you have any filling left over you can shape it into small balls and fry them just before serving, then use them to garnish the joint. Wrap your joint in foil and chill in the fridge until required.

Weigh the stuffed joint and calculate the time required for cooking. You should aim for 15 minutes per 500g. Put the joint onto a rack over a baking pan. Pour 500ml of water into the pan to keep the joint moist. Put the pan into a cold oven, then turn the heat to 200°C/180°C fan/gas 6. At the end of the calculated cooking time, test the internal temperature of your cooked joint with a thermometer: rare is 52°C, medium is 60°C, well done is 70°C. Your joint will continue cooking after you take it out of the oven, so you need to allow for the temperature rising a few degrees while it rests.

When the joint is cooked, remove from the oven and place on a wire rack over a baking tray. Tent with foil, lay a clean towel over the top and allow to rest for 15–20 minutes. Spoon off the excess fat from the cooking pan. Use some stock from the simmering offcuts to deglaze the pan, making sure you get all the meat juices from the bottom. Use to make gravy (see page 50), adding a stock cube if you think it necessary. Quickly fry any extra stuffing meatballs and place them around the joint to serve.

MUTTON SQUAB PIE

Charles Carter, 1730

A squab is a small domesticated pigeon bred for consumption, back in the days when many wealthy households could boast a dovecote. Although some early recipes for squab pie do actually call for pigeon, the more well-known version is of pie with a filling of meat, onions and apples. Mrs Sarah Harrison, of Devonshire, published the following description of the pie in her cookery book of 1733:

'Squab Pye, or DevonShire Pye, made with Mutton or Beef Stakes, season'd with Pepper and Salt, with some Apples and Onions shred in it.' [5]

Other variations call for a mixture of pork and mutton alongside the onions and apples. A similar pie is also popular in Shropshire. Known as Fidget or Fitchett pie, it consists of a mixture of rabbit, fat pork or bacon, alongside the onions and apples.

Charles Carter's recipe expands on Sarah Harrison's description by including some herbs and a few raisins for sweetness, which are a pleasant contrast against the onions and apples.

SERVES 4

400g lean mutton, thinly sliced
4 tbsp chopped fresh parsley
2 tbsp chopped fresh thyme
¼ freshly grated nutmeg
½ tsp salt
1 tsp ground black pepper
1 × batch Hot Water Crust
(page 328)

30g cold butter, sliced very thin
150g raisins
4 dessert apples, peeled, cored and
* finely chopped*
4 onions, finely chopped

For the lear
250ml strong lamb stock (or make
   with 250ml hot water and a
   lamb stock cube)
2 spring onions, chopped
12 sprigs fresh thyme
1 anchovy fillet or 1 tsp anchovy
   essence

4 tsp mushroom ketchup
2 tsp Worcestershire sauce
1 level tbsp cornflour mixed with
   a little cold water (optional)
course ground black pepper

Equipment
20cm pie tin

Preheat the oven to 180°C/160°C fan/gas 4.

Cut the meat into bite-sized pieces. Sprinkle over the herbs, nutmeg, salt and pepper and toss to coat. Set aside.

Set aside a third of the dough and roll out the rest. Use it to line your pie tin using the method on page 59.

Put a thin layer of the sliced butter in the bottom of the pie. Next, lay in the meat and scatter over the raisins. Add the apples, then the onions and finish with another layer of sliced butter.

Roll out the remaining pastry for the lid. Dampen the edges with water, lay over the top of the pie and press firmly to seal. Trim any excess and crimp the edges, using any offcuts to make decorations and attaching them to the pie with a little water. Cut a vent in the middle of the lid and brush the pie with the beaten egg. Bake for 50–60 minutes, turning the pie around after 30 minutes to ensure even colouring, until the pastry is cooked and the top crisp and golden.

While the pie bakes, put all the ingredients for the lear into a small pan and bring to the boil. Reduce the heat, cover and simmer gently for 30 minutes. Strain through a sieve, return to the pan and add the cornflour slurry to thicken if liked.

Remove the pie from the oven and allow to stand in the tin for 10 minutes to firm up the pastry. You can serve it a number of ways:

—Serve the pie whole with the lear alongside for people to pour as they like.

—While the pie is still in the tin, pour the lear into it through the vent and gently shake from side to side to distribute it evenly thoughout the filling. Remove from the tin and transfer to a serving dish.

—While the pie is still in the tin, sandwich it between 2 wire racks and turn it upside down, over a bowl—tricky! Let all the accumulated cooking juices drain out, then turn the pie the right side up again. Skim the fat from the pie juices, and add the remainder to the lear. Thicken the lear with the cornflour slurry then pour into the pie as above.

—Cut off the pastry lid in a neat circle. Cut it into wedges and tuck it back into the pie rim at an angle to decorate. Add the thickened lear—or not—and serve.

5

PORK

The flesh of a pig is probably the most versatile of any domesticated animal raised for human consumption, which is why it alone warrants two chapters in this book: this chapter on fresh pork and another chapter on its uses once cured. Practically everything on a pig can be turned into a dish. Some, admittedly, are less elegant and refined than others, but all have a richness and depth of flavour that has been celebrated for centuries and should be again.

ELIZABETH RAFFALD'S ROAST PORK
1769

Elizabeth Raffald was a remarkable woman. Merely reading of her achievements renders you breathless with admiration as well as exhausted and shame-faced at your own slovenliness. Born in Doncaster into a family of modest means, Elizabeth Whitaker entered service at the age of 15. By the age of 30, she had risen to become housekeeper at Arley Hall in Cheshire. She married the head gardener, John Raffald, and moved to Manchester where, over the next eighteen years, she opened a confectionery shop, ran a register office for domestic servants, then a cookery school, wrote a best-selling cookery book, managed two public houses, had nine (although sometimes cited as sixteen) daughters, established a second Manchester newspaper (*Prescott's Journal*) and wrote and published Manchester's first directory. Mrs Raffald also wrote a book on midwifery, but at the time of her sudden death at the relatively young age of 48, one suspects due to a desire for a bit of a rest, it was unpublished. If her widower later sold the manuscript, it was never published under her name.

This recipe is interesting because Mrs Raffald titled it 'To barbicue a leg of pork'. Along with the preceding 'To barbicue a Pig', these are two of the earliest printed recipes for this method of cooking. Of course, it is nothing like the style of barbecue that is popular today, being roasted before direct heat and basted with copious quantities of red wine. Nevertheless, it does have an interesting treatment for the crackling, which I have immediately appropriated. The stuffing has been imported from Mrs Raffald's other barbecue recipe and is robustly flavoured with sage and liver, but it can be omitted if you think it too strong. The joint you choose is entirely up to you: leg and loin are leaner, and thus require slightly more care in the preparation and cooking, shoulder has a higher quantity of fat and can, to a large extent, be plonked in the oven and forgotten.

SERVES 4

1 large joint of boned pork loin, leg
or shoulder with skin attached
salt and pepper

Equipment
butcher's twine
roasting tin with a rack

For the stuffing (optional)
500g pig's liver
150g breadcrumbs
100g butter
200ml red wine
4 anchovy fillets, rinsed
6 sprigs fresh sage
½ tsp cayenne pepper

If you are stuffing your joint, blitz all the stuffing ingredients to a paste in a food processor. Lay your meat out skin-side down and spread the stuffing generously over the insides. Roll up and tie firmly with butcher's twine.

Using your sharpest knife, score the skin of the joint and most of the fat almost to the depth of the meat in parallel lines 1cm wide. For every other strip of skin, slice through the fat underneath and then twist the strip so that the fat lies uppermost and the skin is underneath. This helps both with the rendering of the fat and the crisping of the skin into crackling. Sprinkle with salt and pepper.

Weigh the joint to help determine cooking time and place it on a rack over a roasting tin. If your joint is either a loin or a leg, tent some foil over the pan to prevent the meat from drying out. A shoulder of pork can be left uncovered. Place the meat in the cold oven and set the temperature to 150°C/130°C fan/gas 2.

Cook the joint for 30 minutes per 500g, then remove it from the oven and discard any foil. Turn up the heat to 220°C/200°C fan/ gas 7. Transfer the meat to a fresh pan, still on its rack. The meat is going back into a hot oven to crisp the skin, so you want as little oil in the pan as possible to avoid a smoky kitchen. You can use the juices in the first pan to make gravy (see page 50). Return the joint to the oven and bake uncovered for a further 30–40 minutes.

Remove the joint and cover with foil. Allow to rest for 30 minutes or so while you prepare the rest of the meal.

Serve with: Spiced Apple Sauce (page 36), Clapshot (page 310), Braised Red Cabbage with Sausages (page 170), Roasted Parsnips (page 295) and green beans.

ADOBADO PORK

Lady Ann Fanshawe, 1664–5

This is yet another recipe from the splendid manuscript of Lady
Ann Fanshawe, loyal supporter of Prince Charles (later Charles II)
during the English Civil War, who travelled with her ambassador
husband throughout Europe, giving birth to and, tragically, burying
nine of her fourteen children along the way. This recipe dates from
the couple's time in Spain, where freshly killed pork had to be
prepared and either cooked or preserved promptly. Modern Spanish
recipes for this dish contain substantial quantities of chillies, so the
use of sage is unusual, while at the same time being stoutly British.

SERVES 4

1 joint of pork, doesn't matter   *Equipment*
* what size or which joint, skinned*   *sealable plastic bag or box large*
450ml red wine   *enough for your joint*
450ml red wine vinegar
1 bunch fresh sage, leaves removed
* and finely chopped*
2 garlic cloves, sliced
2 tbsp sea salt

Place the pork into a large sealable plastic bag or box. Mix together
the wine, vinegar and 450ml water and add the sage, garlic and
salt. Stir well. Pour the mixture over the pork, seal the bag and
refrigerate for 2 days to marinate. If the meat isn't covered by the
marinade, turn it regularly.

Preheat the oven to 180°C/160°C fan/gas 4.

Remove the meat from the marinade, weigh the joint and place in a
roasting tin. Roast for 30 minutes for every 450g, plus an additional

30 minutes. Test for doneness with a thermometer, which should read a minimum of 80°C.

Serve hot with mustard, or cold with baked potatoes, a selection of pickles and an oil and vinegar dressing.

MEDLEY PIE
Eliza Melroe, 1798

I found this useful recipe in a slim volume entitled *An economical, and new method of cookery; describing upwards of eighty cheap, wholesome, and nourishing dishes*, a title sure to strike dread into the hearts of any dinner guest. Individually, 'cheap', 'wholesome' and 'nourishing' are all admirable adjectives when describing a recipe, if a little earnest, but to list all three together conjures up images of gruel, beadles and dancing waifs. Happily, this is far removed from the reality of this dish. It uses cooked pork, which drastically shortens the cooking time compared with other pork pies, but combines it with onion, apple and herbs to deliver a hearty and comforting pie that is refreshingly bright. It requires no additional liquid, as the moisture from the onion and apple is more than enough, however, you could certainly add a little gravy if you have some to hand.

SERVES 4

1 Bramley apple, peeled, cored and finely chopped
1 tsp caster sugar
300g cooked pork, chopped into small pieces
1 onion, finely sliced
½ tsp salt

½ tsp ground white pepper
1 tsp dried marjoram
1 tsp dried sage
1 tsp dried thyme
250g chilled Cornflour Shortcrust Pastry (page 326)
1 large egg, beaten

Equipment
20–25cm ceramic or enamel pie dish

Preheat the oven to 200°C/180°C fan/gas 6.

Put a layer of chopped apple into the bottom of a pie dish and sprinkle over a light dusting of caster sugar. Cover with a layer of onion and a dusting of salt and pepper, followed by a layer of chopped pork sprinkled with the mixed herbs. Repeat the layers until the pie dish is full, finishing with a layer of apples and sugar.

Roll out the pastry to about 5mm thick. Wet the edges of the pie dish with water and lay the pastry over the top, pressing the edges to make a firm seal. Trim the excess pastry. Cut a vent in the middle of the lid and use any pastry trimmings to make decorations, which can be attached to the lid with a little water. Brush liberally with beaten egg and bake for 30 minutes, until the pastry is cooked and golden and the filling thoroughly hot.

PORK FRICASSEE
1695

As the concept of nose-to-tail eating returns to our tables as the fashionable way to dine, it is gratifying to see unusual cuts of meat become more widely available. Pork cheek is just such a cut. Similar in shape to the chicken oyster, but about ten times the size, they are perfect for the long, slow braising of this dish, being small enough to require no further trimming, yet large enough to withstand the long cooking time without falling apart. Contrary to modern casserole methods and also, interestingly, to the acknowledged definition of a fricassee, the pork here is fried in butter *after* cooking in the braising liquid, which adds a hearty caramelisation to the outsides and enriches the thick herbed sauce.

SERVES 4

*1kg pork cheek pieces or 1kg
  skinless pork leg, preferably in
  1 piece
4 onions, peeled
1 bunch fresh parsley
1 bunch fresh thyme
1 tbsp dried marjoram
1 tsp salt, plus extra to season
80ml vinegar or caper pickling
  liquid*

*1–2 anchovy fillets or 1–2 tsp
  anchovy essence
150ml good quality oyster sauce
4oz unsalted butter
2 tbsp capers
pepper
Sippets, to garnish (page 333)*

*Equipment
muslin*

Put the cheeks or thickly sliced pork into a large pan. Add the onions, herbs and salt and pour over cold water until the meat is submerged by about 3cm. Cover and simmer on a low heat for 2 hours, until the meat is tender. Remove the meat from the cooking liquid and set aside to drain.

Strain the cooking liquid through a fine mesh sieve lined with muslin. Measure out 1 litre and store or freeze the remainder for use in soups or stews. Finely chop the onions and parsley from the pot and add to the litre of stock together with the vinegar, anchovy and 100ml of the oyster sauce. Blend to a purée and then simmer over a medium heat to allow the flavours to mingle and develop while you finish off the pork.

Cut each slice of pork into strips about 2cm wide. Melt the butter in a large pan and add the meat. Braise over a medium-low heat, turning often but carefully to avoid breaking it into pieces, until most of the butter has been absorbed and the meat is delicately browned.

Remove 1 cup of the stock mixture and set aside. Transfer the pork to the stock, then use the cup of liquid to wash around the buttery pan to pick up all the nuggets of flavour. Pour this mixture back in with the rest of the meat and sauce and continue to simmer, uncovered, as the liquid reduces and thickens, skimming off any impurities that rise to the surface. When you're happy with the consistency, taste and add salt and pepper, capers and the rest of the oyster sauce as liked.

Transfer the meat to a warmed serving dish and garnish with sippets. Serve with boiled rice.

HERB SAUSAGES
Jane Parker, 1651

There are some people who just love to ruin a tasty morsel by expounding, usually inaccurately, on all the unmentionable ingredients allegedly contained therein, i.e. "Course, you know what they put in them, don't you? Ears and lips and toes and sawdust...'. Thus it was that for many years I was averse to the humble sausage and went decades without braving black pudding at all. I grew up believing that sausages were made with all the leftover bits and trimmings that were unusable anywhere else, squished together in a homogenous blob so that nothing too suspect could be identified. Recently, the rise of specialist sausage makers has returned sausages to their rightful place as a flavourful yet reasonably priced artisan food. This notwithstanding, it was with some trepidation that I began my hunt through the manuscripts for some seventeenth-century sausage recipes, concerned at what I would find and whether it could, or even should, be updated for twenty-first-century consumption.

Whilst I had, for several months, made notes on where these recipes were located, I had deliberately avoided reading them in detail, not wanting to become enchanted by a recipe and then find that I didn't have the equipment to make it. So I hinted heavily at the suitability of a mincing attachment with sausage funnel and casings for an upcoming birthday and set all other sausage-related plans aside. So I felt quite foolish when the time for experimentation came around, because I discovered not only that it was only the choicest cuts of prime, lean pork that were utilised, but that my funnel and casings were to be redundant. Practically every fresh sausage recipe suggested keeping the finished sausage meat in a jar 'for your use', when it could then be rolled into finger shapes, rounded into balls or flattened into patties. Casings or, in the recipes of the times, hogs guts, were reserved for the type of sausages that were dried in the chimney smoke and enjoyed in the depths of winter. Not only were my new utensils redundant but I could probably have managed without the mincing attachment as well, since the chopping action of the majority of modern food processors is more that enough to create sausage meat of whatever degree of coarseness you like. So don't be discouraged for lack of equipment—you probably already have everything you need.

Make sure the pork belly you buy is on the meaty side, although you can always trim the excess fat from under the skin if it seems a bit much. Aim for a lean-to-fat ratio of about 60:40.

Ideally you should make your sausagemeat at least 24 hours before it is required in order for the flavouring from the spices and seasonings to develop.

SERVES 4

1kg pork belly
2 thick slices white bread, crusts
* removed*
150ml single cream
10g fresh sage leaves, chopped
20g fresh parsley, leaves separated
* and chopped*
2 sprigs fresh rosemary, leaves
* separated and chopped*

½ tsp ground cloves
½ tsp ground mace
½ tsp freshly grated nutmeg
1 large egg
1 tsp ground pepper
1 tsp salt

Break the bread into a bowl. Bring the cream to a boil and pour over the bread and leave to soak.

Remove the skin from the pork belly and discard. Chop the meat small with a knife and then mince, or finely chop in a food processor. Transfer the meat to a mixing bowl and add the herbs, spices, egg and seasoning. Once cool, beat the bread and cream vigorously with a wooden spoon until smooth and pour into the herb and meat mixture. Mix thoroughly by hand. Add a little water if the mixture seems heavy or too dense. Cover with cling film and chill in the fridge for 24 hours.

Take a spoonful of the mixture and cook it in a pan. Once cooked, taste to check the seasoning and adjust as necessary. Make up the remainder into balls, patties or rolls, as liked, and fry gently in a dry pan over a medium heat—there will be more than enough fat from the pork belly to moisten the pan. Alternatively, grill on a wire rack under a medium heat. Drain on kitchen paper and serve.

MRS LUKE'S BEER SAUSAGES
circa 1700

Be not alarmed at the quantity of suet in these sausages. I too had some trepidation, warning my husband as I prepared them, 'These might be a little greasy.' I was, however, joyfully proved wrong, for the purpose of the suet was to gently baste the lean meat as it cooked and then to run clear. By the time the sausages were cooked, the pan was full of the rendered suet and the sausages delicately tender and moist. A quick dab with kitchen paper and they made a wonderful supper. You can vary the beer in this recipe to whatever takes your fancy.

SERVES 4

500g lean pork (tenderloin or leg)   *2 tbsp chopped fresh thyme leaves*
250g fresh suet (or 200g dried)   *1 tsp salt*
200ml ruby ale or other beer   *1 tsp pepper*
100ml oyster sauce   *½ tsp ground mace*
15 fresh sage leaves, finely chopped   *¼ tsp ground cloves*

Chop the meat finely and then mix thoroughly with the rest of the ingredients, either by hand or, for a smoother texture, in a food processor. Cover with cling film and chill in the fridge for 24 hours.

Take a little of the mixture and cook it in a pan. Taste to check the seasoning and adjust as necessary. Make up into balls, patties or rolls, as liked, and fry gently in a dry pan over a medium heat. The suet will slowly melt as the sausages cook, basting the meat from the inside. Alternatively, grill on a wire rack under a medium heat. Drain on kitchen paper and serve.

BRAISED RED CABBAGE WITH SAUSAGES
Hannah Glasse, 1747

I have my suspicions that this is supposed to be a side dish, but when I first made it I was so tempted by the bright colour of the cabbage and the piquancy of the dressing offsetting the richness of the sausagemeat that I served it for supper, which is how it has earned a spot in this chapter. You could also serve it as a side dish to richer meats such as roast pork, turkey and goose.

SERVES 4

500g good quality pork sausages
1 red cabbage, finely shredded
500ml beef stock
1 tbsp cornflour mixed with a little
  cold water

2 tbsp vinegar
salt and pepper
chopped fresh parsley, to garnish

Remove the skins from the sausages and discard. Cut each sausage into 4 or 5 pieces, rolling it into balls, if liked.

Put the sausages, cabbage and stock into a pan over a low-medium heat, cover and simmer for 20–25 minutes, until the sausages are cooked and the cabbage is tender but still with some bite to it.

Strain off the stock into a separate pan and add the cornflour slurry. Bring to a simmer, stirring until the mixture thickens and becomes translucent. Taste and add salt and pepper as required. Add 1 tablespoon of the vinegar.

Pour the thickened gravy over the cabbage and sausages and stir to coat. Taste again and add more vinegar and seasoning if required. Pour into a warmed dish to serve, sprinkled with a little chopped parsley.

MRS BALL'S TURKEY PORK
1935

I found this recipe of interest because of its curious title. After months of being immersed in seventeenth-century manuscript recipes where disguise was fashionable (beef like red deer, collops like bacon, mutton like venison, cucumbers like mango), I was curious as to the alchemy involved to effect such a transformation. Practically none, as it turned out. Lean pork is encased in a rich dripping pastry and baked in a moderate oven until done, then, 'Break off the crust; and you will find your pork beautifully white and tender',[1] the inference being that, with the suggested accompaniments of stuffing balls, bread sauce and gravy, the flavours can approximate that of a turkey dinner.

I found this recipe in the 1935 first edition of *Farmhouse Fare*, a book created from recipes submitted by readers of *Farmers Weekly*, usually the wives of farmers. Trying to envisage the origins of the recipe, I could well imagine the exasperation of the farmer's wife, at pig-killing time, at having to serve up yet another piece of pork, due to lack of available storage space and/or suitable refrigeration. As Benjamin Disraeli once wrote, desperation is sometimes as powerful an inspirer as genius, and thus we have this unusually titled, but demonstrably toothsome, dish.

The secret to the success of this recipe is having the pastry completely sealed around the meat in order to both preserve the colour and keep in all of the meat juices. The original recipe suggested wrapping an entire joint in pastry, but after several failed attempts I decided I needed to have a re-think, as it was extremely difficult to make the pastry remain close-wrapped around the joint during baking without holes forming. The compromise of baking a smaller piece of pork in a loaf tin as a form of pie is detailed below. A long, narrow tin is ideal, so that the tenderloin can lie in one piece, but a shorter, wider tin can also be used, and the tenderloin cut in half as required.

SERVES 4

1 pork tenderloin
pepper and salt
1 × batch Beef Dripping Pastry
(page 327)
1 large egg, beaten

Equipment
a 1kg loaf tin

Set aside a third of the pastry and roll out the rest to about 1cm thick. Use it to line a greased loaf tin, easing the pastry into the corners of the tin rather than pushing or stretching it. You want to try to keep an even depth of reasonably thick pastry to avoid it splitting during baking. Allow the excess pastry to hang over the edge of the tin for now. Cover lightly with cling film and chill in the fridge for 30 minutes. You can skip this step if you're short of time, but it does give the pastry time to relax and shrink, which will help the pie to be sealed properly when adding the lid.

Preheat the oven to 180°C/160°C fan/gas 4.

Trim the tenderloin of any fat, silverskin and sinew and season with pepper and salt.

Remove the chilled pastry from the fridge and place the tenderloin inside pressing down gently but firmly. Roll out the reserved pastry to 1cm thick for the lid. Wet the top edges of the pastry in the tin and drape over the pastry lid. Again, ease the pastry into place rather than stretching it or you run the risk of the steam from the cooking blowing a hole in it and then you will lose all the lovely juices inside to evaporation. Press the edges together firmly and trim the excess pastry and crimp the edges. Use the pastry trimmings to make decorations and attach them to the lid with a little water. Cut at least 3 narrow vents along the length of the pie lid. You can incorporate them into the decorations if you want to disguise them. Brush the pastry with the beaten egg to glaze.

Bake for 30–40 minutes, until the pastry is golden brown and slightly shrunken from the sides of the tin and the meat's internal temperature is at least 80°C when measured with a meat thermometer. Allow to cool in the tin for 10 minutes before easing the pie out and transferring to a warmed serving dish. The pie will be full of moisture when you cut into it, so make sure the dish is deep enough to keep it from spilling.

Serve with: Bread Sauce (page 41), Stuffing (page 319) or Savoury Pudding (page 323) and Gravy (page 50).

6

GAMMON, HAM & BACON

Ask anyone what distinguishes gammon, ham and bacon from each other and even the most ardent foodie will probably need a few moments to collect their thoughts, since all three are preserved with salt or brine and all three can also be smoked. Bacon refers to cured pork meat, and can come from any part of the side, or flitch, of the pig. Historically, gammon is the fleshy part of the thigh and a 'gammon' referred to the hind leg joint, which was removed *after* curing. Thus, in many old manuscript books it is possible to find references to 'a gammon of bacon'. A ham was the same joint, removed from the flitch *before* brining and cured or smoked separately. Nowadays the distinctions have narrowed—bacon is generally the thinly sliced meat of the back or belly, gammon is raw cured lean pork, and ham refers solely to cooked and preserved meat.

BACON & HERB PASTIES

William Ellis, 1750

This recipe originates from the pen of Mr William Ellis, gentleman farmer of Little Gaddesden, in Hertfordshire. Mr Ellis was an enthusiast for all things agricultural, publishing numerous tracts and treatises on a whole range of subjects concerning animal husbandry, gardening, cooking, food storage, brewing, shepherding, production and storage of grains, design of various farm implements, etc.

In his *The Country Housewife's Family Companion* (1750) he advised housewives against shopping at country chandlers' shops run by scurrilous rogues and instead recommended the honest tradesmen of London. He especially counselled against buying bacon from anyone, since it was so easy to feed a pig at home:

'For if Servant's cant live upon a Piece of Bacon or pickled Pork, and a Pudding or Apple Dumplins for Dinners and Suppers, let them fast I say.'

Mr Ellis was a great believer in thrift, fending for oneself and trusting no one. Brewing one's own beer and baking one's own bread were also recommended, not only to save money, but to prevent gossiping shopkeepers from learning your business and then using it to their advantage. Even the servants in the household did not escape his mistrust, Ellis counselling to always keep them busy and to prevent them from late-night drinking, dancing and general carousing and thus guard against wasting money. As he noted:

'To rise at five is the way to thrive.'

For all his suspicions and predilection for repeating gossip as cautionary tales, Ellis's work is also scattered with eminently practical tips and advice, as well as numerous simple and choice country dishes. These wholesome pasties are just such a recipe. Made with bread dough instead of the fattier and more friable— and as far as Mr Ellis was concerned, needlessly expensive—pastry, they were a sturdy and practical solution to feeding labourers in the fields. I can come up with no better description of their refreshing taste than Mr Ellis's own:

'For as the Gravey of the bacon is here intirely kept within the Paste with the Juice of the Herbs, the Mixture of them all renders these Pasties a pleasant, wholesome, satiating Victuals, and serves for a delightful Change of Diet among Children and Servants in particular.'

Use whatever bacon you like. Personally, I chop up the lean meat from some cooking bacon. For a richer flavour, include some bacon fat in the mix.

SERVES 4

*400g brown or wholemeal bread
  flour, plus extra for dusting
1 × 7g sachet fast-action yeast
1 tbsp salt
warm water, to mix
250g bacon, chopped small*

*6 spring onions, chopped
6 tbsp chopped fresh parsley
3 tbsp chopped fresh thyme
1 tsp coarse-ground black pepper
1 large egg, beaten*

Put the flour, yeast and salt into a bowl and gradually add the warm water until the dough comes together. Dust the work surface with flour and tip out the mixture. Knead for 10 minutes until smooth and elastic, then return to the bowl, cover with cling film and a clean cloth and set aside to rise for 1 hour, or until the dough has risen to twice its original size.

Mix together the bacon, spring onions, herbs and pepper.

Tip out the risen dough and knock it back by gently pressing out the air. Divide both the dough and filling into 8 equal portions. Line a baking sheet with baking parchment.

Roll out each portion of dough into a circle, not too thin, and dampen the edges with a little water. Put a portion of the filling in the middle and fold the dough over the top. Press the edges together firmly, making sure that there's no air trapped inside, then crimp the edge with the tines of a fork and lay on the prepared baking sheet. Cover lightly with a clean cloth. When all 8 pasties are assembled, preheat the oven to 200°C/180°C fan/gas 6.

When the oven is at temperature, lightly brush the pasties with the beaten egg and bake for 15–20 minutes, until the dough is cooked and browned. Cool on a wire rack.

BACON & PORK SQUARES
William Ellis, 1750

Another of William Ellis's simple country recipes that is nevertheless packed with flavour from a surprisingly short list of ingredients. Effectively a sausagemeat, you can, of course, shape them into any form you please. Equally enjoyable at any time of day, they make a substantial meal in themselves or can form part of a larger breakfast or brunch. In this instance you may wish to make up just half the recipe.

SERVES 4

300g pork tenderloin, cut into chunks
300g rindless streaky bacon, cut into chunks, or unsmoked lardons
2 tsp dried sage

1 tsp coarse-ground black pepper
100g soft breadcrumbs

Equipment
20cm square tin

Finely chop the pork and bacon in a food processor and then tip into a mixing bowl. Add the sage, pepper, breadcrumbs and 150ml water and mix thoroughly until well combined.

Line a 20cm square tin with cling film and tip in the mixture. Press even and flat. Fold over the edges of the cling film to completely wrap the mixture and chill in the fridge overnight.

When you are ready to cook the meat, remove the cling film and cut the meat into 4cm squares. Heat a frying pan over a medium heat. Add the squares and cook, uncovered, until browned on both sides. There's no need to add any fat as it will melt out of the squares as they cook.

BACON FROISE WITH APPLE SAUCE

Seventeenth century

There is mention of a *Froyse* in the *Harleian Manuscript 4016*, dating from the fourteenth century, although that recipe is more of a meat omelette seasoned with saffron. Over the centuries it evolved into a thick bacon pancake, ideal hearty fare for farm labourers, with the William Ellis seal of approval. With the bacon pre-prepared and the batter mixed and resting, it could then be quickly cooked and served hot when the men returned from the fields. I've substituted the original batter for one of oatmeal by Mrs Elizabeth Cleland, a Scottish cook from the eighteenth century, as the saltiness of the bacon complements oats very well. Rather than serve a large and potentially heavy single pancake, I suggest rasher-sized pancakes with a narrow zigzag of batter over the top so that the crispy bacon remains visible. It's fairly straightforward to ladle the batter but, for more control, the easiest way to pour it is from a squeezy bottle; an old ketchup bottle is ideal.

SERVES 4

250g or 16 slices streaky bacon	*½ tsp salt*
250ml milk	*½ tsp coarse ground black pepper*
150g oat flour	*Spiced Apple Sauce (page 36),*
2 large eggs	*to serve*

In a bowl, mix a little of the milk with the flour until it comes to a paste. Heat the rest of the milk in a saucepan over a high heat until it comes to boiling point and pour it into the batter, whisking all the while, until fully combined. Pour the mixture back into the pan and set aside to cool.

Grill the bacon until crisp and browned and blot with kitchen paper to absorb the excess grease.

Whisk together the eggs and seasonings and then whisk these into the cooled oatmeal mixture. The consistency should be like double cream—thick but pourable.

Heat a pan over a medium heat, greasing lightly if necessary. Pour or squeeze the batter into the pan in oval shapes slightly longer than the strips of bacon. Depending on the size of your pan, you can probably get 3 or 4 pancakes cooking at one time. Lay one strip of bacon into each pancake and allow to cook for a minute or two until the surface of the pancake has dried out. Squeeze a zigzag of batter over the bacon strip and turn it over to cook the top. When both sides are cooked and lightly browned, transfer to a dish and keep warm while the rest of the pancakes are cooked.

Serve with the Spiced Apple Sauce on the side.

GAMMON & PEASE PUDDING

Fourteenth century

The pairing of dried peas and salt pork is a tradition that goes back over 600 years. Little has changed with this dish for centuries. A manuscript in the library of the Royal Society lists the following recipe, which is remarkably similar to the modern version below:

'Grene pesen wyth bakon

Take old pesen, and boyle hom in gode flesh broth that bacon is sothen in, then take hom and bray hom in a morter and temper hom wyth the broth, and strayne hom thurgh a streynour and do hom in the pot, ande let hom boyle tyl thai alye homself, and serve hyt forthe wyth bacon.'[1]

This made an excellent winter meal, when fresh produce was difficult to come by. The bacon came from the annual butchering and preserving of the family pig, the dried peas from the harvest of the summer. Nowadays we can choose from a range of pulses, but I like the complimentary colours of green and yellow dried peas. You can, of course, just use 500g of one colour.

SERVES 4

2 dry-cured gammon shanks
250g green split peas
250g yellow split peas
2 large onions, finely chopped
30g unsalted butter
2 tbsp double cream
1 tsp ground white pepper, plus
* extra for seasoning*

Pea Powder (page 326),
* for dusting*
a splash of fruit or white balsamic
* vinegar*

Equipment
2 × muslin bags

Put the gammon shanks into a large dish, cover with cold water and soak for 12–24 hours, to remove excess salt.

Rinse the peas and put them into separate muslin bags. Tie or clip the bags at the top, allowing the peas plenty of room to swell during cooking.

Put the shanks, chopped onions and bags of peas into a large pan and add cold water to cover. Bring to the boil, cover and turn down the heat to a gentle simmer for 3–4 hours, until the meat is coming away from the bones. Remove the shanks from the pan and transfer to a chopping board to cool for 5 minutes.

Lift the bags of peas from the pan and put the bags into a sieve to drain. Discard the cooking liquid and onions. Gently press the bags with a large spoon to squeeze out any excess water, then open the bag of green peas and tip them back into the sieve, rubbing them through using a wooden spoon to remove any tough skins. The resultant purée is wonderfully light and silken. Add half the butter, cream and pepper to the purée and mix thoroughly. Taste, and adjust seasoning if required. Cover and keep warm. Repeat with the yellow peas.

Strip the ham from the bones, remove all connective tissue, skin and fat and break the meat into bite-sized flakes. Serve with the warm pea purée, a dusting of pea powder and a splash of fruit or white balsamic vinegar.

DEJA FOOD
Ham and pease pudding sandwiches make a very enjoyable lunch; simply lay slices of cold pease pudding and ham between fresh buttered bread. To enjoy any extra pease pudding hot, whisk an egg into the pea purée and pour into a well-buttered bowl. Cover with buttered foil and steam for 30 minutes until set.

GAMMON PIE
Gervase Markham, 1623

Gammon originally meant leg or thigh, so it was entirely possible to have a gammon of ham, which we would recognise as the traditional Christmas joint. Nowadays, the term tends to refer solely to the meat rather than the joint itself.

A whole ham can be very impressive, but it requires a lot of care and attention to prepare and is not really a budget menu item. Additionally, if you're not entertaining banqueting level numbers of people, it is also a lot of meat to deal with at once. This recipe is an alternative way of serving ham for a special occasion, with just one or two smaller joints prepared in a much less stressful manner and presented in the equally traditional fashion of a pie. The rye and wholemeal pastry is both sturdy and crisp and the green of the herbs sets off the pink of the ham in a most appetising way. If you're a fan of savoury jelly in your pies, then by all means feel free to add some as the pie cools, but I feel the less slab-like approach, where the tender meat can just tumble from each slice, is altogether more enticing.

Gervase's original recipe suggests baking an entire gammon, wrapping the pastry around the joint and forming it into the shape of a pig's head. It is certainly an eminently suitable shape, with the snout being formed by the shank end of the joint and the ears shaped from pastry and attached at the larger end. The herbs, butter and ham would then be applied only to the outside of the joint, and the baking time adjusted accordingly. If the occasion warrants it, and your pastry-handling skills are up to the task, it can make for a spectacular centrepiece.

It is important to choose dry-cured gammon in order for the meat to retain some texture after its double cooking. You can cook the pie immediately or cover with cling film and chill in the fridge until convenient to bake. Just brush it again with beaten egg before putting it in the oven.

SERVES 4

1kg boneless or 1.5kg bone-in joint
of dry-cured gammon, to give
700g cooked ham
2 tbsp chopped fresh chives
2 tbsp fresh thyme leaves
2 tbsp chopped fresh sage leaves
2 tbsp chopped fresh rosemary
4 tbsp chopped fresh chervil
8 tbsp chopped fresh parsley
2 tsp coarse ground black pepper
1 tsp cloves
10–12 slices Parma ham

30g unsalted butter, chilled
1 large egg, beaten

For the hot water crust pastry
200g butter, cubed, plus extra for
greasing
150g rye flour
450g stoneground wholemeal flour
1 tsp salt

Equipment
1kg loaf tin

Soak the gammon in cold water for 3 hours to remove excess salt. Drain and rinse, then put the joint into a large pan and cover with cold water. Bring to the boil, turn down the heat and simmer gently until the meat is tender and coming off the bone, if present, about 1½–2 hours. Allow to cool in the water.

Remove the meat from the cooled liquid and strip off the skin. Remove any remaining fat and connective tissue and break the lean meat into bite-sized pieces. Weigh out 700g and set any extra aside for other uses. Toss the 700g of cooked meat with the chopped herbs and spices and set aside.

To make the pastry, put the butter into a saucepan with 400ml water and bring to the boil. Mix together the flours and salt and then pour the boiling fat and water mixture into the flours and mix thoroughly. This can be done in a stand mixer if you have one, using the regular paddle, or in a bowl with a wooden spoon and some elbow grease.

Preheat the oven to 200°C/180°C fan/gas 6. Grease a loaf tin and line it with foil. Generously butter the foil.

While the pastry is still warm, take half and roll it out to 1cm thick. Use it to cut out a lid for your pie. Gather the scraps together with the rest of the pastry and use your hands to press it into the bottom and sides of the greased tin. Keep the pastry about 1cm thick all over.

Line the pie with the Parma ham, reserving some slices for the top of the pie. Add the herbed gammon filling and press down firmly. Slice the butter thinly and layer it over the top of the meat, then sprinkle over the cloves and black pepper, which will drop into the pie as the butter melts and baste the filling. Lay the remaining Parma ham over the top. Add the pastry lid over the top and press firmly to seal. Crimp the edges and cut a vent in the middle of the lid. Use any scraps of leftover pastry to make decorations and attach them to the lid with a little water. Brush with the beaten egg to glaze.

Bake for 40–45 minutes, until the pastry is crisp and brown and has shrunken away from the sides of the tin. Allow to cool in the tin and serve cold.

GAMMON RAGOO WITH SWEET SAUCE

Robert Smith, 1725

Before you flick past this recipe with a shudder, let me reassure you that the sauce is not SWEET sweet, it merely has a sweet note at the end. The combination of salty and sweet has recently become very popular, more usually with desserts.

I especially like this recipe because it is remarkably similar to one I found in a book of farmhouse recipes from the 1950s that used a few crumbled-up ginger biscuits in the sauce. I too was doubtful, but tried it anyway and it was fantastic.

The biscuits in the original recipe were macaroons, similar to modern ratafia or amaretti biscuits, however I really liked the rich caramel notes of the ginger biscuits in the modern recipe. A happy medium was to opt for lightly spiced caramelised Lotus biscuits, which are widely available.

SERVES 4

4 gammon slices, cut into strips
200g streaky bacon, chopped
400ml red wine
1 tsp ground white pepper
4 Lotus caramel biscuits, crushed
1 tbsp sugar
1 tsp ground cinnamon
juice of 2 oranges

1 tbsp cornflour mixed with 1 tbsp
  water (optional)
salt and pepper
250g baby spinach leaves, wilted,
  to serve
250g boiled long-grain or basmati
  rice, to serve

Heat a frying pan over a medium heat and add the gammon. No fat should be necessary. Toss lightly until cooked, 5–10 minutes depending on the thickness of the pieces. Drain and keep warm.

Rinse the pan and return it to the heat. Put the chopped bacon into the pan and stir occasionally to prevent burning. When the fat has melted out of the bacon, add the wine, pepper, crushed biscuits, sugar and cinnamon. Simmer uncovered for 5 minutes and then add the orange juice by pouring it through a sieve to remove any pulp and stir thoroughly. Taste the sauce and adjust the seasoning if required. If a thicker sauce is preferred, add the cornflour mixture and stir until the sauce thickens and becomes translucent.

Return the cooked gammon to the pan and simmer everything for 10 minutes to allow the flavours to combine. Serve with wilted spinach and boiled rice.

HAM TOAST FOR ONE

Charles Herman-Senn, 1894

A hot snack from that prodigious cookbook author and co-founder (with J. C. Buckmaster) in 1885 of The Universal Food and Cookery Association. Charles Herman-Senn was a champion of cookery for the working classes and the association produced affordable cookery pamphlets and sponsored free lectures. Born in Lirstal, Switzerland, in 1864, he received classic training as a chef and worked under renowned cookery writer and chef to Queen Victoria, Charles Elmo Francatelli, at the Reform Club, before finding his true calling in the field of education. He had connections with the National Training School for Cookery and Westminster Technical Institute, creating syllabuses and setting exams, as well as establishing standards for food service in the armed forces, hospitals and prisons. He wrote over 30 cookery books, as well as numerous pamphlets and curated 33 annual cookery exhibitions in London, which were held in great esteem by professionals and public alike. He died, at his desk at 110 Victoria Street, London, on 18 October 1934.

This recipe is basically a rearrangement of the elements of a ham and egg sandwich, but it manages to elevate it to an unusually fresh-tasting lunch or substantial snack. I particularly love the way the filling retains its fluffiness during baking, and thus provides such a great contrast of texture to the crisp toast.

SERVES I

50g lean ham, finely chopped
1 large egg, separated
10g butter
a pinch of ground white pepper
a pinch of cayenne pepper
25ml double cream

1 tbsp chopped fresh parsley
1 tbsp chopped fresh chives
2 slices of bread, toasted
fresh parsley sprigs, to garnish
lemon slices, to serve

Preheat the oven to 180°C/160°C fan/gas 6.

Put the ham, egg yolk, butter, peppers and cream into a small pan and mix thoroughly. Stir over a medium heat until the mixture thickens slightly, then add the chopped parsley and chives and stir.

Whisk the egg white until stiff. Use a balloon whisk to briskly beat in a third of the egg white, then use it less vigorously to fold through the rest. Spoon the mixture evenly on top of the toasts.

Bake for 5–6 minutes, until just set. Garnish with the parsley sprigs and lemon slices and enjoy.

VARIATION
Bake the ham and egg mixture in a buttered ovenproof dish and serve the toast hot, crisp and dry on the side.

OFFAL

Offal generally refers to the internal organ meats of an animal and provides a wealth of savoury and economical dishes. Sadly, not everyone is an offal enthusiast and this collective noun does itself no favours in sounding remarkably like 'awful'. Frequently, and inaccurately, seen as less than desirable, I believe the finger of blame for this low opinion can be pointed at, of all people, a nineteenth-century dictionary compiler.

In his book *The Vocabulary of East Anglia*, Robert Forby gave the following definition of a regional phrase:
  "To make one eat humble pie.'—i.e. To make him lower his tone, and be submissive. It may possibly be derived from the 'umbles' of the deer, which were the perquisite of the huntsman; and if so, it should be written umble-pie, the food of inferiors.'

Quite apart from being contradictory—our modern phrase 'perk of the job' is derived from perquisite, so how would you force humility onto someone by giving him a delicious pie?—with those four final words, Mr Forby effectively signalled the start of the decline of offal in status. In the seventeenth and eighteenth centuries offal had been served with great relish on the very best tables in the land, but in the aspirational nineteenth century, offal was looked down upon, and this has continued into modern times.

Thankfully, there has been something of a revival in offal's fortunes thanks to the modern (although, in fact, centuries old) notion of not wasting anything from a butchered animal.

'If you're going to kill the animal it seems only polite to use the whole thing.' Fergus Henderson, The Whole Beast, *2004*

The recipes I have chosen for this chapter will hopefully convince you to discover and enjoy offal in new and unusual ways.

BLACK PUDDING TOASTS
Mrs Rogers, 1950

Black pudding is considered a delicacy in the West Midlands, the north-west and Stornoway in Scotland, and regarded with varying degrees of horror everywhere else. With the rise in popularity of artisanal butchery and hand-made sausages, black pudding too deserves a revival. Compared to the lower quality, wheat-bulked varieties of regular sausages found in high-street shops and supermarkets, good quality black pudding is practically health food, containing only natural ingredients and spices. Black pudding is also much more varied than one might at first imagine. There are just as many regional variations and jealously guarded recipes for black pudding as for regular sausages. You wouldn't judge the entire range of regular sausages based on just one, so if you haven't enjoyed back pudding yet, seek out a new variety. Stornoway black pudding not only enjoys protected status (PGI), some argue it to be the best sausage of any kind in the UK.

This recipe provides a different way to enjoy black pudding from the fried breakfast rounds with which most people are familiar. The crisped oatmeal and sweetness of the onions are fine complements to the sausage, while the buttery toast adds both richness and crunch. Since black pudding is already cooked when you buy it, it only needs a brief time in the pan to heat through.

SERVES 4

20g unsalted butter or beef
  dripping
500g black pudding, skin removed
2 onions, peeled and finely chopped

100g medium oatmeal
4 slices hot buttered toast, to serve
pea shoots and lamb's lettuce, to
  serve

Heat the fat in a large frying pan, add the onion and sprinkle over the oatmeal. Mix thoroughly. Cook over a medium-low heat until the onion is tender and the oatmeal toasted. Crumble in the black pudding and heat through. Add more fat if the mixture becomes dry.

Put the hot toast on the serving plates and spoon over the black pudding mixture. Add the salad leaves and serve at once.

BRAWN

In the Middle Ages, 'brawn' was a word with quite a broad meaning, derived from the old French for flesh/meat/muscle and could be used equally correctly to describe both a person's thigh and edible flesh.

'His lymes grete, his brawnes harde and stronge.'
Geoffrey Chaucer, The Knight's Tale, *1385*

'Braun and blod of þe goos, bacon and colhoppes.'
William Langland, Piers Plowman, *1393*

Over the centuries and, curiously, peculiar to the UK, the word would come to refer specifically to the meat of the wild boar, and later to pig flesh in general. The modern usage is for a cold cut of cooked meat and spices set in a savoury jelly: think pork pie without the pastry. It can be enjoyed on crackers or toast as a snack, or as part of a more substantial meal with salad and new potatoes. Dorothy Hartley recommends creamy mustard sauce as the perfect accompaniment.

The following recipes are, first and foremost, packed with flavour. I have even recruited two of my local butchers to taste test them, and both agreed they were excellent. They also illustrate the variations that can be used with the base of the cooked meat, which you can then adapt to your own personal tastes. These recipes are not quick but neither are they difficult, involving mostly 'doing things for a long time', such as brining, cooking or reducing. All are most definitely well worth the time.

Ideally, you would make brawn from the pig's head, after removing the eyes and brain. Your local butcher should be able to supply one for you or you could approach your local abattoir directly. Remember to ask them to split the head in half for you, it will make the brining and subsequent cooking that much easier, unless you are blessed with gigantic cookware. Alternatively, you can make equally delicious brawn using the cheaper pieces of meat found in the supermarket—suggested cuts are listed below.

These quantities will give sufficient cooked meat to make both the following brawn recipes, as long as the moulds are on the modest side, or one large brawn of either recipe. Before you consider scaling down the starting quantities, remember that the long preparation time means at least a 5-day wait before you can enjoy some more.

MAKES ABOUT 1.5KG OF BRAWN

1 pig's head or 5kg of cheap, gelatinous pork cuts; I suggest 4 trotters, 1 pork leg shank and 2kg pork belly. This will give about 750g–1kg lean meat
3 celery sticks
2 carrots, sliced
1 onion, cut in half
1 bunch fresh parsley
3 bay leaves
a few sprigs fresh thyme
4 cloves
1 blade mace

1 tbsp black peppercorns
salt and pepper

For the brine
450g salt
450g Demerara sugar
20 bay leaves
2 tbsp black peppercorns
24 cloves
2 tsp saltpetre, not compulsory
4 litres boiling water

Equipment
large cooking pot
brining container, such as a food
  grade lidded plastic box or dustbin

double layer of muslin
suitably sized tin(s) or mould(s)

To begin, check that 6 litres of brine will be enough to cover your pork. The easiest way to do this is to put all of your joints of meat into the container you plan on using and pouring over cold water to cover. Remove the pieces of meat and then measure how much water is in the container. Double the brine recipe if necessary.

To make the brine, put the salt, sugar, bay leaves, peppercorns, cloves and saltpetre, if using, into a large pot. Pour over the boiling water and stir until the sugar and salt have dissolved. Heat gently if required. Add 2 litres cold water and stir. This will help cool the brine quicker. Set aside until completely cold. Put the meat into your brining container and pour over the cold brine. Make sure your brine completely covers the meat. You can keep the meat submerged by putting a weighted bowl or plate on top. Cover and refrigerate or leave in a cool place for 3 days.

Remove the meat from the brine and drain. Discard the brine and rinse the container thoroughly. Fill the container with fresh, cold water and return the meat to soak for 2 hours.

Drain the meat and transfer to a clean pan. Cover with cold water and bring to a boil and simmer for 5 minutes. This will draw out the froth and scum, which would cloud your stock if left, so discard this water and rinse both the meat and the pan. Put the meat back in the pan and add cold water to cover, together with the vegetables, herbs and spices. Bring to a boil, turn down the heat and simmer until the meat is ready to fall off the bone, 3–4 hours. Remove the meat and drain.

Strain the cooking liquid of all solids by pouring it first through a fine mesh sieve and then again through a double layer of muslin.

Set aside to cool completely and solidify into a jelly.

Remove the bones and connective tissue from the meat. Chop the lean meat and add whatever proportion of fat you prefer. I like it lean so I don't add any, but you can choose to add up to an equal weight of fat to the lean meat. Chop everything into neat 1cm cubes. When the cooking liquid has cooled, lift off the top layer of fat and set it aside to use for frying or pastry. Since it will be cold when eaten, taste the jellied stock now to see if it will require more seasoning, as cold food always requires more seasoning than warm. The seasoning should be strong but not overpowering.

To be extra sure of the setting qualities of your stock, chill it in the fridge until set. If the set isn't firm enough, return it to the pan and reduce further. This might seem long-winded, but it's better to test the set of your stock before it is poured over the meat, because a too-loose jelly will not allow your brawn to keep its shape once removed from its mould.

MISS MILNE'S HERB BRAWN
1944

This brawn is glorious to behold, with bright pink and pale white meats offset by vibrant green, fresh parsley and a glistening savoury jelly.

SERVES 4

1 × batch brined, cooked and chopped pork, prepared as above
1 bunch fresh parsley, finely chopped

reduced and seasoned stock, prepared as above
salt and pepper

Fold 4 heaped tablespoons of the chopped parsley into the meat and stir. Add the remainder if liked.

Line your tin or mould with cling film. A loaf tin makes for a neat shape and slices well, especially if you will be serving a cold cuts platter, but you could also use a glass dish or bowl.

Put your meat and parsley mixture into the tin or mould and pour over as much of the seasoned stock as you like. Personally I like it to be just enough to fill in the spaces between the cubes of meat, because it makes for a much more solid finished brawn. You could also add sufficient stock to leave the meat suspended in the savoury jelly once set—you decide. If you would prefer your brawn to be compact enough to slice, cover the top of the mould with more cling film and lay a dish or plate with 1 or 2 heavy tins on top. Leave to chill and set in the fridge.

ABBEY FARM BRAWN
1944, Bedfordshire

Farmhouse recipes tend to conjure up an image of robust heartiness and it is nice to reveal that this is the most elegant brawn recipe I've found. The mould is lined with thinly sliced poached chicken breast, which not only pairs exceedingly well with the pork, but provides a striking contrast against the darker meat. Perfect for an eye-catching make-ahead starter.

SERVES 4

1 × batch brined, cooked and   *500ml chicken stock*
chopped pork, prepared as above   *3–4 boneless chicken breasts*
500ml reduced and seasoned stock,   *salt and pepper*
prepared as above

Bring the chicken stock to a boil, add the chicken breasts, reduce the heat and simmer gently until the chicken is cooked, about 10–12 minutes. Remove the chicken from the stock and cut into thin slices while it's still warm. Line your tin or mould with cling film, and then with the sliced chicken, ensuring the slices overlap without gaps.

Mix the chicken stock with 500ml of the cooking liquid from the pork and simmer until reduced by half. Strain through a muslin to clarify, then taste and season highly, but not overpoweringly, with salt and pepper.

Fill the lined mould with the chopped pork. If your mould is large you could add a middle layer of sliced chicken. Add sufficient reduced stock to your taste—just enough to cover for a firm brawn, add more if you prefer a less sturdy brawn. Cover with cling film and leave to set in a cool place.

DARK HASLET
Seventeenth–eighteenth century

At pig-killing time, the internal organs used to be chopped up and
mixed together to make what was known as 'pig's fry', or haslet.
The mixture could vary in composition and include any or all
of the liver, kidneys, heart, lungs, melt and sweetbreads, as well
as the fattier cuts of meat such as pork belly. It was a cheap and
flavoursome mixture which formed the basis of a number of quick-
cook dishes and was ideal in pre-refrigeration days when a lot of
meat had to be butchered in a short amount of time.

Lincolnshire haslet can still be found in delicatessens and sandwich
shops in the form of a pale meatloaf made with lean pork, sage,
breadcrumbs and seasoning. This is not that meatloaf. This is most
definitely The Other Haslet.

This recipe is very rich and very dark, the coppery flavour of liver
and kidney tempered with the sweetness of lean pork and currants
and enriched with fresh herbs, cream and eggs. Traditionally haslet
was wrapped around a spit, enveloped in sheets of caul fat that
would hold it securely throughout its roasting. The permeable caul
was thin enough to allow the slowly rendering fat to drip through,
yet sturdy enough to hold the chopped meat in place. As it roasted,
the caul would gradually crisp up and shrink around the meat like a
lacy meat corset. When 'done to a turn', the cooked meat would be
cut from the spit in rings, or collars, and dished up. This method is
a challenge to recreate in the modern kitchen, but the recipe below
details a good approximation. As a bonus, the cooking juices are
retained, providing some of the most incredibly flavoursome gravy
I've ever tasted. Serve hot, with mountains of Potato Snow (page
299) to soak up all the gravy, steamed peas and carrots.

SERVES 4

1 pig's kidney

1 pig's heart or 400g ready chopped

250g pig's liver

250g pig's lights

or

1kg pig's fry

1kg pork belly, rind removed

225g fresh suet or 200g dried

1 bunch fresh sage, finely chopped

1 tsp salt

1 tsp ground black pepper

225g currants

1 Bramley apple, peeled, cored and
grated

3 large egg yolks

100ml double cream

pig's caul fat, sufficient to line a
1kg loaf tin

500ml beef stock

1 tbsp cornflour mixed with a little
cold water

Equipment

1kg loaf tin

Slice the kidney lengthways, snip out the white core with a sharp pair of scissors and discard. Roughly chop the kidney, heart, liver and lights.

Bring a pan of water to the boil and add all the meat. Cook for 5 minutes then drain. This serves the purpose of firming up the meat. Chop finely by hand or put through a mincer. Add the suet, sage, salt, pepper, currants and apple. Beat the yolks with the cream and mix with the rest of the ingredients.

Line a large loaf tin with the caul fat, allowing a generous overhang at the sides. If you only have small pieces, then make a patchwork with a double layer of caul. Pour the meat mixture into the tin and smooth over. Bang the tin onto the worktop a few times to help get rid of any air pockets, then fold the caul fat over tightly, securely wrapping the meat mixture inside. Pin the caul in place with toothpicks if necessary. Chill in the fridge for 1 hour.

Preheat the oven to 180°C/160°C fan/gas 4.

Place a wire rack over the loaf tin and turn the whole over so that the loaf tin is upside down on the rack. Carefully remove the tin, leaving the caul-wrapped meatloaf sitting on the wire rack, with the edges of the caul tucked securely underneath. Put the wire rack over a roasting tray and pour in the stock. Cover the whole with foil and bake for 30 minutes, then remove the foil and continue baking for another 30–40 minutes, until the caul is crisp and brown and the internal temperature reaches at least 70°C. Keep the haslet warm while you prepare the gravy. Pour the meat juices from the pan into a jug and put in the freezer to solidify the fat. Lift off the solid fat and reserve for adding flavour to sauces and gravies. Make the remaining juices into gravy by adding the cornflour slurry and/or more beef stock. Pour into a jug and serve.

LIGHT HASLET
1675

This recipe is a similar age to the one above but, in terms of flavour, they are as refreshingly different as can be, despite sharing several ingredients. This is a much lighter, herbier recipe, and probably closer to the Lincolnshire Haslet made today, although the latter contains no offal. Rather than one large meatloaf, this version suggests forming meatballs and is, therefore, much closer to what as a child I knew as faggots. We used to eat them cold sprinkled with vinegar and accompanied by salad and jacket potatoes. The first time I saw a TV commercial for the Other Sort of faggots, eaten hot with gravy, of all things, it seemed perfectly bizarre to my 10-year-old mind. To this day, a part of me secretly labels the hot version not 'proper' faggots.

SERVES 4

300g lean pork, finely chopped or minced

200g pork liver, finely chopped or minced

100g pork fat, finely chopped or minced

3 onions, finely chopped

1 Bramley apple, peeled, cored and   1 bunch fresh parsley
chopped   caul fat, for wrapping
1 bunch fresh sage, leaves separated   salt and pepper
and finely chopped

Preheat the oven to 180°C/160°C fan/gas 4.

Mix together the meats, pork fat, onions, apple, parsley and sage and season generously with salt and pepper. To check the seasoning, fry a little of the mixture in a pan and adjust accordingly. If you plan on eating these cold—they're delicious—remember that the flavour of cold food is muted to a certain extent, so be a little heavy-handed with the seasoning.

Form the mixture into large or small meatballs and wrap in the caul fat. If you don't have caul fat, you can bake them in cupcake tins or in a large loaf tin. Put the wrapped meatballs onto a wire rack over a baking tray with the ends of the fat underneath. Cover with foil and bake. The cooking time will depend on the size of the meatballs you have made: 15–30 minutes for small/medium meatballs, up to 1 hour for a single meatloaf. The caul should be crisp and browned and the internal temperature should reach at least 70°C.

Serve hot with Mustard Sauce (page 46), or cold with a sprinkling of vinegar.

BORDER LIVER & BACON

Mrs M. N., 1732

This recipe appears in Richard Bradley's book on cookery and
household duties.[1] Bradley was not a cook, rather a botanist who,
despite being elected a fellow of the Royal Society at the age of
24 and later becoming the first professor of botany at Cambridge
University, lived in impoverishment for most of his life and left his
wife and child destitute upon his death, aged just 44.

Bradley published prolifically and, like Gervase Markham in the
previous century, his knowledge was wide-ranging. His most
enduring contribution is seen as the formation of a unified theory of
infectious diseases across all forms of life.

He accepted a number of recipe submissions for his cookery book,
including this one from an enthusiastic admirer, Mrs M. N., who
gushed:

> 'IF you would please all People, by the several Receipts you publish,
> you ought to have the particular Dish that is the Favourite of every
> County. In Worcestershire and Shropshire, the following is in esteem,
> and I believe you will oblige several Gentlemen and Ladies of these
> Parts, if you would insert it in some of your Works.'

I think this is a delightful dish, so much fresher and lighter
than the modern mixed grill style of presenting these two pieces
of meat. Liver only requires the briefest of sears in the pan to
cook it to a dainty pink inside. Calf's liver has the most delicate
flavour, however lamb's liver is both more economical and more
readily available.

SERVES 4

400g lamb or calf's liver
200g lean rindless back bacon
hot water, to cover
45g unsalted butter
2 heads Little Gem lettuce, shredded
200g Swiss or Rainbow chard,
   shredded

200g baby spinach leaves
6 spring onions, finely sliced
50g fresh parsley, chopped
juice of ½ lemon
salt and coarse-ground black
   pepper

Cut the liver into slices 1cm thick and remove any connective tissue or unsightly tubes. Lay the bacon flat in a large dish or baking tray and pour over hot (not boiling) water to cover. Soak for 30 minutes to remove the excess salt, then drain and blot dry with kitchen paper.

Heat the grill to medium and lay the slices of bacon flat on the grill pan. Grill gently, turning often, until tinged with brown and cooked though. Set aside in a foil-covered dish to keep warm.

Melt 30g of the butter in a frying pan. Sprinkle the slices of liver with salt and coarse-ground black pepper and quickly fry in the melted butter for 1–2 minutes on each side. Put the cooked liver with the cooked bacon and keep warm.

Turn the heat under the pan to high and melt the remaining butter. Add the chopped vegetables and herbs and toss quickly until wilted, then add the lemon juice and toss to mix. Transfer to a warmed serving dish and top with the cooked liver and bacon.

CHICKEN LIVER RAGOO
Patrick Lamb, 1716

The short title for Patrick Lamb's cookery book was called *Royal Cookery*,[2] and if any author was entitled to be knowledgeable on such matters, it was Patrick Lamb himself. Apprenticed to the royal kitchens at the age of eleven as 'an untitled servant in the pastry' he would eventually rise, in 1683, to the position of master cook to the monarch (at the time, Charles II). He would retain this position until his death in 1708/9 and, thus, was remarkable in serving no less than four monarchs during his lifetime: Charles II, James II, William and Mary and Queen Anne. In recognition of his contribution to the sumptuous coronation feast of James II, Lamb was awarded the princely sum of £50 (the equivalent today of almost £200,000). The first edition of his book was published posthumously and appears to be taken directly from his notes. To modern eyes the recipes appear quite recognisable and, despite originating in the royal kitchens, not overly excessive in ingredients, featuring soups, pies, fish, puddings, cakes and salads. Nevertheless, his publishers must have felt the selection a little too exclusive for general interest, for in 1716 they brought out a completely revised second edition:

'...we have endeavour'd to make it of a more general use than it was before, when it was calculated only for the Kitchens of Princes and Great Men, by adding above five Hundred new Receipts, which not being so expensive as the others, may be useful in those of private Gentlemen likewise.'
From the preface to Royal Cookery: Second edition, *1716*

Chicken livers all too frequently end up as chicken liver pâté, which is rich and savoury and a personal favourite, but a little monotonous. Liver is extremely good for you, providing a wealth of vitamins and minerals. It also cooks quickly, making this a great weeknight or last-minute supper. The robust flavours of this ragoo are complimented by an accompaniment of kale and some crusty bread for mopping up all the sauce.

SERVES 4

400g chicken livers	1 bunch fresh mixed herbs
250g curly kale, tough stalks	½ tsp salt
removed and leaves finely	½ tsp coarse-ground black pepper
shredded	300ml strong chicken or beef stock
60g unsalted butter	1 tbsp cornflour mixed with a little
150g bacon, chopped	cold water
250g mushrooms, sliced or 250g	hot toast or warm crusty bread,
button mushrooms	to serve

Rinse the blood from the livers and pick them over, cutting out any tubes, connective tissue or fat. Cut into bite-sized pieces. Bring a saucepan of water to the boil and drop in the chicken livers for 30 seconds. Remove from the water and keep warm.

Discard the water, wash the pan and fill with cold water. Bring to the boil and steam the kale for 8–10 minutes, until just tender and the colour is still bright. Toss in half the butter until lightly coated and set aside. Keep warm.

Melt the rest of the butter and cook the bacon. (If your bacon is fatty you can omit the butter.) Add the mushrooms and toss lightly until softened, together with the herbs, salt and pepper. Add the stock and simmer for 5 minutes to allow the flavours to mingle. Add the chicken livers and warm through, taking care not to overcook the livers. Add the cornflour slurry and stir gently until the mixture thickens and becomes translucent.

Arrange the kale around the edge of a warmed serving dish and pour the ragoo into the middle. Serve with hot toast or warm crusty bread.

MINCED PIES
Bridget Hyde, 1690

You might be surprised to find a recipe for minced pies in a chapter
on offal, but these are the original, savoury minced pies enjoyed
for hundreds of years from Plantagenet to Victorian times. Also
known as Christmas pies and chewets, they were a heady mixture of
savoury meat, fruit and spices. I have read hundreds of variations of
minced meat pies, the savoury element provided variously by beef,
veal, hard boiled eggs and even, occasionally, fish. Nevertheless,
the consensus, both in terms of sheer numbers of recipes as well as
annotations in the margins, is that the very best minced pies are
made with ox tongue.

Nowadays tongue is usually seen at the delicatessen counter, where
it is still popular cut into wafer-thin slices as a sandwich filling.
You could use deli meat at a push, but it really is worth the effort
to try to source an actual tongue from your local butcher or abattoir
because the result is so much more flavourful. In addition, you get
a wonderfully rich stock for your casseroles and stews. One beef
tongue will provide more than enough meat for this recipe and so
you will have enough to set aside and freeze for later batches. You
won't regret it.

I have had to tweak this recipe to suit our twenty-first-century
palates. The original contained an excessive proportion of suet, more
than the quantity of meat, which made the pies extremely heavy
and cloying. Scaling back the fat content allows the dried fruit, peel
and spices to round out the overall flavour. To enjoy these to the full
you need to set aside your idea of the modern mince pie. These are
very much savoury pies, but with a richness and complexity that is
as delightful as it is surprising. The final addition of a simple sweet
and sharp buttery lear really lifts and brightens the flavours, but you
can try this on just one pie initially, to see if it is to your taste.

MAKES 12–18 PIES

1 fresh ox tongue, about 1kg
3 celery sticks
2 carrots
1 onion
1 tbsp black peppercorns
2 bay leaves
1 bunch mixed fresh herbs
1 × batch Cornflour Shortcrust
  Pastry (page 326)

For the mincemeat
75g fresh suet, finely chopped
170g raisins
30g dark muscovado sugar
zest and juice of 1 orange
zest and juice of 1 lemon
1 nutmeg
1 tsp ground cloves
1 tsp ground mace
½–1 tsp rosewater

1 tsp salt
2 sharp dessert apples, peeled,
  cored, diced and tossed in the
  lemon juice
225g currants
30g candied orange peel, diced
  small
30g candied citron peel, diced
  small
1 large egg, beaten

For the lear
30g clarified butter (page 335)
60ml verjuice

Equipment
individual pie tins or cupcake tins
  (12–18 holes)

Put the ox tongue into a saucepan and cover with cold water. Bring to the boil and simmer for 5 minutes to allow the scum to rise. Drain off the water and rinse the tongue and the pan.

Return the tongue to the pan along with the celery, carrots, onion peppercorns, bay leaves and herbs and cover with cold water. Bring to the boil, cover and simmer for 2–3 hours, until the skin on the tongue begins to blister. Lift the tongue from the cooking liquid and set aside to cool.

Strain the solids from the stock and set aside to cool. When cold, lift off any solidified fat and reduce the stock by simmering until the flavour is well developed. The stock is not required for this recipe so use it another time for gravy, soups or casseroles.

When the tongue has cooled sufficiently to handle, peel off the rough skin covering and discard. You may also wish to discard the tough underside of the tongue, known as the root. Chop the meat finely and weigh out 225g. Store the rest for later use. Add the remaining mincemeat ingredients and stir well to combine. The secret to a good mincemeat filling is to ensure all the ingredients are of a similarly small size, especially if you are making individual pies.

Preheat the oven to 200°C/180°C fan/gas 6 and grease the tins.

Roll out half the pastry and cut lids for your pies. Gather the trimmings with the remaining pastry, roll and cut circles to line your tins. The size is entirely up to you, but cupcake-sized pies are ideal. Fill the pies with the prepared mincemeat. Since the meat itself is already cooked, there will be little to no shrinkage during baking so a filled pie should remain full, even after cooking. Dampen the edges of the pastry and top with the lids, pressing down firmly to seal and crimping the edges. Cut a 1cm vent in the centre of each lid and brush with the beaten egg to glaze. Bake for 15–18 minutes, until the pastry is crisp and golden. For larger or smaller pies, adjust the cooking time accordingly.

While the pies are baking, melt the clarified butter in a pan and whisk in the verjuice. Pour about a teaspoon of this sharp lear into each pie through the vent when they are removed from the oven. Cool on a wire rack.

LIVER & BACON SALAD
Twentieth century

When I was 18 I didn't want a huge birthday party, opting instead to go out for an elegant meal. We dined in Worcester, next to the river and in the shadow of the cathedral, at a restaurant which, alas, is long gone. I don't recall much about the meal itself beyond this dish, which I, and everyone else at the table, chose as a starter.

It was the first dish I can recall where the presentation created a real wow factor. The staff brought what looked like fruit bowls to the table, seemingly piled high with salad. They looked enormous. Of course, it was an illusion; each person had, in reality, only 3 or 4 leaves of Iceberg lettuce, but they had been left whole and cleverly arranged merely to give the appearance of being more substantial. The leaves had been tossed in a light vinaigrette and sprinkled with the tiniest morsels of crisp bacon, sautéed chicken livers and crunchy croutons. Eating it was a delight. The salad leaves were mild, fresh and cool, and the punchy flavours from the hot bacon and liver were a great contrast in temperature, texture and intensity of flavour.

This is my effort to recreate that dish, which I remember across the intervening decades as if it were yesterday.

SERVES I

½ slice bread
2 chicken livers, cut into 1cm cubes
2 rashers streaky bacon
15g butter

Salad Dressing (page 49)
3–4 Iceberg lettuce leaves, rinsed
and blotted dry

Toast the bread on both sides and cut into cubes. Keep warm.

Grill the bacon under a high heat until crisp, chop into small pieces and keep warm. Melt the butter in a pan and quickly fry the chicken livers. They will take only a few seconds.

Drizzle the salad dressing over the leaves and toss to coat. Sprinkle with the bacon, toast cubes and chicken livers. Arrange the leaves in a large dish and serve at once.

HOTCHPOTCH OF OXTAIL
1828

I was surprised at what a challenge it was to find a recipe using oxtail that wasn't soup. Not that there's anything wrong with oxtail soup but, according to old cookery books, it seems to have been the number-one usage for over a century. I thought it would be more interesting to try to find something different, and it took some fairly persistent searching before I discovered this recipe in *The Cook and Housewife's Manual*, purportedly written by the fictional Meg Dods, but in reality penned by Christian Isobel Johnstone. Ms Johnstone's recommended accompaniment is a Haricot of Root Vegetables (page 313).

SERVES 4

1 oxtail, separated into joints or
  8–10 large oxtail joints
8–10 bacon slices
4 onions, chopped
2 carrots, chopped
1 bunch mixed herbs
1 bay leaf
3 cloves

2 garlic cloves
beef stock, to cover
salt and pepper
flavourings, to taste (page 21),
  (optional)
1 tbsp cornflour mixed with a little
  water, or 1 tbsp flour and 1 tbsp
  butter

Put the oxtail joints into a large pan and cover with cold water. Slowly bring to a boil and simmer for 5 minutes. Skim off the scum that rises to the surface, then drain the water from the joints. If you don't skim off the scum first it will stick to the meat as you pour off the water and you will then need to rinse each piece by hand. Scrub the pan clean.

Put a layer of bacon in the bottom of the pan (or you could use a slow cooker) and lay the joints on top. Add the onions and carrots to the meat together with the herbs, cloves and garlic. Lay slices of bacon over the top and then pour in enough beef stock to cover. Bring to a boil and then simmer over a very low heat for 4–5 hours, until the meat is falling from the bones. For a slow cooker, cook on low for 6–8 hours.

When the meat is tender, pour the mixture through a colander to separate the liquid from the rest of the ingredients. Discard the herbs and vegetables. Strain the cooking liquid a second time through a fine mesh sieve or colander lined with wetted muslin to remove any small particles of solids. Set aside to cool.

Chop the bacon and set aside.

Separate the oxtail meat from the bones and connective tissue. The long, slow cooking will mean that the meat falls easily from the bones and it will also have softened the connective tissue, which can simply be pulled away. Nevertheless, this is quite a fiddly job, especially with the smallest joints, so switch on the radio and take a seat while you work. Discard the bones and debris. Store the meats in sealed containers in the fridge. Let the cooking liquid get cold, then chill overnight in the fridge.

The following day, remove the stock from the fridge and lift off all the fat. Set it aside for other uses, such as in the pastry for Oxtail Pies (page 225). Pour the now fat-free stock into a pan and set over a low heat. When it has warmed up, taste and if the flavour is not strong enough, simmer and reduce until you're satisfied.

There has been no mention of salt or pepper until now due to several reasons:

—The bacon will naturally leech some salt into the braising liquid.

—If you used a commercially prepared stock or stock cube then it will likely already have had salt added.

—If you decide to reduce the stock at all, this will further concentrate any salt already in the liquid.

So, all in all, the salt level is possibly fine but, as always, adjust to your own personal taste. The same goes for pepper.

Oxtail is very flavourful in itself, but there are a range of sauces and flavourings you can choose from to really bump up the flavour, if desired (see page 21). It's purely a matter of trial and error: add a tablespoon and then taste, then add more, or something else, if you think it needs it. My own preference for this dish consists of 1 tablespoon each of Worcestershire sauce, mushroom ketchup and oyster sauce. If the flavour seems a little cloying I might add a little balsamic vinegar, just to sharpen it up.

If the liquid needs thickening, use a cornflour slurry or a butter and flour roux, which will need to be simmered for at least 5 minutes in order to cook out the floury taste.

When you're happy with both the flavour and consistency of your gravy, add the oxtail meat and bacon and warm gently.

Use a skimmer to lift the warmed meat from the sauce and pile it into a serving dish. Spoon a little of the gravy over the meat and pour the rest into a gravy boat. Serve immediately, with warm, crusty bread to mop up the gravy.

Serve with: Haricot of Root Vegetables (page 313).

OXTAIL PIES
Twentieth century

If you've got any extra oxtail hotchpotch then this is a fabulously tasty way of using it. In fact, this recipe will work with almost any cooked meat with either a sauce or gravy. If there's not much meat available then stir in some cooked vegetables to make it stretch a little further, but these pies are at their most indulgent with purely meat and gravy as filling.

The pastry is a new version of shortcrust that I have adapted from a Victorian bakers' book. Regular shortcrust pastry is usually made with a 50:50 mix of butter and lard (all-butter shortcrust tastes lovely but isn't very robust; all-lard is tremendously crisp but lacks flavour). Unfortunately, this traditional lard and butter mix puts regular shortcrust pastry beyond the reach of vegetarians. But, although the filling for these particular pies is also unsuitable for vegetarians, the pastry isn't. It is an all-butter shortcrust and includes roughly a quarter of the flour content as cornflour, which makes the pastry extra crispy with a smooth, silky feel that means it's very easy to handle. I like to make these pies a little more special by adding a puff pastry lid, but all shortcrust is tasty too.

MAKES 4

cold oxtail hotchpotch, or any cooked meat and sauce/gravy
1 × batch Cornflour Shortcrust Pastry (page 326)
cooked vegetables (optional)
1 × sheet or block puff pastry (optional)
1 large egg, beaten

Equipment
individual foil pie dishes

Preheat the oven to 200°C/180°C fan/gas 6 and grease the pie dishes.

Separate two thirds of the chilled shortcrust pastry. If you're using puff pastry for the lid you can disregard this step. Roll out the shortcrust to 3–4mm thick and use it to line your pie dishes, making sure there is enough pastry hanging over the edges to attach the lid to.

If you're including vegetables, cut them into 1cm cubes. Warm the meat slightly, just enough for the gravy to become liquid, and stir the vegetables into the meat so that they are coated with the sauce.

Fill the pies with the mixture. Don't add too much gravy or you run the risk of it bubbling out through the top of the pie as well as making the base soggy. Smooth the filling so that it is level with the pastry edges.

Roll out either the reserved shortcrust or the puff pastry for the lids, wet the undersides with water and press them firmly onto the pies. Trim off the excess pastry with the back of a knife and crimp the edges.

If you want to save the pies for another day, cut vents in the tops and then stop. Arrange on a baking sheet and freeze, then wrap each pie in a separate plastic bag. You can then glaze with egg-wash and cook from frozen, adding an extra 5–10 minutes to the cooking time, until the pastry is cooked and golden and the filling hot. Otherwise, wash the tops of the pies with the beaten egg and cut small vents in the lids to let out steam. Bake for 25–30 minutes, depending on the size and shape of your pies, until the pastry is crisp and golden. Cool on a wire rack.

8

CHEESE

'Poets have been mysteriously silent on the subject of cheese.'
G. K. *Chesterton*, Alarms and Discursions

*"Marooned three years agone," he continued, "and lived on goats since then, and berries, and oysters. Wherever a man is, says I, a man can do for himself. But, mate, my heart is sore for Christian diet. You mightn't happen to have a piece of cheese about you, now? No? Well, many's the long night I've dreamed of cheese—toasted, mostly—and woke up again, and here I were."'
Robert Louis Stevenson, Treasure Island

Poor Ben Gunn. I can absolutely sympathise with him dreaming of cheese; it is one of my favourite foods. We are blessed with an astonishing number of cheeses in the UK. Even an ardent cheese fan such as myself was surprised to discover that, according to the British Cheese Board, there are over 700 named cheeses in the UK. With such a vast number available there can be no occasion imaginable that cannot be served with some cheese. However, our most frequent uses tend to be to select cheese either to put on or in something. The recipes I have chosen for this chapter go some way, I hope, towards making cheese the star, rather than merely a supporting act.

HONEYSOME
1930s

In the 1930s, Mrs Arthur Webb was tasked by the BBC with collecting farmhouse recipes from around the country 'in order to secure something which was characteristic of its cooking and preparation of food'. Her travels took her into working farmhouses, where she took notes as the women of the house baked and cooked, salted and preserved the produce of the countryside. Honeysome is a simple summer breakfast that's ideal for children yet can be enjoyed at any age. Mrs Webb called it 'fascinating', but did not elaborate on why. Made with the very best four ingredients you are able to find and served with a tall glass of cold milk, I would even go so far as to call it just about the perfect meal.

SERVES I

1 slice fresh bread, hand-cut
fresh farmhouse butter
wildflower honey

vintage farmhouse Cheddar, thinly
sliced
a glass of cold milk, to serve

Spread the bread generously with the butter and drizzle over the honey. Top with thin slices of cheese and enjoy with a glass of cold milk.

CHEESE STEWED WITH ALE

Maria Eliza Rundell, 1842

Mrs Rundell describes this recipe as employing the Welsh method of stewing cheese. It is meant to be served hot, with slices of hot toast on the side for either dipping or spreading. In this regard it differs from a Welsh Rarebit, where the cheese (and mustard) is placed on hot buttered toast and toasted under a hot grill.

The secret to a smooth and creamy mixture here is baking in the oven: made on the stove top, the direct heat would invariably render the cheese into a hard lump. You can vary the flavour by using different ales and cheeses, even mixing several cheeses together.

SERVES 4

200g strong cheese, or a mixture of any cheese you have to hand
2 tsp mustard powder

200ml golden ale
salt and pepper
8 slices wholemeal toast, to serve

Shave the cheese thinly and lay it on the bottom of an ovenproof dish. Sprinkle over the mustard powder and then slowly pour the ale into the dish until it barely covers the cheese. Cover with a lid or foil and place in the cold oven. Set the temperature to 180°C/160°C fan/gas 4 and bake for 20 minutes, then season and serve with the hot toast.

CHEESE & PEA PASTIES

Robert May, 1660

Despite the title, this recipe is actually for a kind of filled dumpling, similar to Italian ravioli or tortellini. It came with the instruction to 'make a piece of paste of warm or boiling liquor', which was intriguing since there is no 'warm water pastry' in use today, and hot water crust is generally used for raised pies that are eaten cold. Experimenting with just-warm water and a hot water crust recipe produced a wonderfully delicate paste, halfway between pastry and pasta, which could be rolled ethereally thin—perfect, in fact, for dumplings. Rolled thin enough, the filling becomes visible through the cooked pastry.

MAKES 18–20 MINI DUMPLINGS

100g frozen garden peas
65g unsalted butter
75g onion, finely chopped
50g hard goats' cheese, finely grated
20g finely grated Parmesan or
Grana Padano cheese, plus extra
for sprinkling
¼ nutmeg, grated, plus extra for
dusting

¼ tsp ground cinnamon
¼ tsp coarse ground black pepper
a pinch of cloves
200g plain flour
½ tsp salt
2 litres water, stock or milk, for
cooking
30g clarified butter (page 335),
melted, for drizzling

Bring a small pan of water to the boil and cook the frozen garden peas for 5 minutes. Drain and set aside to cool.

Melt 15g of the butter in a frying pan and cook the chopped onion for 5–8 minutes, until softened and translucent. Transfer to a food processor and add the peas, spices and cheese. Pulse briefly until the peas are chopped and the mixture forms a dry paste. Set aside.

Mix the flour and salt in a bowl. Put the remaining butter into a pan with 100ml water and heat until the butter has melted. Pour the warm mixture into the flour and salt and mix until it comes together in a ball. Transfer to a clean work surface and knead smooth.

This has to be rolled extremely thin, so just cut off small pieces at a time and roll the paste out until it is translucent, between 1–2mm thick. There's no need for any additional flour, especially if you're working on a silicone mat. Cut out 7–8cm circles for your pasties. Add a teaspoon of filling to each circle, moisten the edges and fold over. Crimp the edge by hand or use the tines of a fork. Continue until you run out of filling and/or pastry, then cover the pasties with cling film and chill until ready to cook.

Bring your chosen cooking liquid to a simmer and drop in 6 or 7 of the chilled pasties. Don't overcrowd the pan. Cook for 5–8 minutes depending how thin you managed to get your pastry. Remove, cover and keep warm while you cook the next batch.

Serve with a drizzle of melted butter, a sprinkling of Parmesan and a dusting of nutmeg.

POTTED CHEESE
Susanna, Elizabeth and Mary Kellet, 1780

The Kellets published their cookbook in Newcastle upon Tyne in 1780 and there's practically nothing else known about them at all. Titbits gleaned from their book inform us that these ladies, probably mother and daughters, ran a cookery school. Their recipes were taught for more than fifty years and they financed the publication of their book through subscriptions; the names of their patrons are listed at the front. And that's it. Part of me wishes there were more details, while another part of me likes the freedom to use my imagination to manufacture lives for them: perhaps they were the culinary Brontës of the north-east, all wild and windswept, pale and interesting. We shall never know.

Their collection of over 400 recipes is an interesting read in itself, with fashionable dishes spelled in entertaining ways ('An Olly Doub' for *à la daub*, 'Beef Treng Blange' for beef *à la Tremblade*, and the mysterious 'To Smut a Hare'). Their novel approach to recipe classification appears to favour method over ingredient, which means, for example, that everything stuffed is listed together. The 'to make…' section is gloriously haphazard, including bread, ketchup, green colouring from verdigris, cream curds, brawn of a swine's head and macaroni, to name but a few of its entries.

Nowadays, potted cheese is seen as a tasty way of using up odd fragments of cheese, and that's both eminently sensible and practical. The Kellet ladies' recipe, however, is purposely made, using simple but flavoursome ingredients. The clarified butter on top has the dual role of preserving the cheese and becoming a built-in spread when served. It's ideal for a light lunch or supper, or an easy make ahead starter.

SERVES 4

150g farmhouse Cheshire cheese,
  finely grated
60g unsalted butter, softened
30ml cream sherry
½ tsp ground mace
½ tsp mustard powder
clarified butter (page 335), melted

oatcakes or wholemeal toast,
  to serve
celery sticks and pickles, to serve

Equipment
2 large or 4 small ramekins

Mix together the cheese, butter, sherry, mace and mustard powder to make a moist paste. Divide between the ramekins, pressing the mixture down firmly to eliminate any air pockets and smoothing over the tops. Pour over the clarified butter to seal. When the butter has solidified, chill in the fridge.

Allow to come to room temperature before serving with oatcakes or wholemeal toast, celery sticks and pickles.

RAMKINS
Susanna, Elizabeth and Mary Kellet, 1780

Despite the name, this is actually an elegant version of cheese on toast. You can make several variations using this cheese mixture, depending on the formality of the occasion. This one, with the filling baked in hollowed-out rolls, is ideal for a snack. I've suggested rolls as it is in keeping with the Kellet ladies' original recipe, but you could just as easily use it on slices of toast.

SERVES 4

2 bread rolls
20g butter, plus extra for spreading
1 large egg, plus 1 yolk
115g strong cheese, grated

30ml double cream
grated fresh nutmeg, to taste
coarse-ground black pepper

Preheat the oven to 160°C/140°C fan/gas 3

Cut the rolls horizontally through the middle and remove some of the soft crumb. Spread the insides with a little softened butter and bake for 2–3 minutes until lightly crisped. Put the 20g of butter and rest of the ingredients into the bowl of a food processor and blitz until smooth. Divide the paste among the 4 halves of the rolls and return to the oven. Bake for 10 minutes until golden.

RAMAKINS

Elizabeth Philipps, eighteenth century

This is much closer to a soufflé than toasted cheese. The addition of breadcrumbs gives it just enough substance to hold its shape when cooked. If you have some decorative moulds, preferably silicone, they make ideal portion sizes.

SERVES 4

115g strong cheese, grated
1 large egg, plus 1 yolk
20g butter
30ml double cream
grated fresh nutmeg

coarse-ground black pepper
60g fresh white breadcrumbs

Equipment
6-hole silicone mould or cupcake tin

Preheat the oven to 200°C/180°C fan/gas 6 and grease the silicone moulds or cupcake tins.

Blend all the ingredients except the breadcrumbs to a smooth paste in a food processor, then stir in the breadcrumbs. Divide the mixture evenly between the moulds and smooth the tops. Bake for 10 minutes, until golden and bubbling, then turn out and serve with salad and oatcakes or crisp wholemeal toast.

CHEESE PATTIES
Elizabeth Marshall, 1777

SERVES 2 (OR MORE IF MADE SMALLER FOR CANAPÉS)

1 sheet puff pastry	*30ml double cream*
2 large eggs, plus 1 yolk	*60g fresh white breadcrumbs*
115g strong cheese, grated	*grated fresh nutmeg*
20g butter	*coarse-ground black pepper*

Preheat the oven to 200°C/180°C fan/gas 6.

Cut out 4 squares from the pastry, then cut out 2 smaller squares from the centre of 2 of the pieces. Beat one of the eggs and use it to moisten the edges of the whole squares. Lay the pieces with the holes cut out on top, aligning the edges. Brush the tops, making sure none of the egg drips down the sides as this would impede the rise in the oven.

Blend the rest of the ingredients in a food processor to a smooth paste and divide between the pastry holes. Bake for 12–15 minutes, until the pastry is puffed and golden and the cheese mixture risen.

WHITLEY GOOSE
Northumberland, twentieth century

Whitley Goose is another dish where the name implies that the ingredients are richer and more expensive than they actually are. Just like Scotch Woodcock (scrambled eggs on toast with anchovies), Glasgow Capon (salted herring) and Savoury Duck (pork and liver meatballs), Whitley Goose hasn't the merest whiff of the titular goose about it. The common elements are cooked

onions and cheese, and while many modern recipes enrich it almost
to fondue level with the addition of cream, this recipe from the
1950s uses fresh sage and breadcrumbs to make a satisfyingly
savoury supper dish that isn't overly rich. A simple fresh salad is
the ideal accompaniment.

SERVES 4

250g strong Cheddar, grated
8 large onions, peeled
1 tsp salt
1–2 tsp ground black pepper
4 tbsp chopped fresh sage
15g unsalted butter, softened

160g dried breadcrumbs
200ml milk
1 tbsp mustard powder
crusty bread or oatcakes, to serve
salad, to serve

Put the onions into a large saucepan, add cold water to cover and
bring to the boil. Simmer for 30 minutes until soft, drain and chop.
Season with the salt and pepper and stir in the sage and cheese.

Use the butter to grease an ovenproof dish and sprinkle with
breadcrumbs. Add a layer of the onion mixture and cover with
a layer of breadcrumbs. Continue layering until the dish is full,
finishing with a layer of breadcrumbs. Mix together the milk and
mustard powder and pour over the top. Put into a cold oven and
set the temperature to 200°C/180°C fan/gas 6. Bake for 20–30
minutes, until bubbling and golden.

Serve with crusty bread or oatcakes and salad.

MRS RAFFALD'S MACARONI WITH PARMESAN

1769

There is something extremely comforting about soft-cooked pastry and cheese, and this has been recognised for over 600 years. As far back as the Middle Ages, the cooks of Richard II recorded a recipe for Makrows in *The Forme of Cury* (1390),[1] which consisted of thin sheets of paste cut in pieces, cooked in water and then layered with butter and cheese, in the manner of a simple, free-form lasagne. Three hundred years later, in Thomas Blount's *Glossographia* (1661), 'Marcaroni' was described as 'lumps or gobbets of boiled paste, served up in butter, and strewed over with Spice, and grated cheese'.

Elizabeth Raffald is credited with the first recognisable recipe for macaroni cheese as we know it, in her book *The Experienced English House-keeper* (1769). It is extremely simple, if a little rich, consisting solely of cooked macaroni, a little cream and a little floured butter, topped with crisp, toasted Parmesan.

Over the years, macaroni's popularity has caused the basic recipe to be tweaked and embellished to such an extent that modern recipes now contain lengthy lists of ingredients and such startling quantities of cheese and cream that the main ingredient, the macaroni, gets swamped. This, and the following recipe, mark a return to the dish's simple, though no less flavoursome, origins. Both can be enjoyed either as an accompaniment or as the basis of a light meal. The quantities may seem small, but the dishes are rich.

This dish is more accurately macaroni in a cream sauce, served both in and with toasted Parmesan. The contrast between the delicate flavour and texture of the creamy macaroni and the crisp and punchy cheese is delightful, the mild taste of the sauce providing an excellent foil for the Parmesan. The overall sensation is of extreme cheesiness without requiring huge quantities. I've made crisp Parmesan baskets in which to serve the macaroni but you could also serve it in individual ramekins sprinkled with the Parmesan crumb. To shape the baskets you will need a small pudding basin or tumbler. They will gradually soften once filled, so assemble just before serving.

SERVES 4

100g freshly grated Parmesan   *150ml double cream*
115g macaroni   *salt and ground white pepper*

Divide the Parmesan into 5 equal piles. Sprinkle one pile of cheese into a non stick pan to make a 12cm circle. Place the pan over a medium heat and melt until golden and bubbling. Remove the pan from the heat and allow to cool for about 30 seconds. When the cheese is cool enough to move, lift it from the pan and drape it over the upturned pudding basin or tumbler. Press the warm cheese close to the mould to shape the bowl. Leave to cool while you make the next bowl and continue until you have 4 Parmesan baskets. Set aside.

Melt the last pile of cheese in the same way, remove the pan from the heat and allow to cool, then crush the Parmesan wafer into small crumbs.

Bring a pan of water to the boil and cook the macaroni until tender, 12–15 minutes. Drain and then return to the pan with the cream and heat through. Season generously with salt and white pepper.

Spoon the macaroni into the Parmesan baskets and sprinkle over the crisp Parmesan crumbs. Serve at once.

MRS FRAZER'S DISH OF MACARONI
1791

I've always been a fan of adding a little dry mustard powder to anything flavoured with cheese. Nothing too noticeable, perhaps a quarter of a teaspoon or so, but it can really boost the savouriness and flavour of the cheese. When working with old recipes I have a personal rule to follow a recipe, exactly as it is written, for the first time of making. After that, I might decide that it requires a little tweak here or a nudge there but, the first time, out of respect to the author that recorded it, I make it their way. And so this is why my new absolute favourite seasoning for cheese is fresh nutmeg. Whether it is the cheese, the baking, or even the freshness of the nutmeg itself, I can't be sure. I just know that the combination is extraordinary and truly transforms this humble recipe into something spectacular. I have included Mrs Frazer's original detail of a puff pastry border and a sprinkling of Parmesan crumb.

SERVES 4 AS A SIDE

50g Parmesan, freshly grated
½ sheet puff pastry
1 large egg yolk
600ml whole milk
115g macaroni
60ml double cream
120g mixed grated cheese

fresh nutmeg
salt and ground white pepper

Equipment
small flower and leaf cutters
20cm pie dish

Sprinkle the Parmesan over a non-stick pan and cook over a medium heat until melted, golden brown and bubbling. Remove the pan from the heat and allow to cool. Break into crumbs. Set aside.

Preheat the oven to 220°C/200°C fan/gas 7 and line a baking sheet with baking parchment. Butter the pie dish.

Halve the pastry sheet and cut small strips of pastry, about 2cm wide, from one half. Cut out a selection of flowers and leaves from the other half. Arrange in groups of 1 flower and 2–3 leaves. Moisten the strips with a little water and stick on each flower/leaf arrangement. Make sufficient pieces to form a border around the dish you're using to bake the macaroni. Pastry will shrink during cooking, so make 2 or 3 more than you think you will need. Mix the egg yolk with a tablespoon of water and brush the decorations to glaze. Bake for 7–8 minutes until puffed and golden. Set aside to cool on a wire rack.

Put the milk and macaroni into a saucepan, bring to a simmer and stir over a medium heat until the pasta is al dente and the milk slightly thickened, about 15 minutes. The milk will have the consistency of single cream, but it will thicken up further when the dish is baked. Season generously with salt and pepper. Add the cream and stir.

Put a third of the macaroni into the greased pie dish and sprinkle with a third of the mixed grated cheese. Repeat this layering, finishing with the remaining cheese and the Parmesan crumbs. Grate a generous amount of nutmeg over the top, cover with a tent of foil and put into the cold oven. Set the temperature to 180°C/160°C fan/gas 4 and bake for 25 minutes. Check that the dish is heated though and the cheese has melted, then remove the foil and cook for a further 10 minutes to brown the top. Alternatively, place under a hot grill until browned. Put the pastry decorations in the oven for the last 3 minutes to heat through.

Arrange the warm pastry decorations around the edge of the dish and serve at once.

VARIATIONS
To turn this into a main meal dish, multiply the recipe by 1½, except for the Parmesan—50g is plenty for a topping. If you have some to hand, add cooked cauliflower, cooked chicken or turkey to the cheese layers to lighten the richness.

TART FOR EMBER DAYS

circa 1390

'Fasting days and Emberings be
Lent, Whitsun, Holyrood, and Lucie.'

Old English rhyme

The Ember Days were the four periods of fasting, one for each
season, nominated by the Church following the Council of
Placentia in 1095. Each fasting period lasted three days—
a Wednesday and the following Friday and Saturday—and
followed the first Sunday in Lent (spring), Whitsun (summer), 14
September, Holy Cross Day (autumn) and December, in the week
following St Lucia's Day (winter). Meat was generally forbidden
on these days, but cheese and eggs were permitted. As with many
recipes, this tart may be varied according to personal taste or
variety. The dried currants add a very pleasant sweet-sharp note to
the rather rich filling, but can be replaced with alternatives such
as cranberries, blueberries, apricots or barberries. If you're feeling
indulgent, replace the cream cheese with some feisty farmhouse
Cheddar or, for a more pious experience, 200g breadcrumbs.

SERVES 4

4 onions, peeled
4 sprigs fresh sage, chopped, or
  2 tbsp dried
4–6 tbsp chopped fresh parsley
300g cream cheese
5 large eggs
60g currants
½ tsp salt

1 tsp coarse-ground black pepper
1 tsp ground ginger
½ nutmeg, grated
1 × batch Cornflour Shortcrust
  Pastry (page 326)

Equipment
20cm tart tin

Put the onions into a saucepan of water, bring to the boil, cover, turn the heat down and simmer gently for 30 minutes, adding the fresh herbs for the last 10 minutes. Drain and allow to cool, then chop the onions and strip the herb leaves from the stalks and finely chop.

Whisk together 4 of the eggs with the cream cheese. Stir in the herbs, onions, currants, salt and spices.

Preheat the oven to 200°C/180°C fan/gas 6 and grease the tart tin.

Roll out the pastry to about 4mm thick and lay it in your tart tin. Make sure the pastry is tucked neatly into the corners, without stretching it. Leave the excess pastry hanging over the sides of the tin and chill for 20–30 minutes. The pastry will shrink a little. Trim the edges and then line the pastry case with baking parchment and fill it with baking beans or rice.

Bake for 10 minutes, then remove from the oven and lift out the parchment and baking beans. Return to the oven for 5 minutes while you beat the last egg, then remove and use the beaten egg to brush the inside of the tart case. Return to the oven for 5 more minutes to allow the egg to set. This will prevent the pastry becoming soggy from the wet filling.

Reduce the heat to 160°C/140°C fan/gas 3. Pour the filling into the case and smooth it over. Bake until the filling is just set but still jiggles when shaken, about 25–30 minutes. Allow to cool for 10 minutes, then remove from the tin and serve.

9

EGGS

Eggs have been a conveniently packaged source of food for thousands of years and have become an integral part of our culinary and symbolic lives. Eggs can be seen as representing life, a means of divining the future, seasonal celebrations of spring and symbols of fertility. They can lighten cakes, enrich sauces, glaze pastries, thicken custards, create airy meringues and soufflés and fill tarts and pies. As with cheese, they can be the forgotten ingredient. The recipes in this chapter are a reminder of their delicacy and their worth.

EGGS & LETTUCE —AKA FARCED EGGS

John Nott, 1723

John Nott was head cook to the Duke of Bolton and his book *The Cooks and Confectioners' Dictionary* (1723) is, unusually, arranged in alphabetical order. Alas, hunting for specific recipes is somewhat of a challenge due to Mr Nott's rather capricious notions of organisation. Recipes, for the most part, are listed by their main ingredient, so beef, for example, comes under B, but also appears under O for Olio and P for Plum Potage. What larks!

Eggs are reassuringly listed under E, which nevertheless leads me to a slight digression. In resurrecting these old recipes, wherever possible I have tried to retain the original title, for provenance as well as authenticity. This recipe, however, has me torn, because not only does the original title contain a word that has fallen into obscurity, it also does not do justice to the dish itself. 'Farced' is an obsolete word meaning stuffed, and I get the feeling that calling this dish Stuffed Eggs would have you hastily flipping past the page with images of platters of 1970s 'horse's doovers' flashing before your eyes. Which would be a shame because the eggs aren't stuffed at all and this dish is actually a rather substantial riot of herbs, salad leaves and eggs that is simple and quick to prepare and tastes both fresh and light. It can be arranged on a platter for maximum impact, or on individual plates for that dainty touch.

SERVES 4

8 large hard-boiled eggs
30g unsalted butter
250g chestnut mushrooms, sliced
4 heads lettuce, any mix of Little
  Gem, Cos, Romaine or O'So,
  finely shredded
100g baby spinach leaves, finely
  shredded
4 tbsp chopped fresh parsley

4 tbsp chopped fresh chervil
4 tbsp chopped fresh dill
juice of 1 lemon
150ml double cream
½ tsp salt
¼ nutmeg, grated
coarse-ground black pepper
bread and butter or toast, to serve

Cut the eggs in half and separate the yolks and whites. Chop each separately into roughly 1cm dice. Put the diced egg whites in a dish and cover with foil. Keep warm in the oven.

Melt the butter in a pan and cook the mushrooms gently over a medium-low heat until softened and any juice has evaporated. Add the shredded leaves and allow them to wilt, stirring gently.

Sprinkle over half of each of the chopped herbs and add the yolks. Squeeze over the lemon juice, and add the cream, salt, nutmeg and pepper. Heat through, folding the ingredients together gently.

When hot, taste and adjust the seasoning if necessary. Pour into a warmed serving dish.

Retrieve the warm egg whites and toss in the remaining chopped herbs. Spoon round the edge of the serving dish. Serve with bread and butter or fresh toast.

EGG PIE
1905

This is a simple yet satisfying dish that can be made as a single pie or in individual servings. I must confess that, given the choice, I always opt for individual dishes, not only for the reduced cooking time, but for the sense of personal attention you get when served with your own miniature version of a recipe. Although most enjoyable in itself, this recipe can also be embellished with additional ingredients, either to make it stretch a little further or for sheer hedonistic delight.

SERVES 4

8 large hard-boiled eggs, peeled and sliced
4 slices bread, in breadcrumbs
2–4 tbsp chopped fresh Parsley Sauce (page 43)

salt and pepper

Equipment
1 × 20cm ovenproof dish or
4 × gratin dishes

Preheat the oven to 160°C/140°C fan/gas 3. Line a baking sheet with baking parchment and grease your dish or dishes.

Sprinkle the breadcrumbs over the baking sheet and bake for 8–10 minutes until crisp and light brown.

Stir the parsley into the white sauce and taste. Add extra seasoning if liked. Spoon a thin layer of sauce over the bottom of the dish. Add a layer of sliced egg, and sprinkle with breadcrumbs. Continue layering sauce, eggs and crumbs until all the ingredients have been used up, finishing with a layer of breadcrumbs. Transfer the dish to a baking sheet and bake for 15–20 minutes, until hot and bubbling.

VARIATIONS
You can make the dish go further by adding layers of cheese, ham,

wilted spinach, cooked mushrooms, caramelised onions, etc. Vary the sauce by replacing the parsley with cheese or make a curry sauce by frying 2 tablespoons of curry paste until aromatic, then adding 300ml double cream.

BROCCOLI & EGGS
J. Williams, 1767

An ideal dish for a quick supper or light lunch. Make sure you have everything to hand before starting as this dish comes together very quickly.

SERVES 4

2 large heads of broccoli, separated
  into florets
10 large eggs
60ml double cream or low fat
  crème fraîche

60g salted butter
salt and coarse-ground black pepper
4 slices crusty wholemeal or
  sourdough toast

Arrange the broccoli florets, stalks down, in a steamer and steam for 8 minutes.

Crack the eggs into a bowl, making sure there is no shell. Melt the butter in a pan and add all the eggs. Stir with a spatula or wooden spoon (a whisk would break them up too much). When the eggs are three quarters cooked, remove the pan from the heat; the residual heat will finish cooking them. Add the double cream or crème fraîche and fold into the eggs. Season with salt and coarse-ground black pepper. Lay the toast on plates or a large serving dish. Spoon over the eggs and arrange the broccoli florets around the edge. Serve immediately.

KITCHERIE
1845

The following two recipes are from Anglo-Indian cookery books, each published at different times during British rule in India. Both are delightful vegetarian meals in themselves, but can also be served as part of a larger spread of dishes, or indeed at the more traditional times of breakfast or brunch.

This one, from *The Practical Cook, English and Foreign* (1845), comes from the twilight years of the hugely influential British East India Company. Granted a royal charter by Queen Elizabeth I in 1600, the company would dominate trade for more than 250 years, and assumed administrative powers for over a century before the Government of India Act ushered in the era of the British Raj in 1858.

SERVES 4

300g basmati rice
4 large eggs
2 tbsp plus ½ tsp salt
60g unsalted butter
4 onions, sliced into half moons

½ tsp coarse-ground black pepper
1 × 400g tin green lentils, drained
*   and rinsed*
chopped fresh parsley, to garnish

Put the rice in a bowl and pour over cold water. Swirl the rice around with your fingertips; the water will become cloudy from the dust and flour on the grains. Pour off the cloudy water and repeat the washing until the water runs clear. This will require 4 or 5 rinses. Cover the rice with fresh water and add the 2 tablespoons of salt. Stir well. Leave to soak for at least 30 minutes, preferably an hour.

Bring a pan of water to the boil, add the eggs and reduce the heat to a simmer. Cook for 15 minutes. Pour off the water and add cold water to cool the eggs.

Melt the butter in a pan and add the onions. Toss in the butter and sprinkle over the remaining salt and pepper. Fry gently over a medium heat until the onions are golden and crisp at the edges. Set aside.

Drain the rice and rinse under running water to wash away the salt. Bring at least 2 litres of water to the boil, tip in the rice and cook for 3 minutes. Tip in the rinsed lentils and cook for a further minute. Taste and check for done-ness. Turn off the heat and drain the rice and lentils through a sieve. Put the sieve back over the pan and cover with the lid. Leave to steam dry for 10 minutes.

Fluff the rice and lentils with a fork and add to the pan with the onions. Toss gently to mix.

Remove the shells from the eggs and cut into quarters. Transfer the rice mixture to a warmed serving plate and tuck the egg quarters around the dish. Garnish with a little chopped parsley and serve.

KEDGREE
1891

This recipe is from the closing years of both the nineteenth century and Queen Victoria's reign as Empress of India.

SERVES 4

300g basmati rice	*seeds from 12 green cardamom*
4 large eggs	*pods*
1 tbsp plus 1½ tsp salt	*2 blades mace*
2 onions, peeled	*a pinch of saffron*
3 garlic cloves, peeled	*60g unsalted butter*
3 bay leaves	*60g sultanas*
2 cinnamon sticks	*30g flaked almonds*
24 cloves	*½ tsp coarse ground black pepper*

Prepare the rice as for Kitcherie (page 262), up to and including the 30-minute soaking and using just 1 tablespoon salt. Boil the eggs as above.

Put the onions, garlic, bay leaves, spices and 1 teaspoon of salt into a pan and add 2 litres cold water. Cover, bring the water to a boil and simmer for 30 minutes to allow the spices to flavour the water. Drain the rice and rinse under running water to remove the salt. Tip the rice into the boiling onion water and cook for 4 minutes. Taste and check for done-ness. Turn off the heat and drain the rice through a sieve. Put the sieve back over the pan and cover with the lid. Leave to steam dry for 10 minutes.

Melt the butter in a pan and add the sultanas and almonds. Stir over a medium heat until the almonds are golden and the sultanas crisp and puffed.

Pick out the onions, garlic, mace, cinnamon and bay leaves from the rice, leaving the cardamom seeds and cloves. Tip the rice into the pan with the sultanas and almonds and toss gently to mix. Sprinkle with the remaining ½ teaspoon salt and the pepper and transfer to a warmed serving dish. Remove the shells from the eggs and cut into quarters. Tuck the pieces of egg into the rice and serve.

GREENS, EGGS & HAM
John Nott, 1723

I've taken a little liberty with Mr Nott's recipe and must confess to adding the slice of ham. Ham and eggs is such a classic pairing, but it's also quite heavy on the digestion. The addition of this profusion of fresh greens and mushrooms boosts a rather pedestrian snack into a meal.

SERVES 4

8 hard-boiled eggs, peeled and quartered
30g unsalted butter
100g mushrooms, sliced
2 heads lettuce, finely shred
1 bunch spring onions, green and white parts thinly sliced

1 bunch parsley, finely chopped
½ tsp salt
1–2 tbsp vinegar
100g sliced ham
2 shallots, finely chopped
6–8 slices hot buttered toast
freshly grated nutmeg, for dusting

Melt the butter in a pan and cook the mushrooms gently over a medium-low heat until softened and any juice has evaporated. Add the lettuce, onions and parsley and allow to wilt, stirring gently. Add the hard boiled eggs, salt and sharpen with a little vinegar at the end.

Lay the ham on the toasts. Spoon the egg mixture over the top and grate over a little nutmeg to serve.

TRIPE OF EGGS
1905

This is a variation on a recipe that has been popular—or, possibly more accurately, has been appearing in recipe books—for over 200 years. The cooked egg whites to some extent resemble tripe in its traditional onion sauce, but the use of eggs instead makes it much more agreeable. You can use as many egg whites as you like, but two per person is a good guide if you wish to make this dish the main part of the meal.

SERVES 4

egg whites
1 × batch Onion Sauce (page 44)
100ml double cream (optional)

2 tbsp chopped fresh parsley
salt and pepper
hot buttered toast, to serve

Whisk the egg whites until loosened and frothy. Pour a thin layer into a non-stick pan over a low heat and heat until cooked through and completely set. You may need to grease the pan. Slide the egg 'pancake' onto a board and cut it into strips. Set aside and keep warm while you repeat until you've used up all the egg whites.

Taste the sauce and season generously with salt and pepper. Add the cream if it appears rather thick. Pour the onion sauce over the egg whites and fold through gently. Serve over hot buttered toast, sprinkled with the parsley.

10

VEGETABLES

The British Isles are not naturally over-endowed with indigenous vegetables, however a combination of introduced plants from various conquering nations and international trade, which now flourish in our temperate climate, mean that there is a wide variety of fresh, local produce that can be enjoyed at its seasonal best practically year round.

The best way to enjoy vegetables is, I believe, simply: fresh and lightly cooked, by either boiling or steaming. However, in times past, we enjoyed a much wider variety of vegetable accompaniments, some of which nowadays play only a minor role in the production of meals. In this chapter you will find recipes that are not only flavoursome, but that also present familiar ingredients to be enjoyed in some not so familiar ways.

SUMMER CAWL
1880

'Cawl' is Welsh for soup, and the modern usage generally refers
to the Welsh winter soup/stew of lamb or mutton, leeks, root
vegetables and potatoes. It was made with either salt beef or bacon,
but lamb has, to a large extent, become synonymous with Wales
and so the dish has evolved.

A paper by Bobby Freeman from the 1981 Oxford Symposium on
Food and Cookery points out that cawl was seen as a year-round
meal, made using fresh and store-cupboard produce from season
to season. Ms Freeman also mentions Cawl Ffa, a summer version
featuring broad beans and bacon. I haven't been able to find a recipe
with this specific title, however I did find something similar in an
old Victorian Welsh-language cookery book I bought a few years
ago. After painstakingly transcribing and translating the faded
text letter by letter, I discovered a Soup of Summer Herbs, which,
although vague on the specifics, had enough detail, together with
Ms Freeman's description, to reveal a light summer soup bursting
with the flavours of tender, new-season vegetables.

Use whatever combination of vegetables and herbs you like, the
following is merely a guideline. The quantities are for a soup of
the meal-in-a-bowl variety. Consider halving the quantities for
starter portions.

SERVES 4

50g unsalted butter
2 turnips, peeled and cut into 1cm dice
1 unsmoked gammon steak or large piece of bacon, diced small
6 spring onions, thinly sliced
1 bunch mixed fresh herbs

6 sprigs fresh parsley
50g broad beans, blanched and skinned
12 asparagus spears, cut into 3cm lengths
1 head Romaine lettuce, finely shredded

*1 head Little Gem lettuce, finely
shredded
½ cucumber, peeled, seeded and cut
into 1cm dice
50g frozen garden peas
50g French beans, blanched and
cut into 3cm lengths
1 litre chicken, veal or ham stock*

*200ml double cream
2 tbsp cornflour mixed with a little
cold water (optional)
freshly grated nutmeg, to season
cayenne pepper, to season
50g baby spinach leaves
salt and pepper
chopped fresh parsley, to garnish*

Melt the butter in a large pan, add the turnips, gammon or bacon and spring onions and fry gently until softened. Add the rest of the herbs and vegetables, except the spinach, and toss to coat in the butter. Pour in the stock and bring to a simmer. When the vegetables are tender, add the cream and cornflour slurry, if using. Stir until thickened slightly, then taste and season generously with salt and pepper, nutmeg and a little cayenne pepper, if liked. Stir in the spinach leaves. The heat of the soup will be enough to wilt them without losing their vibrant colour. Remove the sprigs of parsley and discard, then sprinkle with chopped parsley and serve at once.

CELERY IN A CREAM SAUCE

Hannah Glasse, 1747

Celery has so many uses in the kitchen. It is one of the triumvirate of vegetables necessary for a well-flavoured stock (the others usually being carrot and onion), and as such forms the basis of the majority of soups, stews, casseroles and gravies. For a vegetable that plays such a big part in adding flavour to cooked dishes, celery doesn't really get many starring roles. It is a stalwart of the dieter's salad, of course, but its loud crunch means that its consumption in public forces you to look unnecessarily sanctimonious—Hear that crunch? Yes, I'm eating celery! Everybody look at me being so healthy!

This is a variation of a celery ragoo, most suitable for serving alongside plainly cooked meats and fish.

SERVES 4

2 heads of celery, stalks cut into 5cm lengths, leaves retained for garnishing
chicken stock, to cover
80ml white wine

125ml double cream
1 tbsp cornflour mixed with a little cold water
salt and pepper

Put the celery into a pan with a close-fitting lid and add just enough stock to cover. Bring to the boil then cover and reduce the heat to a gentle simmer for 20 minutes, or until the celery is tender. Remove the celery with a slotted spoon and set aside. Keep warm

Boil the stock briskly to reduce it to about 125ml. Remove from the heat and add the wine and cream. Stir thoroughly. Return to a low heat and warm through. Taste and adjust the seasoning as required. Add the cornflour mixture to the cooking liquid and bring to a boil, stirring until the sauce thickens. Return the cooked celery to the pan and toss it gently in the thickened sauce. Spoon into a warmed serving dish and garnish with celery leaves.

CELERY & BARLEY BAKE
Dorothy Hartley, 1954

This slow-cooked dish resembles a baked risotto, but requires only a fraction of the attention. You can use any flavour of stock you like, depending on what you are going to be serving it with, as long as it's nice and strongly flavoured, but Miss Hartley recommends mutton stock.

SERVES 4

1 large head of celery, cut into 2cm slices, leaves retained for garnishing
50g unsalted butter
100g pearl barley

600ml strong stock
1 bay leaf

Equipment
1 litre ovenproof dish or casserole

Preheat the oven to 150°C/130°C fan/gas 2 and grease the pudding dish or casserole thickly with the butter.

Sprinkle the barley over the base of the dish and top with the celery. Pour over the stock and bay leaf and cover the whole dish with foil, then place on a baking tray and bake for 1½–2 hours, giving it a stir every 30 minutes. The barley will absorb the flavour from both the stock and the celery, and there should be little liquid left at the end of cooking.

When both the barley and the celery are done to your liking, remove from the oven and fluff with a fork. Garnish with celery leaves and serve.

DEJA FOOD
Both the above celery recipes can be enjoyed a second time round
by turning them into a lunchtime bake served with fresh salad
and/or crusty bread or toast. Arrange your celery—or celery and
barley—in an ovenproof dish. Mix together 4 tablespoons each
of wholemeal breadcrumbs, grated cheese and freshly chopped
parsley and scatter over the top, then put into a cold oven. Set the
temperature to 150°C/130°C fan/gas 2 and bake for 20 minutes,
or until heated through. Brown the breadcrumbs under the grill,
if liked.

To transform these dishes into a light evening meal you will need to
add some protein. Diced ham or bacon quickly cooked in a pan go
especially well, as does chicken, either with or without a generous
handful of grated or cubed cheese. Stir through your additions
before sprinkling over the breadcrumb topping.

MANDRANG SALAD
Charlotte Mason, 1773

I was drawn to this recipe because the name sounded so unusual
and exotic, which was no wonder since it comes from the West
Indies. Quite how it got into Charlotte Mason's book is a bit of a
puzzle, because I have found no earlier reference to it in any other
cookery books and it does not appear to have been plagiarised by
any of her contemporaries. Edward Long makes mention of it in
Volume 3 of his *History of Jamaica* (1774) and, more than seventy
years later, Eliza Acton includes two recipes under the name
Mandram, but I have found nothing to predate Charlotte's recipe.
Although the novelty of finding a recipe in an eighteenth-century
English cookery book with such an exotic name and ingredients
was what originally piqued my curiosity, the following line from
Edward Long's book also intrigued:

'The mixture, called man-dram, seldom fails to provoke the most languid appetite.'

Could a cucumber salad, albeit a spicy one, really stimulate a jaded appetite? In short, yes, it can. When I first made the recipe I tried a spoonful, merely to see what it tasted like; the combination of the coolness of the cucumber, the sharpness of the dressing, the sourness of the shallot and the fire of the chilli was so unique and pleasurable that I genuinely thought, 'Well! I do believe I could have a little more of that!' Refreshingly surprising and surprisingly refreshing.

I've substituted Charlotte's vinegar and lemon juice mixtures for lime, which is in keeping with the ingredients identified by Edward Long, who also records that the most popular types of chilli pepper for this salad were either bird's-eye or scotch bonnet. Both of these, even seeded, are much too fiery for my palate, so I've selected the much less inflammatory jalapeño, but if you worship the heat, then swap them back in!

SERVES 4 AS A SIDE OR STARTER

1 cucumber
2 red jalapeño chillies, seeded and
  finely chopped
4 shallots or 8 spring onions, finely
  chopped

juice of 2 limes
100ml Madeira
½ tsp salt
lettuce leaves, to serve

Mix together the chillies, onions, lime juice, Madeira and salt, cover and set aside to marinate for about an hour. Just before serving, cut the cucumber into small dice and transfer to a mixing bowl. Pour over the marinade and toss to coat. Spoon into a serving dish lined with lettuce leaves.

REGALIA OF CUCUMBERS
Sarah Harrison, 1733

Three hundred years ago, raw fruit and vegetables were generally viewed with mistrust, so this dish of cucumbers braised in a richly flavoured stock was one regularly seen on eighteenth-century tables. Rather incongruously, for such a mild-flavoured vegetable, it was most often served alongside the strong-tasting joints of mutton and lamb.

SERVES 4 AS A SIDE

*2 cucumbers, peeled, seeded and cut
  into 1cm slices
½ tsp salt
1 tbsp cornflour
½ tsp ground white pepper
50g unsalted butter
300ml strong lamb stock*

*150ml red wine
1 tsp Savoury Spice Mix 1 or 2
  (page 329)
1 tbsp cornflour mixed with a little
  cold water
chopped fresh parsley, to garnish*

Sprinkle the cucumber slices with the salt and leave for 20 minutes, then pat dry with kitchen paper. Mix the cornflour with the pepper and sprinkle over the cucumber.

Melt the butter in a large frying pan and cook the cucumbers until golden brown. Add the stock, wine and spices and bring to a boil. Turn down the heat to a simmer and cook until tender, 15–20 minutes. Pour in the cornflour slurry and stir until the sauce boils and thickens. Transfer to a warmed serving dish and garnish with chopped parsley.

STEWED LETTUCE & PEAS

Hannah Glasse, 1747

Cooked lettuce is an incredibly speedy side dish to prepare, taking only minutes to wilt to a delicate texture that appeals to both children and adults, and providing an interesting alternative to the more robust cabbage family. Whether adding interest when baked in a pie or whizzed up in a delicate soup, lettuce deserves more than its usual supporting role as merely a backdrop to a salad.

This recipe is great as a quick side to whip up if time is short and it can be ready much sooner than a sturdier green vegetable such as cabbage, which is likely to be both less popular and less vibrant in colour.

SERVES 4 AS A SIDE

15g unsalted butter
100g lean bacon, diced small
4 spring onions, thinly sliced
2 heads Little Gem lettuce, cut into
  1cm slices

300g frozen garden peas
1 tbsp shredded fresh mint
  (optional)
salt and pepper

Melt the butter in a pan and add the bacon and onions. Stir for 2 minutes. Add the lettuce and peas and cover with a lid. Reduce the heat to low and let the vegetables stew gently for 8–10 minutes until the peas are tender and cooked and the lettuce wilted. No additional liquid is necessary as there is more than enough in the vegetables themselves. Taste and adjust the seasoning, then sprinkle over the mint, if using, and stir though.

HERB PIE FOR LENT
Elizabeth Raffald, 1769

This recipe was probably intended as the main part of a Lenten meal, but it serves admirably as an accompaniment to a major protein. It can be made ahead and baked just before serving and can also be enjoyed cold in the following days, with a side salad and baked potato.

SERVES 4 AS A SIDE

200g pearl barley
3–4 onions, peeled
1 tsp salt
30g unsalted butter, plus extra for greasing
1 head Little Gem lettuce, shredded
100g baby spinach leaves
1 leek or 6 spring onions, sliced
150g Swiss chard, shredded
2 sharp dessert apples, such as Jazz, Braeburn or Granny Smith, peeled, cored and thinly sliced

100g fresh parsley leaves, chopped
1 × batch Cornflour Shortcrust Pastry (page 326), chilled
1 egg yolk whisked with 1 tbsp water
salt and pepper

Equipment
24cm loose-bottomed flan tin

Put the barley into a pan and cover with cold water. Make sure there's at least 4cm of water above the barley. Add the peeled onions and salt. Bring to the boil then cover and reduce the heat. Simmer until the barley is cooked but not mushy, about 30–40 minutes. Drain the barley and onions. Chop the onions finely.

Melt the butter in a large pan and tip in the prepared lettuce, spinach, leek, Swiss chard and apples. Stir briskly over a medium heat until the leaves are wilted and the apples slightly softened.

Mix together the wilted greens, barley and chopped onions and stir through the parsley. Add salt and pepper to taste. Set aside to cool. If the mixture is warm when you add it to the pastry-lined tin, it will melt the butter and toughen the pastry.

Preheat the oven to 200°C/180°C fan/gas 6 and grease and line the tin with a circle of parchment paper.

Roll out the pastry and cut a circle large enough for the lid of your pie. Cut any decorations—leaf shapes are nice for such a leafy filling —from this first rolling. Gather the trimmings together and roll out again, this time lining the base of the tin. If the tin is fluted, make sure you ease the pastry into each flute. Leave any excess pastry hanging over the sides.

Spoon the cooled barley mixture into the case and smooth the surface. Moisten the pastry on the rim of the tin and lay the pastry lid over the top. Press the edges of the pastry together firmly to seal and crimp them. Cut a vent in the middle of the lid to let out steam. Attach the decorations using a little water. Brush the pie lid with the egg glaze and bake for 30–40 minutes, until the pastry is cooked and golden brown. You will see it shrink away slightly from the edges of the tin. Allow to cool in the tin for 10 minutes before removing and transferring to a serving plate.

HERB SOUP

circa 1700

It is only relatively recently that the word 'herb' has come to refer exclusively to the aromatic leaves used to season our food. Three hundred years ago, herbs, or 'pot herbs', referred to any edible soft, leafy vegetable. This makes this recipe both seasonal and customisable, as the mixture will vary with the seasons and what is to hand, as well as according to the personal taste of the cook. The delicate nature of the suggested greenery contributes to the speed with which this soup can be prepared.

SERVES 4 AS A SIDE

50g unsalted butter
500g green leaves and herbs, such
  as lettuce leaves, salad burnet,
  lamb's lettuce, beet greens, celery,
  chervil, spinach, sorrel and
  parsley, finely chopped
1 onion or 6 spring onions, finely
  chopped
1 cucumber, finely chopped

200g fresh or frozen garden peas
600ml lamb stock, or any flavour
1 tbsp cornflour mixed with 2 tbsp
  cold water (optional)
salt and coarse ground black pepper
celery tops, a few sprigs of fresh
  parsley and chervil, to garnish
crusty bread, to serve

Melt the butter in a large saucepan over a medium heat and cook all the vegetables for 5–6 minutes, stirring, until the leaves are wilted. Pour in the stock and bring to a simmer. Taste and add salt and pepper as required. Add the cornflour slurry, if using, and stir gently until the liquid thickens and becomes translucent. Sprinkle over the reserved leaves and herbs to garnish and serve with crusty bread.

SALMAGUNDY
Derived from various eighteenth-century recipes

I love this mellifluous word, and I am not alone. Although its original usage has faded into obscurity, it has stayed with us in the form of the nursery rhyme 'Solomon Grundy':

'Solomon Grundy,
Born on a Monday,
Christened on Tuesday,
Married on Wednesday,
Took ill on Thursday,
Grew worse on Friday,
Died on Saturday,
Buried on Sunday,
That was the end,
Of Solomon Grundy.'

The word has the same origins as Salmi (see page 124), meaning a seasoned mixture. In the eighteenth century it referred to what we would now call a mixed salad, although it was much more complex and substantial than a bunch of vegetables tossed in a bowl. Frustratingly, the word's pleasant sound also makes it difficult to investigate, as early recipes were written phonetically and therefore spelled in a number of varied and colourful ways, including: Salmagundy, Solly Magundi, Salmagundi, Sallad Magundy, Salmigundy, Salamongundy and Solomon Gundy.

An analogy for the evolution of the dish is that of a culinary version of the schoolyard game 'Broken Telephone', where the original message is transformed, through cumulative error, into something altogether weirder and more wonderful. Except, in this case, the transformation hasn't been to the dish's advantage. The earliest recipe I have found[1] doesn't sound too bad: 'Sollomy Gundy' is a delicate dish of chicken, ham, onion and herbs served with a sharp salad dressing and seasoning. However, in less than fifty years it somehow morphs into a veritable hotchpotch of minced everything, and the main culprit would appear to be Ms Sarah Harrison. Her *Housekeeper's Pocketbook* of 1733 lists two different recipes. Her Sallad Magundy, or Cold Harsh, consists of cold turkey, anchovies, pickled oysters and cucumbers all minced together and arranged on a dish with a border of pickles. Her Salmigundy, listed much later in the book, comprises cold veal, pickled herring or anchovies, and a chopped mixture of an onion and two apples, arranged in three separate piles on a dish. Although the instructions for each recipe are similar, the dishes themselves are distinctly different. When the recipe has appeared in subsequent books, having been either borrowed or plagiarised, the instructions have become jumbled together, the chopping and the mixing applied to all the ingredients from both recipes, resulting in a very unappetising mishmash. It is time to reinstate Salmagundy as it was originally conceived: a simple yet carefully presented banqueting dish.

Having read umpteen recipes across numerous decades and spanning several centuries, the most definitive statement I can make on this dish is that there are no hard and fast rules by which one must be constrained. It can be comprised of whatever you have to hand in terms of salad, proteins and pickle garnishes. Consequently, I have devised this recipe more as guidelines for you to create your own. As long as you include items from all three categories, your salad will be very close to authentic.

DIY '3P' SALMAGUNDY

Pick at least 3 ingredients from each list and arrange in groups on a serving platter.

PROTEINS

These will remain naked and unadorned on your platter, so you should take care to present them to their best advantage. Some items can be laid out whole, while others will appear better sliced thinly and fanned out, or cut into even dice.

chicken
turkey
veal
ham
hard boiled eggs, whites and yolks
  chopped separately
anchovies
pickled herrings

smoked mackerel
rollmop herrings
crayfish tails
prawns
brown shrimp
smoked salmon
smoked trout

PRODUCE

Attention to detail should also be made when displaying your salad produce. Whether you are serving individually plated dishes or a grand platter, you should bear in mind the daintiness of your presentation. If your guests will be helping themselves from a large platter, make sure each individual item can be easily served both in terms of the size of the items and the utensils you provide. The following are merely suggestions; feel free to elaborate.

shredded lettuce
mixed lettuce
salad leaves
lamb's lettuce
baby spinach leaves
watercress
rocket
celery

cucumbers
radish
parsley
dill
olives
peppers
apple and spring onion, chopped
  and tossed in lemon juice

PICKLES

The sharpness of pickled vegetables adds a real piquancy to the other elements of your platter so be generous in the range and strength of the varieties you provide. Suggestions include, but are not limited to, the following.

beetroot, sliced, whole or baby
red cabbage
silverskin onions
gherkins

cornichons
jalapeños
artichokes

PATRICK LAMB'S SALLAD MAGUNDY

Patrick Lamb, 1710

Patrick Lamb's more formal arrangement is a visual delight and
perfect for a summer luncheon. It is simple to prepare and the work
of only a few minutes to arrange on a suitably sized platter. You can
drizzle the completed dish with oil and lemon juice, a light fruit
vinegar or, alternatively, serve Salad Dressing (page 49) on the side.

SERVES 4

16 round shallots, peeled
300ml milk
300ml water
200g slender French beans,
 trimmed
2 or 3 heads Cos lettuce, or a
 mixture of salad leaves, finely
 shredded
2 cooked skinless chicken breasts,
 sliced into strips
4 cooked skinless chicken thighs,
 diced
100g marinated anchovies, cut
 into fillets, or a jar of anchovy
 fillets in oil or salt, rinsed

4 large hard-boiled eggs, yolks and
 whites separated
3 tbsp chopped fresh parsley
zest of 1 lemon
juice of ½ lemon
100g seedless green grapes
100g seedless red grapes
100g seedless black grapes
salt and pepper
vinegar or lemon juice and oil
 dressing, to serve

Put the shallots into a pan with the milk and water. Slowly bring to a boil, then reduce the heat and simmer until the onions are tender. Drain and set aside to cool.

Bring a small pan of water to the boil over a high heat and cook the French beans for 7 minutes, then drain and drop into iced water to arrest the cooking process. When cold, drain a second time and set aside.

Cover your serving dish with the shredded lettuce leaves and lay the chicken strips around the rim, with the ends pointing towards the centre of the dish. Set aside one of the anchovies and lay the rest of the fillets around the dish, between the strips of chicken.

Finely chop the remaining anchovy fillet and add it to the diced chicken thigh meat. Crumble the egg yolks over the top together with the parsley, lemon zest and juice. Toss this mixture together and season with salt and black pepper. Arrange in a mound in the centre of the platter. Place the cooled shallots around the edge of the chopped meat. Finely chop the egg whites and scatter neatly around the circle of shallots.

Cut the beans into 2cm lengths and scatter, along with the grapes, into any remaining spaces on the serving dish.

Serve with a simple vinegar or lemon juice and oil dressing, seasoned with salt and pepper.

DRESSED MUSHROOMS
Penelope Humphreys, circa 1700

I can't remember the last time I saw a mushroom that wasn't either a garnish or stuffed with cheese. This is a little disappointing when we are really spoilt for choice when it comes to the sheer range and variety of mushrooms available to us with so little effort. A single recipe can be transformed merely by changing the type of mushroom used. I've deliberately not specified any particular type in the following recipes, so feel free to experiment.

The following recipes can be served as accompaniments, but they also make hearty lunches or light suppers with some crusty bread or a small salad. Both are ready in just minutes and so great for meals at short notice.

SERVES 4 AS A SIDE OR 2 FOR LUNCH/SUPPER

500g mushrooms
1 tsp salt
50g unsalted butter
250ml red wine or port
250ml strong lamb stock
2 garlic cloves, sliced

1 tbsp black peppercorns
1–2 tbsp vinegar
2 tsp cornflour mixed with 2 tsp
  cold water
fresh parsley, to garnish

Simmer the mushrooms with the salt in a pan of boiling water for 10 minutes until tender. Strain and put into a fresh pan over a low heat to evaporate the excess moisture. Add the butter and toss gently until the mushrooms are coated and have absorbed some of the butter. Add the wine, stock, garlic, peppercorns and 1 tablespoon of the vinegar. Simmer gently for 15 minutes. Taste the sauce and add the remaining vinegar if necessary. Add the cornflour slurry and stir until the sauce thickens and becomes translucent. Pour the mushrooms into a warmed serving dish and add a sprig of parsley to garnish.

MUSHROOMS IN A CREAM SAUCE

Jane Newton, 1675

SERVES 4 AS A SIDE OR 2 FOR LUNCH/SUPPER

1 large sprig fresh thyme
1 small onion, peeled
2 slices back bacon
4 cloves
500g mushrooms
150ml white wine
25g unsalted butter

2 tbsp double cream or 1 rounded
  tbsp crème fraîche
½ tsp ground nutmeg
2 tsp cornflour mixed with 2 tsp
  cold water
juice of 1 orange
salt and pepper

Poke the sprig of thyme through the centre of the onion and pierce each bacon slice with 2 cloves.

Put the mushrooms in a pan with the wine, butter, bacon and onion. Cover and stew over a low heat until the mushrooms are tender and the flavours mingled, 10–15 minutes. Remove the bacon and onion from the pan, then remove and discard the thyme stalks and cloves. You can choose to discard the onion and bacon also, but they are full of flavour, so I like to chop them finely and stir them back into the sauce. Stir in the cream or crème fraîche and nutmeg. Taste and add seasoning as required. Add the cornflour slurry to the pan and stir until the sauce thickens. Just before serving, stir in the juice of an orange.

DEJA FOOD

Both mushroom recipes above reheat well and the flavours only get better over time. Make sure you only warm them through, as extreme heat may cause the sauces to curdle or split. You can add some texture by spooning into blind-baked shortcrust pastry cases, sprinkling with breadcrumbs and warming gently in a 150°C/130°C fan/gas 2 oven for 15–20 minutes.

SUPPLE ONIONS
Martha Hodges, 1680

SERVES 4 AS A SIDE

800g onions, about 8 medium,
peeled and thinly sliced
750ml lamb stock, or water and
2 stock cubes
250ml white wine

½ tsp ground ginger
30g butter
2 tbsp chopped, fresh parsley,
to garnish
salt and pepper

Put the onions, stock and wine into a pan and bring to the boil.
Turn down the heat and allow to simmer for 30 minutes, until the
onions are tender. Taste and season with the ginger, salt and pepper.
Simmer for a further 15 minutes. Add the butter and stir until
melted. Transfer to a warmed serving dish and sprinkle with the
chopped parsley.

DEJA FOOD
Either reheat as is or turn into a soup by blitzing in a liquidiser.
Heat gently and serve with wholemeal toast and a sprinkling of
cheese.

BAKED ONIONS
Elizabeth Raffald, 1808

It isn't strictly necessary to use cupcake cases and trays for this recipe—you could just put the onions on the rails of the oven if you like, but they do tend to ooze a bit of juice, which takes only moments to caramelise and blacken into the darkest, hardest, stickiest substance, which is a devil to scrub off. You could, of course, just use a baking sheet lined with parchment, but the cupcake tin keeps the onions upright and stops them rolling around.

1–2 medium brown onions per   *Equipment*
person, choose ones about the size   *1 cupcake case per person*
of an apple   *6 or 12-hole cupcake tin*

Leaving the skins on, put an onion into a cupcake case and drop into the holes of a cupcake tin. Bake for 1 hour, until the outsides are crisped and the insides soft.

DEJA FOOD
Remove the skins and chop the cooked onion. Use for Season or Savoury Pudding (pages 321–324).

MANY WAYS WITH PARSNIPS

Parsnips are one of the few native British vegetables, yet they don't enjoy much interest individually, more often than not being lumped together in a roast of mixed vegetables or a root vegetable soup mix. Parsnips used to form part of the grand trio of vegetables used for stock (alongside celery and onions), until supplanted by the more mellow carrot. They have a natural sweetness, something well recognised by the oldest recipes I've found, as they were used for desserts, much as carrots are today, to make sweet pies, fritters and cakes. While this may be a bit of a leap to begin with, the recipes below are all ways in which you can enjoy the unique flavour of this under-appreciated vegetable.

The simplest way of cooking parsnips still allows for a fair degree of scope in what can be achieved once they are boiled. Regardless of how you choose to serve them, butter is a must. Although the British came to be despised by the French for their predilection for butter on everything, on parsnips it brings out their sweetness and adds richness to a humble root. Due to their hardness, the easiest way to prepare parsnips is to leave them whole and simmer them long. You can scrape or peel them before cooking or rub off the skin once they are cooked and then trim to your liking.

SERVES 4

500g parsnips, scrubbed
1 tsp salt

50g clarified butter (optional, page 335)
butter and seasoning (optional)

Add the parsnips to a pan of cold water with the salt. Bring to a boil, cover and simmer for 15–20 minutes, until tender. Drain then return the parsnips to the pan and cover with a lid to steam for 5 minutes. If you've not yet peeled your parsnips, the thin skin will be easy to rub off.

You can now serve your cooked parsnips as ribbons, slices, long quarters or dice. Simply toss in some butter and seasoning, or roast in a pan by tossing over a medium heat with 50g clarified butter and then reducing the heat to low, tossing occasionally, for 15–20 minutes, until they have crisped at the edges. Alternatively, cut into rough chunks, add some butter and seasoning and mash vigorously or purée using a stick blender.

PARSNIP SOUP WITH APPLE

This is a creamy and comforting soup that can be made and served in about 30 minutes, or less if you begin with cooked parsnips. The addition of sharp apple just before serving really freshens the flavour of the soup.

SERVES 4

500g fresh or cooked parsnips, peeled and roughly chopped if fresh
1 onion, chopped
1 celery stick, sliced
1 carrot, peeled and roughly chopped

40g clarified butter (page 335)
500ml chicken or vegetable stock
salt and pepper
1 small Bramley apple, peeled, cored and grated
sippets or crisped onions, to serve

Put the onion, celery, carrot and fresh parsnip, if using, into a food processor and chop finely. You do not need to add cooked parsnip at this stage.

Melt the clarified butter in a pan and tip in the chopped vegetables.

Stir over a medium heat until coated with butter and slightly softened. Pour in the stock, cover and simmer for 10–15 minutes, until the vegetables are tender. If you are using cooked parsnips, add them now, together with the grated apple.

Purée the mixture thoroughly until smooth using a stick blender or liquidiser. Pour the smooth soup back into the saucepan and warm though. Taste and adjust the seasoning with salt and pepper. Don't heat to high or too long or you will lose the freshness of the apple. Serve with sippets or a sprinkling of crisped onions.

VARIATION

Parsnips pair well with warm spices, so to turn this into a curried parsnip soup, try adding 1 teaspoon each of ground cumin and ground coriander to the butter before adding the vegetables.

HOW TO BOIL POTATOES
Samuel Hayes, 1795

Early in 1795, concern at the rising cost of food and the threat of
low wheat crops prompted the Board of Agriculture to investigate
the feasibility of promoting the planting and harvesting of potatoes.
Although the Board had aspirations to become a government
department, at that time it was a private society concerned with
improving and disseminating knowledge on agricultural topics.
The report, published in June of that year, detailed the combined
wisdom and very best advice concerning potato cultivation and
usage for both man and animals. Nevertheless, the very necessary
details of how to cook potatoes were relegated to an appendix,
written by the barrister Samuel Hayes of Avondale, County
Wicklow, pioneer and champion of the re-afforestation of Ireland,
in response to a number of queries by the Board. The essence of his
guidance is detailed below.

Boiling potatoes in their skins helps prevent them disintegrating
into a watery soup. Sort them by size and only boil those of a
similar size together. Plan on allocating 250g of raw potato per
person. Scrub your selected potatoes free of dirt and place in a
large saucepan in a single layer. Add sufficient water to almost
cover; when the water boils it will cover the potatoes, but you don't
want to waterlog them. Add 1 teaspoon of salt. Bring to the boil
and simmer, uncovered, until cooked through. The 'uncovered' is
important, since a covering would raise the temperature too much
and the skins would split. You might need to top up the water if
they are taking longer than expected to cook through. If so, do it
with boiling water, and just enough to submerge the potatoes.

The length of time to cook will depend on the size of the potatoes,
but a general guide for a potato the size of a small apple would be
20–30 minutes from cold. Larger potatoes will take proportionally
longer. You can test whether your potatoes are done by inserting a
wooden cocktail stick into the thickest part of the potato: if it passes

through with no resistance the potatoes are cooked. Since you're cooking potatoes of a similar size, there is no need to go poking holes into all of them. Gently drain the water from the potatoes; try to avoid the violence of avalanching them into a colander in the sink, as this runs the very high risk of breaking the skins and turning them to mush—doubly disappointing after all your care and attention. Keep, or return the potatoes to the saucepan and switch off the heat. Cover with a clean tea towel and the saucepan lid and steam dry for 10 minutes.

JACKET POTATOES & POTATO SNOW

Jacket potatoes are top of my personal potato preparation list, in part due to the extremely low amount of preparation required. I don't bother with anything other than a clean skin. The result is crisp, parchment-dry outside and a mound of fluffy, dry (in a good way) cooked potato on the insides. Be sure to cut a steam vent in them when removed from the oven, otherwise the steam stays inside and turns the potato soggy.

Scrub one potato per person free of dirt and pat dry. Using a sharp knife or skewer, poke a few steam holes in the skin to prevent the potatoes from bursting. Put directly onto the oven shelf bars, turn the heat to 200°C/180°C fan/gas 6 and bake for 1 hour. There is no need to add salt or oil.

POTATO SNOW

The insides of baked potatoes are ideal for Potato Snow, provided they are scooped out as soon as they come out of the oven. Pass the cooked potato though a ricer, straight into a warmed serving dish. It is very important that the riced potato is allowed to fall directly into the dish and remain untouched, making a pile of feather-light flakes.

ROAST POTATOES
1817

Roast potatoes are the classic accompaniment to Sunday lunch and are extremely straightforward. With a little preparation, you can even wait until the joint is removed from the oven and is resting on the side before cooking them.

The earliest recipe for what we would recognise as roast potatoes I found in William Kitchener's *Apicius Redivivus Or The Cook's Oracle*. That recipe calls for parboiled potatoes to be placed under the spitted meat so that they are both cooked in the heat of the fire and flavoured by the meat juices and fat from the joint. I suspect the result would probably be closer to a confit potato, but the notion of cooking potatoes in the fat of the meat is one that has endured through the years.

You can choose any number of fats in which to cook your roast potatoes, the most flavourful option being either the fat from the joint of meat being cooked or the clarified fat from a previous joint.

SERVES 4

1kg floury potatoes, such as *Maris Piper or King Edward*	*120g fat*

Peel the potatoes and cut into large pieces, about the size of half an apple. Put into a saucepan of cold water and place over a high heat for 10 minutes to parboil. When the time is up, drain the water and return the potatoes to the pan. Cover with a clean cloth and allow to steam dry for 5 minutes.

When the potatoes are dry, shake the saucepan gently to roughen the edges of the potatoes. This will make for a much crunchier outside once fully cooked.

Heat the oven to 200°C/180°C fan/gas 6.
Put some fat in a roasting tin and put into the oven for 5 minutes until hot. Remove the pan from the oven and gently place the roughened parboiled potatoes into the hot fat, basting the potatoes fully, ensuring that all sides have a coating of the hot fat. Return to the oven and bake for 15 minutes, then turn over the potatoes in the fat and bake for another 15 minutes. Drain on a metal sieve before transferring to a warmed serving dish.

VARIATIONS

The easiest way to vary your roast potatoes is to alter the fat in which you cook them. You can opt for one of the fats readily available in the supermarket: beef dripping and lard are both excellent for crispness, although the refining process will have stripped out much of their individual flavours. Goose and duck fat are both rich in flavour and are becoming more readily available. Marrow fat provides a deliciously savoury roasting medium and is well deserving of it's nickname of beef butter. Scoop the marrow from some beef bones and allow it to melt slowly, either in a pan on the stove top or in the oven. Pour off the rendered fat and allow to solidify. Store in the fridge.

If you pine for crunchy roast potatoes but prefer something less fatty, you can achieve a pleasing degree of crispness by just brushing the outsides of the potatoes with fat using a silicone pastry brush, then baking them on parchment paper instead of half-submerged in the fat.

A third, fat-free option is to toss the peeled, uncooked potatoes in lightly whisked egg white before baking on parchment. The egg white forms a seal around the potatoes which becomes deliciously crisp and crunchy during baking. Since the potatoes will not be partially cooked they will require longer in the oven, or you can choose to cut them into smaller pieces. As a general guide, this method will require 30–40 minutes' cooking time. Parboiling and shaking the potatoes to roughen the edges actually makes for a less crisp potato using this method, so be clear on which method you're following before you start preparing your potatoes.

BOXTY
County Sligo, 1930s

This is derived from some recipes I found online dating from the 1930s. As part of a social studies syllabus, Irish children would, through conversations with parents and neighbours, record various aspects of Irish culture, including food. Interestingly, I found that the Boxty recipes varied between geographical areas, both in ingredients and method. The proportions of this particular recipe are the most popular style of Boxty from this region.

MAKES 4 FARLS

200g dry cooked potatoes
200g raw potatoes, peeled
100g plain flour

1 tsp bicarbonate of soda
½ tsp salt

Mash the cooked potatoes until they are free of lumps.

Grate the raw potatoes and squeeze out as much liquid as possible, either by pressing firmly in a sieve or by rolling in a dry cloth and twisting hard.

Mix all of the ingredients together into a soft, scone-like dough and shape into a disc about 3cm thick. Cut into quarters, or farls.

Put a large frying pan over a large ring on the lowest setting and warm for 2–3 minutes. Lay the farls on the dry pan and cook for 10 minutes on each side.

BUBBLE & SQUEAK

'Then slice the Beef, and souce that and the Cabbage both in a Frying-Pan together, and let it bubble and squeak over a Charcoal Fire'
The Midwife or Old Woman's Magazine, *1753*

The original bubble and squeak was a dish of cooked cabbage and thin slices of beef tossed in a pan with melted butter until heated through and slightly caramelised. The name originated from the sound of the cabbage and beef in the pan as they were reheated. Over time, the dish evolved into a more spartan, but to my mind just as flavourful, dish without meat.

Bubble and squeak is the quintessential 'day after' dish, using both cooked cabbage and cooked potatoes. In fact, I would go so far as to say that it is not possible to make the best bubble and squeak unless the cooked vegetables are a day old.

SERVES 4 AS A SIDE

400g cold boiled potatoes
400g cold cooked cabbage

50g beef dripping or rendered beef marrow

I have two different ways of making bubble and squeak, depending on whether I'm in the mood for a crunchy or a smooth texture. For the crunchy version, melt some flavoured fat in a pan—beef dripping or beef marrow, for preference. Cut your cold potatoes into bite-sized pieces and toss gently in the melted fat to coat. Set over a low heat, turning the potatoes every 10 minutes until the edges are well coloured and crisp. Don't rush this stage or be tempted to increase the heat as you might burn the potatoes. It will take abut 30 minutes or so. When the potatoes are crisped, remove from the pan and keep warm. Shred the cabbage and add to the pan. Increase the heat to high and toss the cabbage vigorously until heated through and starting to caramelise. Remove from the heat, stir in the crisped potatoes and serve.

For a softer version, melt a little butter or, preferably, beef dripping or goose fat, in a pan and add equal quantities of cooked cabbage and cooked potato. Press the ingredients gently but firmly into the pan to form a solid 'cake'. Allow to cook slowly over a low heat so that the potatoes can become crisp and golden brown. When the underside crust has formed, you can either slide the cake out of the pan onto a plate and turn it over or use a spatula to turn the cake over in pieces in the pan. This mixes the crust into the middle of the cake and is delicious. Sprinkle generously with salt and pepper and add a little more of whatever fat you are using to help the crust form again. When heated through and crispy underneath, serve at once.

SWEET & SOUR SPINACH
Gervase Markham, 1623

This side dish can be made with any spinach, but my preference is for baby spinach leaves because their tenderness means it can be cooked and served in less than 5 minutes.

SERVES 4 AS A SIDE

200g baby spinach leaves
20g unsalted butter
2 tbsp vinegar

1 tsp icing sugar
75g currants
salt and pepper

Melt the butter in a pan, add the spinach, cover and shake over a medium heat for 2 minutes, until the leaves are just wilted. Remove the lid and add the vinegar, sugar and currants. Toss together. Taste and add salt and pepper as required. Transfer to a warmed serving dish and serve.

TARTS OF SPINACH
& CHEESE
Martha Hodges, 1680

Martha Hodges' manuscript household book is a riotous jumble
of handwriting styles, poems, anecdotes, doodles and medical
receipts, in addition to well-laid-out recipes.[2] Buried in the jottings
are hints that many of the recipes originated in the Middle Ages.
Recipes such as Manchet, Vottes, Marchpane Collops, Leach
Royal and Powder Douce all echo the grand dishes described in
the very earliest recorded recipes. Despite their noble origins, I get
the impression that not everyone through whose hands this book
passed was comfortable with the more elaborate recipes. 'A Grand
Dish For The Summertime' describes a substantial centrepiece
of leg of lamb garnished with six stuffed chickens, lamb stones,
sweetbreads and candied sweetmeats. A disapproving later hand has
added 'For Grand Folks' next to the title. The recipe for Olio (an
anglicised version of *olla podrida*, a Spanish stew of mixed meat and
vegetables) has garnered the later comment 'a foolish French dish'.

This recipe, however, is delightful in its simplicity. The pairing
of spinach and white cheese in the filling of these little pies is
reminiscent of the classic Greek spanakopita, but the spices make it
a little more unusual. Fantastic for packed lunches and picnics, they
can also be served as a light summery lunch.

MAKES 4 PIES

400g baby spinach leaves
¼ tsp ground mace
¼ tsp ground cloves
30g unsalted butter, melted
125g mild white cheese such as curd
cheese, goats' cheese, feta, cream
cheese, Lancashire or Cheshire

1 large egg yolk, plus 1 large
beaten egg
¼ tsp ground nutmeg
¼ tsp ground ginger
½ × batch Cornflour Shortcrust
Pastry (page 326)

½ × sheet ready-rolled puff pastry
salt and pepper

Equipment
4 mini loaf tins

Heat a large lidded pan over a medium-high heat and add the spinach. Cover and let the leaves steam and wilt for 2 minutes, then remove and drain, pressing gently to get rid of as much of the liquid as possible. Sprinkle over the ground mace and cloves and add the melted butter. Toss thoroughly.

Put the cheese, egg yolk, nutmeg, ginger, salt and pepper into the bowl of a food processor and blitz until smooth.

Preheat the oven to 220°C/200°C fan/gas 7 and grease the mini loaf tins.

Roll out the shortcrust pastry to 5mm and use it to line the mini loaf tins. I find the easiest way to do this is to roll it out into a 15cm square and cut it into even quarters, then roll each piece individually to the required thickness. Make sure you ease the pastry into the corners of the tin rather than stretching it, for well-defined pie edges.

Add a layer of spinach to each pastry case, then a layer of the cheese mixture, followed by more spinach and so on until the pie is full, finishing with a layer of spinach. I managed 5 layers in the mini loaf tins: 3 spinach and 2 cheese. You want the filling to come nearly level with the top of the tin. If you're baking these freeform, a 3-layer spinach 'sandwich' is probably best.

Roll out the puff pastry and cut out rectangles for the lids. Moisten the top edges of the pies with a little water and press on the puff pastry lids. To trim the edges, carefully turn the loaf tins upside down and lay them on the counter, then cut around the edges of the tins with a sharp knife or pizza wheel. You want a nice, sharp edge so that the pastry can puff up. Turn the pies the right way up again and pinch and crimp the edges. Brush with the beaten egg to glaze. Using your sharpest knife, cut the outline of a leaf—or whatever

pattern you like—into the lid. Be careful not to cut all the way
through the pastry. If you do this before you glaze, the egg
just gums up the lines and inhibits the rise. Cutting the design
afterwards makes for a fabulous contrast, once cooked, between
the shiny brown glazed pastry and the unglazed cuts. Put your pies
onto a baking sheet and bake for 10 minutes, then turn the baking
sheet around and reduce the heat to 200°C/180°C fan/gas 6 for
a further 8–10 minutes. Allow to cool in the tins for 10 minutes
before removing and cooling on a wire rack. Serve warm or at room
temperature.

JOHN EVELYN'S MIXED SALAD

John Evelyn, 1699

As a contrast to the formality of an arranged salad such as Salmagundy (pages 285–287, this recipe from John Evelyn's classic book on salads, *Acetaria: A Discourse of Sallets* (1699), is delightfully freeform and haphazard. Relying mostly on store-cupboard ingredients, it requires only the addition of a couple of fresh items to come together. If you've ever thought the concept of a salad could in any way be encapsulated in a limp mix of lettuce, tomato and cucumber, I thoroughly recommend perusing John Evelyn's book for a fabulously refreshing peek at the sheer number and range of late seventeenth-century salad ingredients.

SERVES 4 AS A SIDE

100g fresh samphire
2 handfuls mixed salad leaves,
  such as spinach, lamb's lettuce
  and rocket
a selection of pickled/marinated
  vegetables such as cornichons,
  capers, olives, silverskin onions

50g flaked almonds
50g chopped, candied peel
50g currants
50g colourful raisins
oil and vinegar dressing

Bring a pan of water to the boil and cook the samphire for 2 minutes. Drain and then drop into a bowl of iced water to cool. Drain again.

Arrange the salad leaves on a serving platter and scatter the samphire over the top. Sprinkle over the rest of the ingredients and serve with the dressing on the side for everyone to help themselves.

CLAPSHOT
F. Marian McNeill, 1929

The 'bashed neeps' beloved of many a Burns Night feast are actually
Swedish turnips, now more often referred to as swedes. This
version of a wonderfully comforting side dish from famed Scottish
folklorist Florence Marian McNeill is a mixture of mashed swede
and potato, generously seasoned and sprinkled with chives. It is also
made delicious by substituting other root vegetables such as turnips,
celeriac, carrot, parsnip, etc., for the swede and mixing with the
mashed potatoes.

SERVES 4 AS A SIDE

1 swede, scrubbed and cut into
    thick slices
an equal weight of potato
60g salted butter or meat dripping

½ tsp salt
coarse-ground black pepper
4 tbsp snipped chives

Boil or steam the swede and potatoes separately. If you have a
saucepan with a steamer layer then this is ideal: cook the swede
in the water in the bottom and steam the potatoes above. When
tender, remove the skins of both and mash thoroughly or, for an
even smoother consistency, first blend the swede using a stick
blender. Mix in the butter and seasonings and stir until the fat
has melted, then stir in the snipped chives. Taste and adjust the
seasoning as necessary. Add more butter/dripping/chives, if liked.
Pile into a warmed dish and serve.

SWEDE & BACON BAKE
1940

The smokiness of the bacon really complements the earthy flavour of the swede and the simplicity of both preparation and cooking make this a firm winter favourite.

SERVES 4

1 swede   *coarse-ground black pepper*
200g smoked bacon, either thin
  slices or lardons

Peel the swede (this is easiest with a sharp knife rather than a peeler) and slice thinly, or use a mandolin to cut it into matchsticks.

Put a layer of bacon into the bottom of a pan with a close-fitting lid. A sauté pan is ideal. Add a layer of swede and a dusting of black pepper. Continue layering until the ingredients are used up or the pan is full. Drizzle over 30ml cold water and cover with the lid. Put on a low heat and stew gently until cooked through and tender, about 45–60 minutes. Alternatively, layer the bacon and swede in an ovenproof dish, cover tightly with foil and bake in the oven at 180°C/160°C fan/gas 4 for 1 hour.

TURNIPS ROASTED IN PAPER

John Evelyn, 1699

1 turnip per person

Preheat the oven to 200°C/180°C fan/gas 6.

Cut a 20cm square of parchment paper for each turnip and wrap each one, crumpling the paper around and then twisting the top to seal. Bake for 45–60 minutes until tender.

HARICOT OF ROOT VEGETABLES

1856

The following is just a suggestion of vegetables you could use for this recipe, but it offers a pretty range of colours and textures. The quantities seem large, but some of this will be lost in the preparation, and these amounts will mean that nothing further is needed for the meal, apart from your meat. To make this humble dish extra special you can use mini cutters in a variety of shapes to cut out the vegetables, a different shape for each one.

SERVES 4 AS A SIDE

400g large carrots, scrubbed
400g parsnips, scrubbed
400g swede, scrubbed and cut into
* 2cm slices*
400g small round shallots, peeled

400g celery, trimmed and cut into
* 10cm lengths*
400g cooked beetroot
400g radishes, red skin scraped
50g butter

Cook or steam each vegetable until tender, but still with a little bite. If you're planning on using cutters to shape your vegetables you can leave them unpeeled. Wherever possible, I prefer steaming and cooking as whole as possible to keep in the flavours. The celery and radishes will need the least time to cook, the swede the longest.

Preheat the oven to 110°C/90°C fan/gas ¼.

When your vegetables are cooked, cut into even sizes. The shallots and radishes should be your guide. Cut the carrots, parsnips and cooked beetroot into 2cm slices and then, together with the swede, cut them into suitable shapes, or use mini cutters. Slice the celery in 2cm slices and leave the radishes and shallots whole.

Put all the vegetables into a large casserole. Add the butter and a little water to prevent them from drying out, and cover with a lid or foil. Rest in the warm oven while you finish preparing the rest of your meal. Gently toss in the now melted butter before serving.

TRACKLEMENTS

I love the word 'tracklements'. Dorothy Hartley used it in her 1954 classic book *Food in England* to describe the traditional accompaniments to mutton. I've appropriated the word for this chapter as an umbrella term for all those little bits and pieces that don't really fit in anywhere else. As well as recipes for various 'trimmings' to accompany the best Sunday lunches, there are also a number of pastry recipes, garnishes and spice mixes with which to embellish your cooking.

HORSERADISH BUTTER
Mrs Carr, 1682

A traditional accompaniment to beef.

MAKES 120G

2 tbsp peeled and grated fresh   *100g unsalted butter, softened*
horseradish   *salt and pepper*

Blanch the grated horseradish in a pan of boiling water for 2
minutes then drain and tip onto kitchen paper to absorb the
excess water. Cream the softened butter with a wooden spoon. Stir
through the blanched horseradish and add salt and pepper to taste.
Mix thoroughly. Smooth into butter dishes and chill in the fridge
until required. Alternatively, allow to firm up a little in the fridge,
then shape into a cylinder, wrap in cling film and chill until firm.
You can then slice off as little or as much as you want, as required.

LIGHT BAKED PUDDINGS
Seventeenth century

There's no named author for the manuscript in which I found this
recipe,[1] so we'll never know to whom may be attributed these early
ancestors of Yorkshire puddings. What drew me to this recipe, quite
apart from the speed at which the fantastically billowy puddings
are baked, is the small quantity of ingredients and no mention of
standing the batter for hours before baking, which is so common
in modern recipes. I found this so unusual I actually put it to the
test and mixed two batches, baking one immediately and one

after letting the batter stand for 2 hours. I found no discernible difference in the result, which is such a boon for busy cooks who, like me, tend to get distracted by the whole meal process so that we only remember about the batter as the joint comes out of the oven to rest.

One detail that did emerge from the testing of this recipe was the importance of the shape of the tin the puddings are baked. Traditionally, the batter was poured into the tin beneath the roasting joint so that it could catch the fat and meat juices as they fell. The more popular method nowadays is for individual puddings of various sizes. If you like your puddings to have a nice bowl shape to them, you might have to rethink your baking tin or tins as they must have straight vertical sides. My own Yorkshire pudding tins slope outwards at an angle. The puddings baked in them are wonderfully puffed, but not bowl shaped. To achieve a beautifully rounded bowl shape I use four mini layer or sandwich-cake tins, about 9cm in diameter. If you can't find similar, use a straight-sided cupcake tin for miniature puddings or 2 × 20cm sponge-cake tins. The secret to getting your puddings to puff is not to peek into the oven for at least 20 minutes, as this lets out all the heat and steam that make the puddings rise.

MAKES 4 SMALL OR 2 LARGE PUDDINGS

110ml milk	*Equipment*
60g plain flour	*4 × 9cm, or 2 × 20cm round*
1 or 2 large eggs	*straight-sided tins*
salt and pepper	

Preheat the oven to 200°C/180°C fan/gas 6 and lightly grease the tins, if necessary, with just a teaspoon of the fat from whatever joint you're cooking. Put the tins onto a baking sheet and heat in the oven.

Whisk all the ingredients to a smooth batter. If you like your puddings crisp then just add 1 egg, if you like them moist in the middle, add the second. Pour the batter into a jug. When the tins are hot, remove from the oven and use a pastry brush to spread the hot fat all over the surface of the tin. Quickly pour in the batter to no more than half full. Return to the oven and bake for 20 minutes, without opening the oven door. After 20 minutes, check for doneness. I prefer them crispy so I usually allow another 5 minutes or so, but if you prefer them soft, 20 minutes is usually fine. Serve hot.

STUFFING
Traditional

Traditional stuffing is so simple—breadcrumbs, onions, herbs and stock—yet it can really enhance a main meal. When it comes to the traditional roast, though, I have a problem with where it goes and how it is usually gets served up.

I understand that, packed inside the poultry of your choice it is supposed to both impart flavour and absorb the meat juices as they run free, but what invariably gets dished up is a big glop of solid stodge to eat alongside some dried-up old bird, and I'm not just referring to myself here. Stuff stuffing the stuffing, I say! Cook it separately and both the meat and the stuffing can be cooked to perfection and everything is right in the world.

You can bake stuffing in a big slab or roll it into balls and let it cook around the outside of the meat. Personally I like to cook it in individual portions in a bun tin so that the outside gets crispy and crunchy, while the inside remains light and moist. Traditionally, stuffing contains suet, but I prefer to replace it with butter for two reasons: it means vegetarians can enjoy it as well (make sure you use vegetable stock), and it still tastes great when cold in a sandwich. Cold, congealed suet is not a good taste in anything. So today's handy hint is: avoid suet if you'd like to continue to enjoy your stuffing cold.

MAKES 12 SERVINGS

2 onions, chopped
50g butter
225g breadcrumbs (from 4–5 slices bread)
1 heaped tsp dried parsley
1 heaped tsp dried sage
1 heaped tsp dried thyme

1 heaped tsp dried oregano
½–1 tsp dried rosemary
1 egg
200ml stock
salt and pepper
Equipment
12-hole muffin tin

Preheat the oven to 200°C/180°C fan/gas 6 and grease the tin.

Cook the onions gently in the butter until softened and translucent and then add to a bowl with all the other ingredients and any butter left in the pan. The mixture should be moist enough to hold its shape when pressed together. If it appears dry, add more stock until you achieve the right consistency. Spoon into the tin and press down gently. I think the crunchy bits on top are the best bits, so I use a fork to rough up the surface. Bake for 45 minutes.

SEASON PUDDING
Florence White, 1932

This old Yorkshire recipe occurs in two variations, one batter-based and this breadcrumb-based version. Served as accompaniments to roast dinners, season puddings not only added a savoury relish, but also provided a filling extra if the joints were small or unexpected guests turned up. In some parts, versions of this dish were served with gravy as a first course. An account from Halifax recorded by Sheila Hutchins told of vast quantities of this pudding being made and sent around to neighbours when the family pig was killed, together with piping-hot portions of cooked pig's fry, a gesture that would be reciprocated when other households killed their own pigs.

SERVES 4

100g stale bread
1 tsp dried sage
1 tsp dried marjoram
1 tsp dried rosemary
½ nutmeg, grated
¼ tsp salt
¼ tsp black pepper
1 small onion, finely chopped

30g oatmeal
1 large egg
200ml milk, for soaking, plus extra
  if required

Equipment
20cm cake tin

Soak the bread in milk for 30 minutes until soft. The quantity of milk will depend on how dry your bread is. If it seems dry after soaking, add a little more until the crumb becomes tender. Mash with a fork to break up any large pieces.

Preheat the oven to 200°C/180°C fan/gas 6 and grease the cake tin.

Add the herbs, nutmeg, seasoning, onion and oatmeal to the soaked bread, then whisk the egg and stir it through the mixture. When thoroughly mixed, pour into the tin and smooth over. The mixture should be around 3cm deep. Roughen the top with a fork to ensure lots of crisp crust and bake for 40 minutes, until cooked through and the top crusty and browned.

VARIATION
Omit the bread and milk and whisk the egg into a Light Baked Pudding batter (page 316). Stir though the rest of the ingredients and bake for 20–25 minutes.

DEJA FOOD
Enjoy cold, otherwise warm gently in a cool oven (150°C/130°C fan/gas 2) for 15 minutes.

SAVOURY PUDDING
Twentieth century

This recipe is something from my childhood. It's a great way to round out the Sunday lunch as it compliments practically any joint or bird. It's not a pudding in the traditional sense, involving suet and hours of boiling, but more akin to a savoury scone. Pre-boiling the onions takes away their harshness, and the use of fresh herbs makes this addition to the meal both incredibly savoury and fresh. You don't have to use the exact mix of herbs suggested, just go with whatever your personal taste is or, as is frequently the case in this household, whatever the cupboard or garden has to offer at the time. Dried herbs work fine too, although you should use just half the quantity of the fresh.

SERVES 6

2 medium onions, peeled
225g plain flour
30g unsalted butter
½ tsp coarse-ground black pepper
½ tsp salt
½ tsp bicarbonate of soda
1 tsp cream of tartar
1 large egg
8 tsp chopped, mixed, fresh herbs, such as rosemary, sage, parsley, savory, chives, thyme, oregano and basil

80ml plain yogurt
80ml milk, plus extra for brushing

Equipment
20cm square or round baking tin

Bring a pan of water to the boil and cook the onions for 10 minutes. Drain and then set aside to cool.

Preheat the oven to 220°C/200°C fan/gas 7 and line the baking tin with parchment paper.

Put the flour, butter, pepper, salt, bicarbonate of soda, cream of tartar and the egg into the bowl of a food processor and blitz until the mixture resembles breadcrumbs. Tip the mixture into a large bowl and stir in the chopped herbs. Roughly chop the cooled onions and add to the mixture. Keep the pieces about 2cm square to add some texture. Mix together the yogurt and milk thoroughly and gradually stir in until the mixture comes together into a soft dough. Tip into the prepared tin and spread evenly. I like to roughen the surface with a fork to give lots of crunchy bits. Brush the surface with milk and bake for 15–20 minutes, until risen and golden, turning the tin around after 10 minutes to ensure even baking. Cool in the tin for 5 minutes before removing and serving hot.

DEJA FOOD
Wrap in foil and warm in the oven for 15 minutes. Enjoy as an accompaniment, or split and spread with butter. Alternately, wrap in foil or plastic and freeze.

PEA POWDER
William Kitchener, 1827

A condiment for use on pease pudding and pea soups.

MAKES 33G

14g dried sage

14g dried mint

4g celery seed

1g cayenne, allspice or black pepper

Grind all the ingredients to a powder in a pestle and mortar or spice mill. Sieve finely and store in a sealed jar. It will retain its aromatic bouquet for several weeks.

CORNFLOUR SHORTCRUST PASTRY
circa 1900

A deliciously crisp all-butter shortcrust for use in both sweet and savoury dishes.

MAKES ENOUGH FOR 1 LARGE OR 4 INDIVIDUAL DOUBLE CRUST PIES

225g plain flour

60g cornflour or rice flour

140g butter

ice-cold water

Put the flours and butter into the bowl of a food processor and blitz until the mixture resembles breadcrumbs. With the machine running, gradually add the cold water, a tablespoon at a time, until the mixture comes together in a ball. Tip onto a lightly floured surface, knead smooth then wrap in cling film and chill for 30 minutes, after which, it will be ready for use.

BEEF DRIPPING PASTRY

1950s

This is a cross between a shortcrust and a flaky pastry, due to the baking qualities of beef dripping when mixed with flour. Simply made using a shortcrust method, the pastry is difficult to handle, rather heavy and incredibly friable. However, combined with the rolling and folding usually associated with rough puff and you get a much lighter and more flavoursome crust. You can make your own dripping by saving and clarifying the fat from any beef roasting joint (page 334).

MAKES 750G

500g plain flour
200g beef dripping

1 tsp salt
ice-cold water

Add the flour, 40g of the fat and the salt to the bowl of a food processor fitted with a blade and blitz until the mixture resembles breadcrumbs. Gradually add the ice-cold water, a spoonful at a time, until the mixture comes together in a ball. Tip onto a lightly floured surface and knead smooth. Form into a flat rectangle.

Roll out the pastry into a long rectangle. Dot 40g of the fat over the bottom two-thirds of the pastry, then fold the top third of the pastry down to the middle and the bottom third up over the top. Turn the folded pastry 90 degrees and repeat. Roll and fold a total of 4 times, then rest in the fridge for 30 minutes. The pastry is now ready to use.

HOT WATER CRUST
Traditional and seventeenth century

This hot water crust recipe is a combination of Dorothy Hartley's 1950s advice to pair the fat of the pastry with the filling, Elizabeth Jacob's seventeenth-century recommendation for including rye flour, and my own experiments with proportions. It can be used for a range of hot meat pies, not just for mutton and lamb. For other fillings, change the fat to that of the meat you are using for the pie: dripping for beef, lard for pork, chicken fat for chicken, etc. The addition of a small proportion of rye flour adds sturdiness to the crust and helps prevent cracks or leaks.

MAKES 500G

100g mutton fat or butter　　　　*225g wholemeal flour*
1 tsp salt　　　　　　　　　　　*75g rye flour*

Put the fat into a pan with 200ml water and the salt and warm over a low heat, just until the fat has melted. Put the flours into a bowl and pour over the warmed liquid. Stir well. The paste will be very soft when it comes together. You can roll it out if you like, but it can also just be flattened and pressed into the tin by hand.

SPICE MIXES

The very oldest recorded British recipes mention two spice mixtures that were in general use: powder douce (sweet or gentle) and powder fort (strong). There is much discussion as to what exactly they might have contained, but the answer is much more straightforward: whatever took your fancy. There were a few standard component spices but the proportions were very much down to personal taste, and households used to mix up their favourite permutations, much in the same way we can mix and use garam masala as a general spice mix today. Below are some suggestions for a few different spice mixes with which to experiment. For maximum flavour, whole spices should be ground together in a pestle and mortar or spice mill, but pre-ground spices can be used to test whether the mixes appeal in the first instance. It is better to mix little and often than to make a large batch and for the flavours to fade before you've had an opportunity to use it all.

Simply grind or mix all the ingredients together thoroughly and store away from sunlight, in sealed jars.

SAVOURY SPICE MIX 1
1656

The original recipe suggested using four times this quantity of salt. That would be just a quarter of a teaspoon of spice to each teaspoon of salt. Having experimented with these proportions, I would suggest something closer to equal quantities of salt and spice, but that's just my own personal taste. Alternatively, you can choose to keep the spices and salt separate and to season with both as the recipe requires.

MAKES 100G

30g dried ginger   2g nutmeg
15g black pepper   2g cinnamon
1g cloves   50g salt
1g mace

....

SAVOURY SPICE MIX 2
1695

MAKES 400G

20g ginger   10g nutmeg
5g mace   60g white pepper
5g cloves   300g salt

....

CHARLOTTE MASON'S SPICE MIXES
1787

Mistress Mason doesn't include any further details on her own spice mix other than the spices that make up each combination. The proportions are very much down to personal taste and experimentation. As a guide, I have rewritten the ingredients in what I believe to be proportion order, with the spice with the greatest proportion listed first.

Sweet: sugar, cinnamon, nutmeg, salt, cloves, mace.

Savoury: salt, pepper, nutmeg, mace, cloves.

VEAL FORCEMEAT

Hannah Bisaker, 1692

Veal forcemeat is incredibly versatile and useful for adding an enriching savouriness to a number of dishes. Due to its mild flavour it can be used to enhance a wide range of other meats, including poultry, as a stuffing, rolled into meatballs for filling gaps in a pie or under the skin of a fowl. In the past it was a popular component of rich mince pies, adding savouriness without overpowering the other ingredients. It can also be rolled into small balls or sausage shapes and served as a garnish. As a general rule, if the meat you are serving these with is pale (veal, chicken, turkey, pork), the forcemeat should be poached in veal or chicken stock until just cooked. For darker meats it should be lightly fried and crisped in a pan. This recipe is savoury and herby, a little bit sharp with a hint of spiciness—ideal, in fact, for serving alongside almost any joint of meat or fowl. You can also bake it in a loaf tin to enjoy by itself, like a meatloaf.

MAKES 600G

250g lean veal or veal mince

100g streaky bacon, minced or finely chopped

2 anchovy fillets, rinsed and chopped

¼ nutmeg, grated

½ tsp ground ginger

a pinch of ground cloves

a pinch of ground mace

¼ tsp black pepper

¼ tsp salt

2 shallots, finely chopped

2 tbsp fresh thyme leaves

2 tbsp fresh marjoram, chopped

2 tbsp fresh savory leaves, chopped

2 tbsp fresh parsley, chopped

30g baby spinach leaves, finely chopped

100g fresh breadcrumbs

50g samphire, finely chopped, or add 20g more spinach

1 tbsp capers, chopped

zest and juice of ½ lemon

2 large egg yolks

Mince together the veal, bacon and anchovies until thoroughly combined. Sprinkle with the spices and salt and mix again. Add the rest of the ingredients, except the yolks, and stir until thoroughly combined. Add the yolks, one at a time, until the mixture will hold together. Roll teaspoons or tablespoons of the mixture into small balls or small sausages and simmer in broth, fry in clarified butter (page 335) or use as directed.

SIPPETS

Sixteenth century

Sippets, the British version of France's croutons, are both an economical way of using up bread that is past its prime and, formerly, an integral part of serving and garnishing dishes of old. Sippets can take many forms: large slices for placing on serving platters underneath roast meats to soak up the juices; small fancy shapes, or cubes, to add crispness and crunch to soups, broths and pottages, or served as garnishes and decoration around larger dishes.

Depending on how you wish to use them they can be prepared in several ways:

—*Dried bread:* retain the pale white of the bread by slicing/dicing/cutting into shapes/blitzing to breadcrumbs and dry in a low oven (120°C/100°C fan/gas ½).

—*Toasted bread:* as above, but toasted under a grill to give both crispness and colour.

—*Fried bread:* the crunchiest option. Dip into the fat of the dish and then toss in a pan until crisped and golden.

TO CLARIFY FAT

Fat is flavour, and the fat that renders out of meat as it cooks is the most flavourful of all. Once cold, it solidifies and can easily be lifted from the meat juices underneath and set aside for use later in a number of delicious ways. Any non-fat particles contained therein will eventually cause the fat to become rancid so remove them by clarifying the fat and it will be practically immortal, although it will probably—and rightfully—be used long before that point is proved for making pastry for meat pies, crisping sippets, searing meat or roasting potatoes.

To clarify fat gleaned from cooking, strain off as much of the non-fat liquid as possible. If you have a fat separator jug, then this makes it a lot easier. Otherwise, refrigerate until the fat becomes solid.

Lift off the disk of fat and warm just enough to melt in a saucepan. When fully melted, pour over a litre of water. Some methods say to use hot, some cold. I've tried both ways and cannot discern any difference, so let's say to use cold water. The water will wash through the fat and the lighter density fat will float on top of the water, while the heavier particles will sink. Set aside to cool, then chill overnight in the fridge (or outside with a weighted lid if your quantities are large and your fridge is too small).

The following day you will be able to lift the solid, clarified disk of fat from the surface of the water. You might have a layer of small meat particles stuck to the bottom, but these can easily be scraped off. Break up the disk of pure, cleaned fat and store in a plastic box in the fridge for use later. You can, if inclined, melt this fat and pour it into a sealed container for a neater look. Use as required.

TO CLARIFY BUTTER

Clarified butter is a great standby item to have in the fridge. Containing neither casein nor milk solids there is nothing to burn or perish, so its shelf life, and that of recipes in which it is used, is extended. I always make my citrus and fruit curds with clarified butter and honey, and they last much longer than those made with regular butter. I usually clarify 500g butter at a time and keep it handy in the fridge for this and other uses.

MAKES 500G

500g unsalted butter

Equipment
1 × clean jar or plastic box with lid

Put the butter into a small saucepan and set it over the lowest possible heat. Leave until completely melted and the milk solids have sunk to the bottom. Turn off the heat and leave to cool for 30 minutes.

Skim and discard the debris from the surface, then either pour or spoon the clarified butter into a jar or sealable plastic box. Don't let any of the milk solids become mixed with the clarified butter. Stop pouring when this looks like happening, but don't throw anything away. Cover the clarified butter and leave it to cool in the fridge.

Pour the remaining butter and milk solids into a glass and leave it to solidify. Once it is set, cut around the butter and remove the disc from the glass. Rinse in cold water, making sure all milk solids are removed. Add the disc of washed butter to the rest of the clarified butter, crumbling it to fit if necessary.

TO MAKE STOCK

Stock is a valuable commodity in the making of soups, casseroles, gravies and sauces. An older term, dating from around the year AD1000, is broth. A broth consisted of the liquid in which other ingredients had been simmered, to extract all their flavour and nutrients. It could be used for making sauces or served on its own as a nourishing liquid for the infirm. 'Stock', to my mind, diminishes it rather, down to the status of an ingredient rather than a dish in itself, but, nevertheless, it forms just as valuable a part of our modern cooking resources as it did a thousand years ago.

Which is odd, considering how little it is made. The availability of the modern conveniences of stock powders, cubes, concentrates and fresh sauces confirm its use is still widespread, but, considering the ease and simplicity of how it is made, it should be a much greater part of the home cook's repertoire.

There is no strict recipe for making stock, but by following a few guidelines, everyone is capable of producing a richly flavoured liquid to enhance their recipes. It is an unhurried process, and can be spread over 2 or 3 days, but the effort required is minimal and the rewards many.

Firstly, if you can count to three, you can make good stock. That three refers to the triumvirate of flavourings that form the basis of any stock: onion, carrot and celery.

1 onion
2 carrots
3 celery sticks

This is the basic ratio. That said, you can switch the carrot and celery around depending on what you are making stock from: beef and lamb both have an affinity with carrots, so a beef/lamb stock might begin with 1 onion, 2 celery sticks and 3 carrots.

If you have no celery, ½ a teaspoon of celery seed per stick of celery can be used instead.

The additional flavourings should consist of:

1 dried or 2 fresh bay leaves
1 tbsp black or white peppercorns
a few parsley stalks, leaves as well
  if you have them, but stalks have
  quite enough flavour
any other fresh herbs to hand

With these few ingredients you can make stock from anything: fish, meat or poultry.

Back in the eighteenth century, cooks such as Hannah Glasse would recommend making stock from raw ingredients and use a mixture of bacon, veal, ham and beef simmered in gallons of water. While no doubt flavourful, a much more economical and, in terms of quantity, more appropriate volume of stock can be made from the trimmings and remains of joints of meat. This has a knock-on effect that you then have stock to hand for the making of the next gravy or sauce.

The best approach to making stock is to start it after any remaining meat has been stripped and trimmed for a subsequent meal. Whether you do this immediately or the next day is entirely up to you. Leaving it until the next day is fine if you have the room to store the ingredients in the fridge overnight. Conversely, preparing the ingredients after the meal means your stock can be simmering overnight.

The following instructions are for a chicken stock, but the principles can be applied to the remains of any cooked joint of meat.

the remains of roast chicken(s),   *2 carrots, roughly chopped*
   (bones, skin, fat and ligaments)   *2 fresh bay leaves or 1 dry*
1 onion, quartered, skin on   *1 tbsp black peppercorns*
3 celery sticks, roughly chopped   *12 parsley stalks*

Put all the chicken parts into a saucepan or, even better, a slow cooker.

Add the onion (there's no need to remove the brown skin as it will add a lovely golden colour to your stock), with the rest of the ingredients, pour over cold water to cover, put the lid on and cook overnight on the lowest possible heat.

The following day, turn off the heat and strain the stock through a fine mesh sieve. Discard the solids. Rinse the sieve and line it with muslin. Strain the stock again to remove the fine particles. You should now have a relatively clear stock covered with a layer of liquid fat. This fat needs to be removed before you reduce the stock, otherwise it will make your stock cloudy.

Pour your stock into a suitable container and allow to cool, then chill in the fridge until the fat, and possibly the stock, solidifies. Remove the solidified fat and set aside. Some fats, especially those from poultry, are still fairly soft even when chilled, so you might need to spoon it off the top of your stock. It is better to take a little stock off with your fat, than to leave the fat on the stock. When your stock is free of fat, return it to the pan and warm it through. Taste and decide if the flavour needs strengthening. If so, simmer uncovered until it develops enough flavour. Allow to cool, then store in the fridge or freezer until required.

NOTES

SAUCES

[1] MS3009, Wellcome Library Collection.

BEEF

[1] MS3547, Wellcome Library Collection.

[2] MS3082, Wellcome Library Collection.

[3] *'In the XIIth year of the reign of Charles II—Written in the Office of the Pantry, the Butler and the Cellar of the Lord King in the year of our lord 1660–1661. Paid Joseph Batailhe for 169 Bls [bottles] 1 parcel wine of Hobriono [Haut-Brion] for himself personally delivering for the Lord King and hospitality at 21s 4d per Bl with full jugs and measures of £180–5–4 and 60 Bls 2 parcels of wine of Graves at 28 (…) per dozen, £32–2–8 in total, in the months of June and January.'*

[4] *The metamorphosis of the town: or, a view of the present fashions. A tale: after the manner of Fontaine*, Elizabeth Thomas, 1730.

BIRDS

[1] MS1325, Wellcome Library Collection.

MUTTON & LAMB

[1] *The art of cookery refin'd and augmented containing an abstract of some rare and rich unpublished receipts of cookery*, Cooper, Joseph, 1654.

[2] *The secret history of clubs: particularly the Kit-Cat, Beef-Stake, Vertuosos, Quacks, Knights of the Golden-Fleece, Florists, Beaus, &c.*, Edward Ward, 1709, London, p361.

[3] Ibid., pp362–3.

[4] *The critical and miscellaneous prose works of John Dryden: now first collected, with notes and illustrations, an account of the life and writings of the author, grounded on original and authentick documents: and, a collection of his letters,*

the greater part of which has never before been published, John Dryden, 1631–1700; Edmond Malone, 1741–1812, 1800, London, vol. I, p526.

5 *The House-keeper's Pocket-book, and Compleat Family Cook*, Sarah Harrison, 1733, London.

PORK

1 *Farmhouse Fare*, 1935, p25.

GAMMON, HAM & BACON

1 *Arundel Collection*, No. 344 p282, cited and quoted in *Antiquitates Culinariae*, Richard Warner, 1791, p53.

OFFAL

1 *The Country Housewife and Lady's Director: In the Management of a House, and the Delights and Profits of a Farm. Containing Instructions for Managing the Brew-house, and Malt-liquors in the Cellar; the Making of Wines of All Sorts. Directions for the Dairy, in the Improvement of Butter and Cheese Upon the Worst of Soils; the Feeding and Making of Brawn; the Ordering of Fish, Fowl, Herbs, Roots, and All Other Useful Branches Belonging to a Country-seat, in the Most Elegant Manner for the Table. Practical Observations Concerning Distilling; with the Best Method of Making Ketchup, and Many Other Curious and Durable Sauces. The Whole Distributed in Their Proper Months, from the Beginning to the End of the Year. With Particular Remarks Relating to the Drying Or Kilning of Saffron*, Richard Bradley, 1732.

2 The full title being the much less succinct, *Royal Cookery; or, the Complete Court-Cook. Containing the choicest receipts in all the particular branches of cookery, now in use in the Queen's palaces of St. James's, Kensington, Hampton-Court and Windsor. With nearly Forty Figures (curiously engraven Copper) of the magnificent Entertainments at Coronations, Istalment, Balls, Weddings, &c. at Court; Also Receipts for making the Soups, Jellies, Bisques, Ragoo's, Pastes, Tanzies, Forc'd-Meats, Cakes, Puddings, &c. By Patrick Lamb, Esq, Near 50 Years Master-Cook to their late Majesties King Charles II, King James II, King William and Queen Mary, and to Her Present Majesty Queen Anne. To which are added, Bills of Fare for every Season in the Year*, 1710, London.

CHEESE

[1] "Makrows. .lxl. Tak and make a thyne foyle of dowh & kerue it on pecys and cast hy on boylyg wat & seeþ it wel. take chese & grate hit & butt most cast bynethen & aboue as loseyns and sue hit forth", *English MS 7*, John Rylands University Library, The University of Manchester, page 46r.

VEGETABLES

[1] MS7892, Wellcome Library Collection.
[2] MS2844, Wellcome Library Collection.

TRACKLEMENTS

[1] MS8097, Wellcome Library Collection.

SOURCES

ACTON, ELIZA, *Modern Cookery for Private Families* (London: Longmans, 1845).

BAILEY, NATHAN, *Dictionarium Britannicum* (London: T. Cox, 1730).

BISAKER, HANNAH, MS1126, Wellcome Library Collection.

BLOUNT, THOMAS, *Glossographia* (London: T. Newcomb for H. Moseley & G. Sawbridge, 1656).

BRADLEY, RICHARD, *The Country Housewife and Lady's Director* (London: Printed for D. Browne and T. Woodman, 1732).

BREGION, JOSEPH and MILLER, ANNE, *The Practical Cook, English and Foreign*, (London: Chapman & Hall, 1845).

CARR, MRS, MS1511, Wellcome Library Collection.

CARTER, CHARLES, *The Complete Practical Cook: Or, a New System of the Whole Art and Mystery of Cookery* (London: W. Meadows & others, 1730).

CLELAND, MRS ELIZABETH, *A New and Easy Method of Cookery* (Edinburgh: Printed for the Author by W. Gordon, C. Wright, S. Willison and J. Bruce, 1755).

COOPER, JOSEPH, *The art of cookery refin'd and augmented containing an abstract of some rare and rich unpublished receipts of cookery* (London: Printed by J.G. for R. Lowndes, 1654).

DAWSON, THOMAS, *The Good Huswifes Jewel* (London: By Iohn Wolfe for Edward White, dwelling at the litle North doore of Paules at the signe of the Gunne, 1587).

ELLIS, WILLIAM, *The Country Housewife's Family Companion* (London: Printed for James Hodges at the Looking-glass, facing St Magnus Church, London Bridge and B. Collins, Bookseller at Salisbury, 1750).

EVELYN, JOHN, *Acetaria: A Discourse of Sallets* (London: Printed for B. Tooke at the Middle Temple Gate in Fleet Street, 1699).

EYTON, AMY, MS2323, Wellcome Library Collection.

FANSHAWE, LADY ANN, MS7113, Wellcome Library Collection.

FORBY, ROBERT, *The Vocabulary of East Anglia* (London: Printed by and for J.B. Nichols and Son, 1830).

FREEMAN, BOBBY, *Is Welsh cookery really there? An examination of Welsh cookery tradtions and their curious denial by the Welsh*, National & Regional Styles of Cooking: Proceedings of the Oxford Symposium on Food and Cookery, 1981, pp. 221–230.

GLASSE, HANNAH, *The Art of Cookery made Plain and Easy* (London: Printed for the Author and sold at Mrs Ashburn's, 1747).

GROSE, FRANCIS, *A Classical Dictionary of the Vulgar Tongue* (London: Printed for S. Hooper, 1785).

HARRISON, SARAH, *The Housekeeper's Pocket-Book* (London: Printed for T. Worrall, 1733).

HARTLEY, DOROTHY, *Food in England* (London: Macdonald, 1954).

HAYES, SAMUEL, in *Report of the Committee of The Board of Agriculture, appointed to extract information from the county reports and other authorities, concerning the culture and use of potatoes* (London: Printed by W. Bulmer and co, 1797).

HEPPINGTON RECEIPTS, MS7997, MS7998, MS7999, Wellcome Library Collection.

HERMAN-SENN, CHARLES, *Recherche Side Dishes for Breakfast, Luncheon, Dinner and Supper* (London: John Haddon & Co, 1894).

HODGES, MARTHA, MS2844, Wellcome Library Collection.

HUMPHREYS, PENELOPE, in MS7851, Wellcome Library Collection.

HYDE, BRIDGET, MS2990, Wellcome Library Collection.

JACOB, ELIZABETH, MS3009, Wellcome Library Collection.

JOHNSTONE, CHRISTIAN ISOBEL, *The Cook and Housewife's Manual* (Edinburgh: Oliver & Boyd, 1828).

KELLET, SUSANNA, ELIZABETH and MARY, *A Complete Collection of Cookery Receipts* (Newcastle Upon Tyne: Printed by T. Saint, 1780).

KIDDER, EDWARD, *Receipts of Pastry and Cookery* (London, c1740).

KITCHENER, WILLIAM, *Apicius Redivivus: Or, The Cook's Oracle* (London: Printed for S. Bagster, 1817).

LAMB, PATRICK, *Royal Cookery; or, The Complete Court-Cook* (London: printed for Maurice Atkins, 1710).

LARWOOD, JACOB, *The Story of the London Parks* (London: Chatto and Windus Publishers, c1872).

LONG, EDWARD, *History of Jamaica* (London: printed for T. Lowndes, 1774).

MARKHAM, GERVASE, *Countrey Contentments, or The English Huswife* (London: By Iohn Beale, for R. Iackson, and are to be sold at his shop neere Fleet-streete Conduit, 1623).

MARSHALL, ELIZABETH, *The Young Ladies' Guide in the Art of Cookery* (Newcastle: Printed by T. Saint, for the Author, 1777).

Mason, Charlotte, *The Lady's Assistant for regulating and supplying her table* (London: printed for J. Walter, 1773).

May, Robert, *The Accomplisht Cook, or The Art and Mystery of Cookery* (London: Printed by R.W. for Nath. Brooke, at the sign of the Angel in Cornhill, 1660).

McNeill, Florence Marian, *The Scots Kitchen* (London: Blackie & Son, 1929).

Melroe, Eliza, *An Economical, and New Method of Cookery* (London: printed and published for the author, by C. Chapple, 1798).

Miller, Mrs Mary, MS3547, Wellcome Library Collection.

Newton, Jane, MS1325, Wellcome Library Collection.

Nott, John, *The Cooks and Confectioners' Dictionary* (London: printed by H. P. for C. Rivington, 1723).

Parker, Jane, MS3769, Wellcome Library Collection.

Pegge, Samuel, *The Forme of Cury: A Roll of Ancient English Cookery Compiled, about A.D. 1390* (London: J. Nichols, 1780).

Philipps, Elizabeth, MS3082, Wellcome Library Collection.

Phillips, Mrs Sarah, *The Ladies Handmaid: Or, A Compleat System of Cookery* (London: Printed for J.Coote, 1758).

Pick, Mrs, attributed in MS8097, Wellcome Library Collection.

Raffald, Elizabeth, *The Experienced English House-keeper* (Manchester: Printed by J. Harrop, 1769).

Rundell, Maria Eliza, *A New System of Domestic Cookery* "By A Lady" (Boston: W. Andrews, 1807).

Slany, Elizabeth, Manuscript D/DRZ1, Essex Record Office.

Sleigh, Eliza, MS751, Wellcome Library Collection.

Smith, Robert, *Court Cookery: Or, The Compleat English Cook* (London: Printed for T. Wotton at the Three-daggers, Fleet Street, 1725).

Switzer, Stephen, *The Practical Kitchen Gardiner* (London, Printed for T. Woodward, 1727).

Thomas, Elizabeth, *Metamorphosis of the Town* (London: J. Wilford, 1730).

Webb, Mrs Arthur, *Farmhouse Cookery* (London: George Newnes Ltd, c1935).

Williams, J. *Primitive cookery; or the Kitchen Garden display'd.* (London: printed for J. Williams, 1767).

Woodforde, Rev. James, *The Diary of a Country Parson*, Editor: John Beresford, (Pub. H. Milford, Oxford University Press, 1924).

INDEX

Items marked with an asterisk are Deja Food dishes, where at least one ingredient has already been cooked.

Stuffing 319–21
sugar 26
Summer Cawl 270–71
Sunday lunch 10
Supple Onions 293
swede
Clapshot 310
Swede & Bacon Bake 312
Sweet & Sour Spinach 304

T

tarts
Tart for Ember Days 250–51
Tarts of Spinach & Cheese 305–7
*Thatched House Pie 108–10
thickenings 18–19
toast *see* bread
tongue: Minced Pies 218–20
Tonson, Jacob 138
tracklements 315
Tripe of Eggs 268
turkey
*Chook Weed 114–15
Lumber Pie 99–102
Modish Turkey 103–5
Turkey in Beef Broth 111–13
turnips
Braised Duck with Turnips 119–20
Turnips Roasted in Paper 313

V

veal
Pontack's Collops 80–83
Veal Forcemeat 331–2
Veal Ragoo 63–4
vegetables 269
Herb Pie for Lent 280–81
Herb Soup 284
Haricot of Root Vegetables 313–14
Summer Cawl 270–71
vegetable side dishes 11
see also individual names and salads
verjuice 25
vinegar 24
Elder Vinegar 77

W

white sauces
Cheese Sauce 44
Egg Sauce 44
Onion Sauce 45
Parsley Sauce 44
Rich White Sauce 44
Traditional White Sauce 42–3
Traditional Bread Sauce 45
Whitley Goose 242–3
wine 25, 80

Y

Yorkshire Puddings *see* Light Baked
Puddings

ABOUT THE AUTHOR

MARY-ANNE BOERMANS was a finalist in the 2011 series of
The Great British Bake Off and is now a successful food blogger.
Mary-Anne has been cooking and baking for more than 40 years.
She is passionate about home cooking and has amassed a library of
over 1,200 cookery books, with an emphasis on traditional, British
recipes. Mary-Anne's first book, *Great British Bakes*, was shortlisted
for the 2014 Fortnum & Mason Food & Drink Awards and won
the Guild of Food Writers Jeremy Round Award for Best First Book
2014. She lives in Worcestershire with her husband and daughter.

ACKNOWLEDGEMENTS

My family, for being supportive as well as live-in taste testers.
Thanks too to all my other taste testers, willing and unwitting:
—Ali, Carole, Pippa, Keith, Pam and Jim in Shropshire;
—Viv in Warwick;
—Neil, Dawn and 'The Lads' at Offmore Road Garage for being
such enthusiastic taste testers.
The following excellent food heroes and heroines:
—Kate Daniels, Little Black Pig at Willow Farm, for beautiful
mutton and ham;
—Anna Franklin, Franklin's Farm Butchers, for miraculously
conjuring goose for me in January;
—Dan Jackson, Hodgehill Butchery, for cheerfully supplying a
variety of unusual beef and pork item requests.
—My *Bake Off* colleague and friend, the accomplished Yasmin
Limbert, for the fantastic food styling and her talented husband,
Sean Limbert, for the beautiful photography.